LABOR IN A CHANGING AMERICA

LABOR IN
A CHANGING
AMERICA

Edited by *WILLIAM HABER*

University of Michigan

BASIC BOOKS, Inc., Publishers
New York   London

The Authors

BENJAMIN AARON is Professor of Law and Director, Institute of Industrial Relations, at the University of California at Los Angeles.

JACK BARBASH is Professor of Economics at the University of Wisconsin.

JOSEPH A. BEIRNE, President of the Communications Workers of America, AFL-CIO, is the author of *New Horizons for American Labor.*

IRVING BERNSTEIN is Professor of Political Science and Associate Director of the Institute of Industrial Relations at the University of California, Los Angeles.

EVELINE M. BURNS is Professor of Social Work at the Columbia University School of Social Work.

NEIL W. CHAMBERLAIN is Professor of Economics at Yale University.

EWAN CLAGUE is former Commissioner of Labor Statistics in the Department of Labor and has recently been appointed to head New York City's new Urban Research Institute.

OTTO ECKSTEIN is a Member of the President's Council of Economic Advisors and is on leave from his professorship in economics at Harvard University.

SIDNEY FINE is Professor of History at the University of Michigan.

CHARLES GREGORY is John B. Minor Professor of Law at the University of Virginia.

WILLIAM HABER is Professor of Economics and Dean of The College of Literature, Science, and the Arts, University of Michigan.

RALPH HELSTEIN has been the President of the United Packinghouse, Food & Allied Workers, AFL-CIO, since 1946.

GEORGE H. HILDEBRAND is Professor of Economics and of Industrial and Labor Relations at Cornell University.

EVERETT M. KASSALOW is Professor of Economics at the University of Wisconsin.

CHARLES C. KILLINGSWORTH is University Professor of Labor and Industrial Relations at Michigan State University.

ROBERT J. LAMPMAN is Professor of Economics, University of Wisconsin.

HAROLD M. LEVINSON is Professor of Economics at the University of Michigan; his primary research has been in the area of collective bargaining.

F. RAY MARSHALL is Professor of Economics at the University of Texas.

A. H. RASKIN is Assistant Editor, Editorial Page, of *The New York Times*.

ALBERT REES is Professor of Economics at the University of Chicago.

CHARLES M. REHMUS is Co-director of the Institute of Labor and Industrial Relations and Associate Professor of Political Science at the University of Michigan.

VICTOR REUTHER is director of the United Automobile Workers International Affairs Department and administrative assistant to the President of the United Automobile Workers.

ARTHUR M. ROSS is on leave of absence as Professor of Industrial Relations at the University of California and is currently Commissioner of the U.S. Bureau of Labor Statistics.

PHILIP TAFT is Professor of Economics at Brown University.

HAROLD L. WILENSKY is Professor of Sociology and Research Sociologist in the Institute of Industrial Relations, University of California, and has previously taught at the University of Michigan and the University of Chicago.

Preface

It would be surprising indeed if the economic and technological revolution that characterizes the United States in the second half of the twentieth century was not to have a large influence on American labor. Rapid, head-long change is reshaping many institutions in our society. The research revolution is creating new products and materials at a fantastic pace and is also speeding up the obsolescence of established ways of working and living. The technological revolution, coupled with the computer and automation, is changing jobs and skills. Employment is declining in many industries. Railroads and mining, for example, provide less than one-half the number of jobs which these industries had only twenty-five years ago. A large proportion of the labor force twenty years from now will be working in occupations that have not yet been created. White collar employment is rapidly growing. Educational requirements, even for relatively low skilled occupations, is expanding. The less educated and marginal workers are already in economic difficulty.

Economic and technological change is not new to American labor. Change has been perennial. What is significant about these times is that change is pervasive. It is affecting every field of endeavor—economic, social, and political. We are growing, and the tempo, if not the rate of growth, is unprecedented. Percapita output is increasing. An average family income of ten thousand dollars, at 1965 prices, is not many years away. Living standards have been improving steadily. We are, in fact, beginning to be concerned with the problems of leisure during working life, as well as with security and activity during retirement.

These conditions of relative affluence prevailing simultaneously with the "war on poverty" coupled with a relatively secure legal position presents some serious challenges to American trade unions. The earlier issues stimulated organization and support for the labor unions. Low wages, the sweat shop, "exploitation" of labor, long hours, the right to organize, the absence of grievance machinery, these were the "fighting issues." The quest for "industrial democracy" and the right to be consulted and represented by representatives "of their own choosing"—these issues were surrounded by a considerable degree of idealism. American labor found allies. Progressive and liberal forces came to its support in critical situations. While it is an exaggeration, in my view, to refer to the present period as "the end of idealism," the issues and challenges are clearly different. The unions are groping to find the present-day equivalent for the slogans and problems which led to mass organization of the basic industries in the 1930's. They are concerned with non-wage problems, with fringe benefits, with economic security, with the organization of the white collar workers, the semi-professional and technical employees, with the well educated, with the organization of teachers and public employees. Their appeal must be made to American employees who are relatively "well off," who own homes and automobiles, and who, on the critical issues of our security, think in "middle class" terms. The earlier methods successful in enrolling low paid and unskilled blue collar workers or those possessing established crafts are less applicable today. The organizer must be a sophisticated and trained person appealing to skeptical employees who do not think in "working class" terms.

Consequently, American unions feel challenged by the fact that their membership is not increasing and that they represent a declining proportion of the American labor force. Support from the "general public" and the traditional "liberal" groups is less certain. Even the strike as an ultimate weapon is now subject to serious question. Automated employment is bound to decrease its usefulness from the viewpoint of the unions. The disruption of public life in our highly integrated and interdependent communities has already given greater force to those who are seeking alternative solutions to the strike weapon.

The purpose of these essays is to portray the position of labor in a changing America. This volume is intended to describe and analyze how the forces of technology and affluence are affecting the conditions of life and how American unions are accommodating to change. One of my purposes was to bring together in a single volume the analysis and reflections of some of the contemporary students of the American labor scene. These essays seek to clarify at least some of the problems which face labor and the American community.

Ann Arbor   WILLIAM HABER
April 1966

Contents

The Authors   v

Preface   **William Haber**   vii

1   The American Labor Force   1
     Albert Rees

2   Class, Class Consciousness, and American Workers   12
     Harold L. Wilensky

3   Changing Living Standards of American Labor   45
     Ewan Clague

4   Income Distribution of American Labor   58
     Robert J. Lampman

5   The Reaction of American Labor to Technological Change   68
     Ralph Helstein

6   Unemployment in the United States   82
     Charles C. Killingsworth

7   Another View of Unemployment   97
     Otto Eckstein

8   The History of the American Labor Movement with Special Reference to Developments in the 1930's   105
     Sidney Fine

9 Forces Affecting the Growth of the American Labor Movement   121
    Irving Bernstein

10 The Philosophy of the American Labor Movement   132
    Philip Taft

11 The Rise of Industrial Unionism   143
    Jack Barbash

12 Unionization of White-Collar Workers   158
    Everett M. Kassalow

13 The Philosophy of American Management toward Labor   171
    Neil W. Chamberlain

14 Work and Leisure in the Round of Life   185
    Arthur M. Ross

15 Wage Policies of American Unions   197
    Harold M. Levinson

16 Disputes Settlement: The Grievance Procedure and the Role of Voluntary Arbitration   211
    Benjamin Aaron

17 Government Regulation or Control of Union Activities   224
    Charles Gregory

18 The Position of Minorities in the American Labor Movement   238
    F. Ray Marshall

19 Labor in American Politics   252
    Charles Rehmus

20 Social Security in America: The Two Systems—Public and Private 268
  Eveline M. Burns

21 The Economic Influence of American Unions 285
  George H. Hildebrand

22 The International Activities of American Trade Unions 298
  Victor Reuther

23 Whither Labor: Recent Developments in the Strength and Philosophy of American Labor 311
  A. H. Raskin

24 American Labor in a Changing World 322
  Joseph A. Beirne

  Index 333

LABOR IN A CHANGING AMERICA

1 THE AMERICAN LABOR FORCE

Albert Rees

DEFINITIONS AND MEASUREMENT

In March 1965, there were more than 75.1 million people in the civilian labor force in the United States. This labor force has been growing steadily; its average size in 1947 was 60 million people, or 15 million fewer than today. It constitutes by far the most important productive resource of the American economy.

The civilian labor force is made up of persons fourteen years of age or older who are either employed or unemployed, excluding the armed forces and inmates of such institutions as prisons or mental hospitals. The employed are those who work full time or part time for wages and salaries plus those employed in their own businesses or doing more than fifteen hours a week of unpaid work in a family business. The unemployed are those who are looking for work or are on layoff from their jobs. In March, 1965, there were 71.3 million persons employed and 3.7 million unemployed.

The size and composition of the labor force are estimated each month from data collected in a sample survey covering approximately 35,000 households in 357 geographical areas, scientifically selected to represent the entire country. Household-survey techniques have been used to measure the American labor force since 1940 and are being adopted by an increasing number of other countries. The monthly data used in this talk have been adjusted by the United States Department of Labor to remove the effects of recurrent seasonal changes.

1

LABOR-FORCE PARTICIPATION

In the period since 1947, the rate of participation in the civilian labor force has fluctuated without trend in a rather narrow range—from slightly over 57 per cent to slightly over 59 per cent of the civilian noninstitutional population of working age. This over-all stability conceals some striking trends in component parts of the labor force.

The most stable participation rates have been those of men in the central ages twenty-five to fifty-five. More than 95 per cent of this group has been in the labor force at all times. Participation is particularly high and stable for married men of these ages living with their wives; they are the heads of households or breadwinners, often called "primary workers." The term "secondary workers" is applied to married women whose husbands are also in the labor force or to younger or older men who are not the main support of their families. Among secondary workers, attachment to the labor force is less firm, entry and exit are more frequent, and trends in participation rates are often pronounced.

From 1947 to 1963, the participation rate for all males declined from almost 85 per cent to about 79 per cent, while that for all females rose from 31 to 37 per cent. The decline in male labor-force participation was concentrated in the youngest and oldest age groups. The rate for males fourteen to nineteen fell from 54 to 44 per cent, largely as a result of an increase in school attendance. The output lost through this deferred entry of young men into the labor force will later be regained from the increase in their productivity contributed by added schooling. At the opposite end of the life span, the participation rate for men sixty-five and over fell from 48 per cent in 1947 to 28 per cent in 1963. Several factors have contributed to this change. One is the decreasing importance of farming and other forms of self-employment in which complete retirement at a particular time is usually replaced by a gradual tapering-off of productive activity. A second force has been the rapid spread and improvement of public and private plans for providing income after retirement, that is, pension plans or social security. Finally, there has probably been an increase in the extent of rules made by employers requiring re-

2

tirement at a fixed age. Such rules are the cause of some concern. The lengthening of life spans and the improving health of those over sixty-five might suggest that an increasing proportion are able to work beyond conventional retirement age and that some of these might be happier at work than in retirement.

Females

Among females, labor-force-participation rates have increased at all ages from twenty upward. However, the rise has been especially sharp in the ages from thirty-five to fifty-four. The rate for women thirty-five to forty-four increased from 36 per cent in 1947 to 45 per cent in 1963; that for women forty-five to fifty-four increased from 33 to 51 per cent. This rise in participation rates has occurred almost entirely among married women.

INDUSTRIAL AND OCCUPATIONAL COMPOSITION

There have also been substantial changes in the industrial and occupational composition of the labor force as shown by statistics of employment. Average annual employment in agriculture fell from 8.3 million people in 1947 to 4.9 million in 1963, or from 14 per cent of total employment to 7 per cent. This drop in farm employment is the continuation of a long-term trend. The particularly sharp drop in the postwar period was caused by the extraordinary increase in farm productivity, resulting largely from improved machinery, seed, chemical fertilizers, and pesticides. In the same years in which farm employment fell by 3.4 million, acreage harvested was also declining, but farm output rose 38 per cent.

The most striking occupational change in the postwar labor force has been the growth of white-collar occupations relative to blue-collar, or manual, occupations. In 1947, there were 23.6 million blue-collar workers (craftsmen, foremen, operatives, and nonfarm laborers) and 20.2 million white-collar workers (professional, technical, managerial, clerical, and sales workers). By 1963, the number in blue-collar occupations had grown only 1.4 million, to 25 million in all, while that in white-collar occupations had risen to 30.2 million—a gain of 10 million.

Within the white-collar occupations, the fastest-growing group has been professional, technical, and kindred workers, who more than doubled in number in sixteen years. There were 3.8 million such workers in 1947 and 8.3 million in 1963. This group includes doctors, nurses, lawyers, accountants, engineers, draftsmen, and teachers—all occupations requiring extensive training. Its growth highlights the improvement in the educational attainments of the labor force. Between 1950 and 1960, the number of persons in the labor force twenty-five years old or over who had completed at least one year of college rose from 7.5 million to 11.3 million, and the number who had completed four or more years rose from 3.8 to 5.8 million. Some of these people attended college to enhance their participation in life as citizens and consumers and received no training directly relevant to their work. However, there can be no doubt that, on the whole, the high level of education of the American labor force represents an investment in human resources that contributes greatly to productive capacity. Physical capital and advanced technology are necessary for a high level of output, but no more so than an educated and experienced work force at all levels from the production worker to the manager, engineer, and scientist.

PARTICIPATION RATES AND AGGREGATE DEMAND

So far, this discussion of the labor force has been largely descriptive, but there are also interesting analytical issues connected with labor-force participation. One of the most important of these concerns the response of labor-force participation to changes in business conditions—that is, the response of labor supply to fluctuations in demand.

During the 1930's a hypothesis was advanced known as "the added-worker hypothesis," which held that a decrease in the demand for labor, as shown by a rise in the unemployment rate, would increase the size of the labor force. The advocates of this position believed that the unemployment of the breadwinner or family head would cause other members of the family to enter the labor force in order to maintain family income. Since the head would continue to seek work, the new secondary workers would be a net addition to the labor force. When this hypothesis was put forward, unemployment was not measured directly, but was estimated by subtracting a measure of employment from a straight-line projection of the labor force. The hypothesis implied that this projection of the labor force was too low because the added workers were not taken into consideration and that unemployment was therefore being underestimated.

After World War II, an opposite hypothesis was advanced, which we may call "the discouraged-worker hypothesis." This held that, when the demand for labor falls and the rate of unemployment rises, secondary workers are discouraged from entering the labor force because of the poor prospects of finding suitable employment. The size of the labor force will therefore decline with the decline in economic activity. As a hypothesis about the typical behavior of secondary workers or about the size of the labor force, this is, of course, the opposite of the added-worker hypothesis. Surprisingly enough, however, it had the same implications for the measurement of unemployment. After World War II, unemployment in the United States was being measured directly. The discouraged secondary worker who withdrew from the labor force was not counted as unemployed, but as out of the labor force. However, it could be argued that he (or she) represented a kind of disguised unemployment that should have been included in the count.

The problems raised by the controversy over added workers have been largely resolved by statistical research carried on in recent years by a number of university and government economists. Some of these studies have compared the labor-force-participation rates of secondary workers among places that differ in their level of unemployment; others have analyzed the movement of participation rates of secondary workers through time; still others have examined data describing the experience of individual families. From this research, two firm conclusions emerge. First, in those families in which the husband is unemployed, there is a strong tendency for the labor-force participation of other family members to increase as predicted by the added-worker hypothesis. The entry of secondary workers into the labor force, like borrowing or the drawing down of savings, is one of the devices that families use to maintain accustomed levels of consumption as nearly as possible intact in the face of unexpected or temporary

5

declines in income from usual sources. The second conclusion, however, is equally firm: in the aggregate, the discouraged-worker hypothesis is true and swamps the effect of the added workers. Labor-force-participation rates of secondary family members are consistently lower in places and at times where the unemployment rate is high. It is easy to understand why, in the aggregate, this effect should be dominant. Suppose that the unemployment rate of family heads rises from 4 to 6 per cent. Then, in about 2 per cent of all families, added workers will tend to enter the labor force. But in the great majority of families whose heads are still employed full time, the discouragement effect will operate. Even if it is rather weak, the numerical importance of these families will cause it to determine the aggregate outcome.

UNEMPLOYMENT AND PUBLIC POLICY

This finding has important implications for public policy. It means that the reduction in output caused by a recession is larger than would be expected from the unemployment rate alone and that the number of new jobs needed to restore full employment will be consistently larger than the excess of unemployed persons over a normal level. It has been suggested that new methods of obtaining current information on the persons not in the labor force might be devised which would give us monthly or quarterly statistics during periods of less than full employment on the size of the group that could be expected to enter the labor force if there were adequate demand.

WOMEN IN THE LABOR FORCE

Another important analytical problem in this general area is the relationship between the incomes of husbands and the labor-force-participation rates of wives. In comparisons among places at a given time, it has consistently been found that the higher the income of a group of husbands, the smaller the fraction of their wives who are in the labor force. This in itself is not a surprising finding. Families in which the wife both keeps house and has an outside job will usually have less leisure than other families. As the income of the husband rises, some of the increase can be used to obtain added leisure through the wife's withdrawal from the labor force. However, during the postwar period, we have seen that there has been a sharp rise in the labor-force-participation rate of married women. At the same time, there has been a large increase in the average incomes of husbands, even after full allowance is made for increases in the cost of living. It therefore seems that the findings from comparisons at a point in time are contradicted by the findings from changes over time.

This paradox has been resolved through the use of more complete models of the factors influencing the labor-force participation of wives. The additional variables considered include the wage that the wife can earn if employed, the presence of children in the home, and the rate of unemployment. It has been shown in comparisons among places at a point in time that the labor-force-participation rate of married women is negatively related to husband's income, the unemployment rate, and the presence of children and positively related to the female wage. The positive effect of a higher female wage is, in general, more powerful than the negative effect of a higher husband's income. Since female wages have also been rising through time, this variable helps to explain the rise in the participation rate of married women. There are, in addition, other forces explaining the changes over time that cannot be easily introduced into statistical analysis. The choices confronting wives are as much those between work in the home and work in the market as between labor and leisure. The labor-force-participation rate will therefore tend to be increased with the greater availability or lower costs of substitutes for the work of the wife in caring for the home and family. This suggests that the widespread use of such products as washing machines, clothes dryers, vacuum cleaners, and prepared foods may contribute to the rising labor-force participation of wives. At the same time, the availability of such products does not differ significantly among places within the United States and therefore would not affect relations between participation rate and husband's income among places at a given time. The possible importance of this factor is suggested by the increase in the percentage of homes wired for electricity having certain home appliances. Between 1947 and 1962, the percentage having vacuum cleaners rose from 50 to 78, the percentage having electric washing machines from 63 to 82, and the percentage having electric or gas clothes dryers from less than 1 to 23.

THE EVIDENCE FOR NONWHITE WOMEN

Studies of labor-force participation in the United States have shown significant and persistent differences in the participation rates of whites and of nonwhites, most of whom are Negroes. The participation rates of nonwhite females have consistently been higher than those of white females, although the difference has narrowed appreciably in recent years. For the past ten years, the participation rate for white males has been slightly higher than that for nonwhite males. The last difference may be related to the somewhat lower educational attainment of nonwhites and to the presence of racial discrimination in employment.

Differences in the labor-force-participation rates of white and nonwhite wives have been analyzed in more detail. The rate for nonwhite wives remains higher even after the income of the husbands is held constant—that is, if the husbands are sorted into income classes, the labor-force-participation rate of nonwhite wives is higher in each income class. In particular, it appears that the presence of school-age children is a less important factor inhibiting the labor-force participation of nonwhite wives. The underlying forces explaining this difference are undoubtedly more sociological than economic. They may include the traditionally more important role of the wife and mother in holding together the Negro family; the presence of discrimination in housing, which reduces the satisfactions possible from work in the home; the greater frequency of part-time work among Negro women; and the higher marital instability in Negro families, which encourages the continued labor-force participation of the wife as insurance against the possibility of separation, desertion, or divorce.

Differences in occupational distribution by color among employed workers are much more striking than differences in participation rates. There is still a strong tendency for nonwhites to be concentrated in the lower-paying and less skilled occupations. In 1963, 21 per cent of employed nonwhite males were nonfarm laborers, as compared with only 6 per cent of employed white males. Of nonwhite females, 34 per cent worked in private households compared with only 6 per cent of white females. At the opposite end of the occupational scale, 5 per cent of nonwhite males were professional, or technical workers, while 12 per cent of white males fell in this category. The difference was even sharper for managers, proprietors, and officials, an occupational group that included 15 per cent of white males but only 3 per cent of nonwhite males.

It is to be hoped that these differences will, along with many others, narrow further or disappear completely as the United States moves toward full economic equality among races. The passage of the Civil Rights Act of 1964 could contribute to this goal. The narrowing of the gap in the educational attainment of the labor force by color will also help to eliminate differences in employment patterns. In 1952, the median number of years of school completed by the white labor force eighteen years old and over was 11.4 and of the nonwhite labor force 7.6. Ten years later, the figure for whites was 12.2 years and for nonwhites 9.6. Thus, a gap of 3.8 years in the median number of years of school completed was reduced by 1962 to 2.6 years. Differences remain, however, in the quality of schooling which cannot be reflected in statistics of educational attainment.

LABOR-FORCE PROJECTIONS

The people who will enter the civilian labor force in the next fourteen years have already been born, and it is therefore possible to make accurate projections of the working-age population through 1978. Projecting the labor force is much more difficult, however, because it involves the projection of participation rates. We cannot be certain whether recent trends in participation rates will continue, will accelerate, or will be reversed. The United States Department of Labor has made projections of the labor force to 1975 on the basis of what seem to its staff to be reasonable assumptions about trends in participation rates. It projects a total labor force, including the armed forces, of 86 million in 1970 and 93 million in 1975. The projected growth is 10 million from 1963 to 1970, and another 7 million from 1970 to 1975.

These projections reflect the high birth rates in the years following World War II; babies born in the immediate postwar years are now beginning to enter the labor force in substantial numbers.

The official projections have been criticized on the ground that they do not allow sufficiently for the depressing effect on labor-force participation of the rather high rates of unemployment experienced from 1958 through 1963. The critics argue that restoration of full employment will lead to a larger growth in the labor force than shown in the official projections. Two private projections for 1970 lie above the official ones by 1 million and almost 3 million persons, respectively.

LABOR-FORCE GROWTH
PROBLEMS AND OPPORTUNITIES

There is, of course, general agreement that the growth of the American labor force will be substantial in the years ahead. From one point of view, this growth represents a problem; jobs must be found or created for the new entrants, and they must be trained to do the kinds of work needed in an economy whose technology is changing rapidly and growing constantly more complex. Those who do not receive enough training or the kind of training suited both to their talents and to the environment in which they will work may receive low incomes or experience substantial periods of unemployment.

From another point of view, the growth of the labor force represents a major opportunity. Despite the progress of labor-saving technology, there is an enormous amount of work left to be done in the United States and in the world in raising the living standard to that now enjoyed only by the most prosperous, in eradicating poverty, in relieving disease, and in easing the congestion and enhancing the aesthetic qualities of life in crowded modern cities. It would not be hard to expand this list of unmet needs or wants at length, and, although people may differ about what to include, few would have difficulty in finding additions. A large and well-trained labor force remains our most valuable resource in meeting the needs of a growing population and in meeting at least some of their aspirations for higher living standards. The 86 million or more people who will be in the American labor force in 1970 can make an important contribution to the economic progress of both the United States and of the other countries with which it trades and to whom it sends capital and technical assistance.

2 CLASS, CLASS CONSCIOUSNESS, AND AMERICAN WORKERS

Harold L. Wilensky

For centuries, social critics and social scientists have given us the images with which we construct our picture of the world. Among the concepts that have done the most to mislead us in our search for an understanding of social reality are "class" and "class consciousness." European students of labor—*théoricien et militant* alike—take for granted the utility of such ideas. In America, academic journals and the press are filled with references to the "middle class" or "working class"; discussions of the affluent worker becoming "middle class" are commonplace. And the constitutions of many American unions only yesterday contained the ringing slogans of class warfare.

This rhetoric—whether it is tolerated by nostalgic exsocialists who head a few modern labor unions or whether it is taken more seriously, as in popular discussions of the affluent worker—obscures more than it reveals of the shape of American society. I should like to ask "Where do the ideas of class and class consciousness fit the situation of American labor well, and where do such ideas fit badly?" I shall argue that, in the United States and in other rich countries, class consciousness among manual workers is a transitional phenomenon—characterizing workers not yet accustomed to the modern metropolis and the modern work place; that a clearly defined working class no longer exists, if it ever did; that much behavior and many attitudes said to be rooted in class are instead a matter of race, religion, ethnic origin, education, age, and stage in the family life cycle. Indeed, almost any of these traditional groupings of the population display more homogeneity of behavior and belief than "labor," if by the latter term we mean all manual workers or even all union members.

Finally, if we want to use economic classifications that yield uniformity in ideology or mentality, we must turn to such categories as "small entrepreneur" (a small part of the lower middle class) or to particular crafts (a small part of the upper working class) and to the established professions (a minority of the upper middle class). Insofar as class categories remain at all useful, the line that divides stably employed, well-educated, well-paid workers from the lower class is becoming more important than the split between upper working class and lower middle class. Whether we are witnessing the *embourgeoisement* of the workers or the sinking of the middle class into the proletariat, the top of one and the bottom of the other seem to form a new middle mass, a population that increasingly shares common values, beliefs, and tastes. And the process goes on in every rich country.

In general, I hope that all this will add up to a more realistic picture of the position, prospects, and mentality of that minority of the urban labor force that we customarily label "manual worker" or "working class" and its relation to other classes.

THE IDEA OF SOCIAL CLASS

All students of stratification are concerned with the distribution of rewards in society—who gets whatever is valued and why. They are also interested in the effect of the distribution of rewards on human behavior.[1] But there is no agreement about

[1] The necessity of specialization—universal differences in role based on sex, age, work, and authority—leads everywhere to social stratification. People classify one another in categories and place these categories above or below one another on a scale of superiority and inferiority. The criteria of ranking vary; anything valued and unequally distributed may suffice: wealth, power, magic, women, and so on. Despite the recurrent dream of absolute equality— for example, the "classless society"—every society past or present has had some system of stratification. Distinctions are made. Some positions are honored, others not. Some are accorded more authority than others. Who is and who is not honored—the priest, the workman, the scholar, or the warrior; the distance between top and bottom positions—the difference between rich and poor, leader and rank-and-file; these and other features of stratification systems vary from place to place, time to time. But power and prestige differences do appear everywhere. Among the reasons are these: (1) Any society

what rewards shared by what strata and what positions held by what groups are significant in explaining social structure and change; for instance, how we decide whether a man is a member of the working class or whether the working class is becoming middle class.

Karl Marx's definition of class, although imprecise, tends to emphasize, not sources of income (wages, profit, rent), not amount of income, not type of occupation, but what he called "the relations of production"—that is, *authority relations rooted in the distribution of property rights,* political power anchored in economic power.[2] Individuals form a class only insofar as they are locked in political combat with another class. Marxist discussion of "class consciousness" has since followed this line, emphasizing three criteria. In the Marxian view, a man is said to be class conscious when he is (1) rationally aware of his own class interests and identifies with them; (2) aware of other class interests and rejects them as illegitimate; and (3) aware of and ready to use collective political means to realize his class interests.[3]

In this Marxian sense, is American labor class conscious?

---

has to distribute people among its different positions and induce them to perform essential duties. (2) Every society has a hierarchy of values based on the fact of scarcity. (3) Differences in the distribution of these values (for example, income, power) move people to go after positions and to perform once they are in them. (4) As long as the family has anything to do with bringing up children and as long as some of the behavior and possessions unequally valued and unequally distributed are learned or acquired in the family, then some inequality will be perpetuated. (5) The various criteria of stratification are related—power differences among men are universal; those with power can use it to obtain for themselves and their kin those things which are valued (a man of power can use connections to get his son a good job; a man of wealth can buy his son a good education). Cf. K. Davis and Wilburt E. Moore, "Some Principles of Stratification," *American Sociological Review,* X (1945), 242–249.

2 For the best recent discussion of Marx's theory of class, see Ralf Dahrendorf, *Class and Class Conflict in Industrial Society* (Stanford: Stanford University Press, 1959), Chapter 1. The task of evaluating Marx is beyond the scope of the present essay. Note, however, that by Marx's own definition of class, the abolition of private ownership of the means of production cannot lead to the "classless society" because authority is obviously neither tied to the legal title of property nor confined to the industrial sphere. For a balanced summary of sociological critiques of Marx, see *ibid.,* Chapter 4.

3 C. Wright Mills, *White Collar* (New York: Oxford University Press, 1951), Chapter 15.

MARXIAN CLASS CONSCIOUSNESS
IN AMERICAN LABOR HISTORY

Surely, for brief episodes, during our most rapid industrialization, American labor displayed a militancy that fits the Marxian model and that has its contemporary counterpart in the labor movements of less developed countries. In the last quarter of the nineteenth century, American labor protest was intermittently tame and violent, economic and political; labor organizations were unsteady, easily diverted to elaborate political programs (from greenbackism to the single tax, from revolutionary anarchism to Marxian socialism, from Owen's "estate guardianship" to producers' and consumers' cooperation). Obstinate employers used private armies; the courts declared unions to be criminal conspiracies (until use of the injunction in the late nineteenth century gave them a better weapon); and the government broke strikes by use of local, state, and federal troops. In the 1880's, especially during and just after the depression of 1884–1885, labor protest began to sweep the land. Skilled and unskilled, women and men, native and foreign-born—never before (and not again until the 1930's) had American labor displayed such a drive to organize.

The peak of immigration was reached that decade, and streams of newcomers caught the enthusiasm. "Labor organizations assumed the nature of a real class movement. . . . General strikes, sympathetic strikes . . . nationwide political movements became the order of the day.[4] Employer associations quickly counteracted with lockouts, blacklists, armed guards, and detectives. When the wave of strikes failed, a consumer-boycott movement of epidemic proportions got under way. This was a time of great upheaval, when the Knights of Labor, an inclusive labor organization espousing the ideal of producers' cooperation, spearheaded a mid-eighties mass movement culminating in an unsuccessful nationwide strike for the eight-hour day. It was the time, too, of the famous bomb explosion on Haymarket Square, which touched off a period of hysteria and police terror in Chicago and resulted

4 Selig Perlman, *A History of Trade Unionism in the United States* (New York: Macmillan, 1928), p. 84.

in the unjust conviction and execution of innocent men.[5] The strength of employer opposition and the unwieldiness of the Knights' own organization threw the labor movement into decline.

As the movement broke up, the American Federation of Labor (AFL) was established to organize workers on straight trade-union lines, for better wages, hours, and working conditions through collective bargaining—foreshadowing the form in which labor protest was to be cast during the next century. The last gasp of nineteenth-century working-class militancy came in the form of the Homestead strike of 1892 (which involved a violent battle between an army of three hundred Pinkerton detectives hired by Andrew Carnegie and armed strikers, including women and boys, who were finally overcome by the militia) and the great Pullman strike of 1894, which was broken with the aid of federal troops, a federal injunction, and the imprisonment of its leaders.

This enormous thrust upward from the people of poverty and low status was again repeated in the early days of Franklin Roosevelt's New Deal and provoked much the same militant fear on the part of the wealthy and well-born. In the 1930's, with almost revolutionary fervor, autoworkers in Flint, Michigan, seized control of corporate property in the famous sit-down strikes.

Marxian class consciousness? Yes, sporadic, loosely organized, and, as America had grown richer, fading into memory. Today, some of those sit-down strikers—or their sons—peacefully negotiate contracts with employers, serve on community welfare council boards, run for municipal office (and occasionally win), and live the modestly comfortable middle-class life of trade-union officials. The spontaneous protest movements of yesterday have become the "business unions" of today—large stable organizations sanctioned by contracts and the law. American labor today has limited goals: better wages, shorter hours, and improved conditions of employment. Its means are mainly economic: the establishment of collective-bargaining agreements enforced in part by arbitration of grievances. Occasional legal strikes over

[5] *Ibid.*, pp. 68–105; and Charles A. Beard and Mary R. Beard, *The Rise of American Civilization* (New York: Macmillan, 1933), II, 220 ff., 73.

the terms of the agreement occur, but these have become the accepted alternative to massive state control of labor relations. A decreasing proportion of union members and of the total labor force is now drawn into strikes. The strike weapon, though not obsolete, has been blunted.

Similarly, in politics, the period of early industrialization saw many efforts to base political parties on distinctive working-class interests and membership. But, in recent decades, American labor has taken its place in the coalition of interest groups that dominates the Democratic party nationally and in the machinery of both major parties at local levels.

ATTITUDES TOWARD CLASS TODAY

The theme that class consciousness in American labor has dwindled is consistent with what we know of the attitudes of the American population toward social class and class conflict. Keeping in view the Marxian sense of class consciousness, what can we say about awareness of classes? Surveys using a variety of questions, leading and neutral, fixed and open-ended, indicate that most Americans think that classes exist, but there is little agreement about their nature and number, and there is great variation in how people on the same income and occupational level identify themselves.

In such research, the pitfalls are many and the results not very gratifying. There is the well-known problem that phrasing affects response: the researcher gets what he asks for. Thus, if you suggest that "Some people say that there are social classes in the U.S.A. They call them lower, middle, and upper social classes," and then ask, "Which would you put yourself in?", the vast majority will choose the comfortable "middle." Add "working class" as one of your alternatives and a third to half of these "middle class" identifiers will switch to "working class." Leave the matter open—"What social classes do you think there are [in this city]" and "which one of them are you in?"—and as many as half the population will either deny the existence of classes or in some way indicate that the idea is meaningless.[6]

[6] Cf. Richard Centers. *The Psychology of Social Class* (Princeton: Princeton University Press, 1949), and Joseph A. Kahl, *The American Class Structure* (New York: Rinehart, 1957), Chapter 6. Using four census tracts in

If you now confine yourself to those who think that classes exist and ask them for the number and characteristics of the classes, you will tap a great range of rather vague ideas. Few Americans see labor and capital as the classes; few see them at war. Various groups and strata emphasize various criteria of ranking—the value of material possessions (house, furniture, cars, clothing), type of job or job opportunities, amount of education, income or economic security (the lower strata emphasize this more), refinement of taste and manners (college people sometimes em-

Minneapolis representing four rental levels, Gross asked 935 subjects all three questions described above. Here is a comparison of percentages using one or another label by form of question, along with results from other studies using roughly comparable questions

Form of Question and Sample

Percentage saying:	UML Minnea- polis*	UMWL Minnea- polis*	UMWL U.S.A.†	UMWL U.S.A.‡	Open Minnea- polis*	Open U.S.A.§	Open Talla- hassee‖
Upper	5	2	3	4	1	3	2
Middle	76	42	43	36	31	47	43
White-Collar	—	—	—	—	—	—	3
Working	—	45	51	52	11	11	6
Lower	10	3	1	5	3	4	2
No classes	2	1	1	—	14	—	25
Don't Know	4	2	1	3	20	28	—
Other classes	3	5	—	—	15	8	9
No Response	—	—	—	—	5	—	10
TOTAL	100	100	100	100	100	100	100
	(935)	(935)	(1,097)	(1,337)	(935)	(5,217)‡	(320)

* Neal Gross, "Social Class Identification in the Urban Community," *American Sociological Review*, XVIII (1953), 398–404. Four census tracts chosen to represent four rental levels.

† Richard Centers, *op. cit.*, p. 77. Centers reports on two national samples. These samples were cross sections of white males. These are the results which Centers obtained in his sample of July 1945.

‡ *Ibid.*, p. 77. This is Centers' cross section of February 1946.

§ "The People of the U.S.—A Self Portrait," *Fortune*, XXI (1940), 14. A national cross-section quota sample.

‖ John L. Haer, "An Empirical Study of Social Class Awareness," *Social Forces*, XXXVI (1957), 117–121. Area probability sample.

Total, not reported in the *Fortune* article, is cited in Haer, *op. cit.*, p. 119.

phasize this), "morals" (the thrift-spendthrift theme is strong here among some members of the lower middle class), or social origins. The number of classes named is similarly variable.

Finally, the context of questioning and the area of life covered by the questions affect criteria for the definition of the classes. If you go to a man in the evening and ask about the neighbors, he will think about status symbols and styles of life—consumption, house, car, leisure uses; if you talk to him on the job and ask about the people there, he will think of authority—the authority of bosses, of skill and expertise.[7] The average American is a Veblenian at home, a modified Marxist at work.

In assessing class consciousness in American labor, it is perhaps more important to examine the types of people who label themselves upper, middle, or working class. By any objective measure, there is considerable cross-class identification. About a fifth of all manual workers call themselves middle class; more than a fifth of all professional, business, and white-collar people identify as working class.[8] The clearest and most consistent awareness of class is at the top; a hard core of business, professional, and technical people plus some of the clerical and sales people call themselves middle class no matter how you ask the question. Among workers, the more skilled are the most class conscious—consistent with the fact that labor organization emerged first among employees in a strategic market or technical position (printers, locomotive engineers, cutters in the garment industry).

What about the rejection of other class interests as illegitimate and the willingness to act out such sentiments politically? The few recent American studies that have looked for this evidence of class consciousness have turned up precious little of it. For instance, a sample of white men in Philadelphia, half Protestant, half Catholic, was asked in 1953: "To which one of these groups do you feel you owe your allegiance—business or labor?" They were also asked whether they agreed or disagreed with six policy statements, three taken from the CIO, three from the NAM. To

---

[7] Cf. Kahl, *op. cit.*, p. 86.

[8] *Ibid.*, pp. 161–162. In my study of the Detroit area, about two in five of the white men in the upper working class (defined by income and occupation) aged 21–55 identify as middle class given the four choices; even one in four of the men on relief say that they are middle class.

be scored class conscious, a man had to choose sides, agree with all his side's policy statements, and disagree with the others. By this measure, only minorities of every group were class conscious: 40 per cent of the big businessmen in the sample, 25 per cent of the small businessmen, 28 per cent of unionized workers, and only 13 per cent of nonunionized workers. On the allegiance question, more union workers were neutral than were pro-labor.[9]

A similar study of unionized textile workers in Paterson, New Jersey, a highly industrialized city with a long history of industrial conflict, showed similar results. "How do classes get along?", these workers were asked. "In general are they like enemies, or like equal partners, or like leaders and followers?"

TABLE 2–1. *Attitudes about Class Relations among Ninety-five Textile Workers in Paterson, New Jersey (including multiple answers)*

Paternalism	27
Enemies	21
Partnership	19
Snobbish or jealous	12
Vague	8
Don't Know	14

As Table 2–1 suggests, the most common responses to this and similar questions reflect more a pattern of paternalism than one of class warfare. One worker said, "If the bosses would treat the working people right, they would get along all the time. It's like a dog with a bone. If you give him food, he will be all right. Just treat us right and we'll follow right along." Another expressed his general approval of the class system in this most un-Marxian way: "The people who have money own businesses, and the rest of the people work for them. If there were no rich people, who would the poor people work for?" Twenty-eight per cent expressed such paternalistic views. One in five saw

9 Oscar Glantz, "Class Consciousness and Political Solidarity," *American Sociological Review*, XXIII (1958), 375–383. The sample of 201 Protestants and 199 Catholics was a multistage sample of households, stratified and purposive at the first stage (precincts of varying occupational and religious composition), and random, with different probabilities, at the second stage.

classes as partners, about one in five, as enemies. Over one in three held some other view, mostly vague. Most of these unionists felt that the class system was both inevitable and desirable. And although one in three thought that the system was becoming more rigid, half thought that it was becoming more open, especially for the next generation.[10]

The most intensive recent survey of the political expression of working-class consciousness was carried out among 375 blue-collar men in Detroit. If we are to uncover Marxian class consciousness anywhere, it would be in this study.[11] The sample was chosen from seven ethnically homogeneous neighborhoods: one of them northwest European, three mainly Negro, three Polish—generally overrepresenting the economically deprived and uprooted. They were interviewed when severe unemployment was a fresh memory—down from a recession peak of 20 per cent of the labor force in 1957–1958 to 6 per cent at the time of the interview in 1960. All but 10 per cent used class imagery in response to at least one of eight unstructured questions designed to elicit spontaneous expressions of class symbolism (who was his favorite president and why, etc.). The closer one pushed these men to a Marxian model, however, the smaller the fraction that one could call class conscious. From mere class verbalization, characterizing 26 per cent of the sample, the measure moved toward militancy as follows: (1) "When business booms in Detroit, who gets the profits?" Answers such as "rich people" or "big business" were considered indicators of moderate "skepticism" and covered 30 per cent. (2) Favoring a statement about picketing a landlord was scored "militant radicalism"; 23 per cent went this far. (3) Agreeing with the statement that the wealth of our country should be divided up equally so that people would

10 Jerome Manis and Bernard Meltzer, "Attitudes of Textile Workers to Class Structure," *American Journal of Sociology*, LX (1954), 30–35. The sample: 200 randomly-selected members of the TWUA–CIO in Paterson, New Jersey. Ninety-five men were interviewed, including sixty-seven operatives, nineteen craftsmen, and nine laborers. Median age: fifty. Median residence in Paterson: forty years.

11 John C. Leggett, "Uprootedness and Working-Class Consciousness," *American Journal of Sociology*, LXVIII (1963), 682–692. Cf. Alfred W. Jones, *Life, Liberty, and Property* (New York: J. B. Lippincott, 1941), a sophisticated study of attitudes among Akron residents on such issues as the sit-down strikes of 1936.

have an equal chance to get ahead counted as militant egalitarianism. Only 10 per cent would go all the way, the same tiny fraction that failed to verbalize in class terms at all.

Do class attitudes affect a man's politics? Do class-conscious union members, however few, act out their militancy?

THE LABOR VOTE

During the presidential campaign of 1948, when President Truman was running for office, I had an opportunity to study political action in a local union of the autoworkers in southeast Chicago. A local officer recounted an incident in a plant across the street that was discussed during the campaign by members of his local. He was telling me about the union shop, not politics, and he said he would give me an example of how important it was "from the standpoint of discipline" that workers be pro-union:

> There was a guy over there who was bitterly against Roosevelt. . . . Then Roosevelt died and the boys in the shop felt pretty bad. They decided that they would have three minutes' silence on the day Roosevelt was buried. Well, this old guy had it all figured out ahead of time. When the bell rang all the fellows stood up at their machines in absolute quiet. . . . And then this old geezer began to . . . make as much noise as he could. . . . The funny thing is that [the workers] didn't do a thing. They just turned away from him and wouldn't even speak to him afterwards. . . . They came over to the union and the first thing was they insisted that he be thrown out of the union or at least suspended for a couple of months. We had a big meeting about that and I told the boys that that wasn't a real punishment, that the agony of having to work with the men would be a lot worse than having a leave of absence. I told them that they should fine him and make him keep on working. So that's what they did. They fined him $100 and the money went for a fund to build a statue of Franklin Roosevelt . . . [When he came to the local meeting to pay the fine, he] stood right up there in front of all his fellow workers and he said that he had been wrong and that he was sorry. . . . It took a lot of courage to admit that he was wrong. That made a terrific difference. You have no idea. He's made a good union man.

The Democratic New Deal tradition was still strong among the union activists in 1948 and—as in the case of the story—they slid easily from problems of discipline on strictly union matters to problems of discipline on strictly political matters. The president of Local 166, one member commented, "can't get it through his head that a guy can be Republican and still be for the union."[12]

For a quarter of a century, studies of voting and political orientation have shown that American labor unions have, with their emphasis on issues rather than man or party, solidified the political direction of those exposed to their influence, helping to keep their active members in the old New Deal–Fair Deal coalition, now revived in President Johnson's "Great Society." The years 1944–1952 saw the emergence of a new postwar, post-Roosevelt political generation—a loosening of the ties that bind ethnic Catholics to the urban Democratic machines[13] and a breakup of the lower-middle-class–working-class coalition that formed the basis of Democratic strength for two decades. There is some evidence that, nationally, the lower half of the working class, including the Negro minority, had politically significant elements that were becoming alienated from both the Democratic party and the political process.[14] For the minority involved directly with unions, however, the old ties to the liberal–labor wing of

12 Harold L. Wilensky, "The Labor Vote: A Local Union's Impact on the Political Conduct of Its Members," *Social Forces*, XXXV (1956), 114. The following discussion of the labor vote is drawn from this article, which also assesses evidence on political behavior of union members and activists up to 1956.

13 Samuel Lubell, *The Future of American Politics* (New York: Harper, 1951) and Seymour M. Lipset, *et al.*, "The Psychology of Voting," in *Handbook of Social Psychology*, Ed. Gardner Lindzey (Cambridge, Mass.: Addison-Wesley, 1954), II.

14 An analysis by Morris Janowitz and Dwaine Marvick of the Survey Research Center data on the 1952 election campaign shows that nonvoting among lower-lowers (defined by income and occupation) reached 45 per cent, and those who voted gave Stevenson only a 5 per cent plurality. Catholics as a whole gave Stevenson a similarly small plurality. Like the farmers, the lower middle class made major shifts to Eisenhower. *Competitive Pressure and Democratic Consent* (University of Michigan, Institute of Public Administration, 1956). President Johnson's even more overwhelming victory over Barry Goldwater in 1964 similarly cut across class lines; every bloc of voters moved to the Democrats because of fear of extremism in domestic affairs and recklessness in foreign affairs.

the Democratic party remained strong. From 1936 to 1952, comparisons between the candidate and/or party preferences and participation of union and nonunion voters on roughly the same socioeconomic level consistently show that the union voters are less apathetic and are more inclined to vote Democratic.[15] For example, Louis Harris, analyzing poll results for 1952, concludes that (1) while the rest of the nation was going 3:2 for Eisenhower, union members were voting over 3:2 for Stevenson ("the labor vote held remarkably well"); (2) fewer than one in ten Catholic union members bolted the Democrats, compared to three in ten of the nonunion Catholics; (3) labor and economic issues were a bit more salient for union members and their families than for the rest of the population; (4) union members were solidly convinced that their economic welfare was tied to continued Democratic rule; but (5) the families of union members voted 9:8 for Eisenhower, slipping from their normal 2:1 Democratic inclination. (Two out of every ten members of union families bolted from the voting pattern of their household breadwinner.)[16] These studies suggest that although labor unions change few votes (the John L. Lewis endorsement of Willkie is

[15] See Gallup poll results reported for 1936, 1940, and 1944, in V. O. Key, Jr., *Politics, Parties, and Pressure Groups* (3rd ed., New York: Crowell Co., 1952), p. 79. On 1948, see David Truman in F. Mosteller *et al.*, "The Pre-Election Polls of 1948," *Social Science Research Council Bulletin*, LX (1949), 229–230; and Angus Campbell and Robert L. Kahn, *The People Elect a President* (Ann Arbor: Survey Research Center, 1952), pp. 27–28. On 1952, see Angus Campbell, G. Gurin, and Warren E. Miller, *The Voter Decides* (Evanston: Row, Peterson, 1954), pp. 72–73.

[16] "Labor Was Not an Issue in the Election," in *Labor and Nation Timely Papers*, Vol. I, No. 1 (1953), 15–25, and Louis Harris, *Is There a Republican Majority?* (New York: Harper, 1954), pp. 148–149. R. W. Dodge, using interviews with an area probability sample of the adult population in Detroit in 1951–1952, found that about 80 per cent of the people in union families who indicated a political preference favored the Democratic party, while the nonunion segment had only a slight Democratic majority. The contrast held for the labor-backed mayoralty candidate in 1951, whose main support, however weak, came from persons in union (especially CIO) families. "Some Aspects of the Political Behavior of Labor Union Members in the Detroit Metropolitan Area" (unpublished doctoral dissertation, University of Michigan, 1953). Only two of these studies—Harris, *op. cit.*, and Bernard R. Berelson, Paul F. Lazarsfeld and W. H. McPhee, *Voting* (Chicago: University of Chicago Press, 1954)—use controls for such politically-relevant social categories as race, ethnicity, and religion.

often cited[17]), they do much to mobilize the committed vote, to activate class disposition, and to reinforce party appeals.[18]

That class consciousness can combine with union activity to yield uniform voting is shown in an analysis of the hard-core supporters of G. Mennen Williams, the liberal Democratic governor of Michigan from 1948 to 1960, now Assistant Secretary of State in charge of African affairs. Recognizing Governor Williams' strong commitment to civil rights, almost all of the Negroes, union and nonunion, militant and tame, voted for him in 1958. But when we look at the Williams vote among whites, we find (1) militant unionists, 81 per cent; (2) moderate unionists, 72 per cent; (3) nonmilitant unionists (the ones who merely mention class in discussing issues or avoid class symbolism entirely), 52 per cent; (4) militant nonunionists (only 5 cases); (5) moderate nonunionists, 50 per cent; (6) nonmilitant nonunionists, 38 per cent.[19] Clearly, that minority of workers who are highly class conscious and are exposed to a lively union act out their ideology in the political arena.

We can see the process by which this takes place. Comparison of the political orientation of members and nonmembers or of union actives and inactives suggests that (1) routine experience in union social and economic affairs leads to a generalized pro-labor orientation; (2) this orientation leads to acceptance of union discipline in strikes and collective bargaining; (3) the younger, more ambitious, better educated and sometimes more skilled workers who become involved in local union activity and take charge of union affairs develop transferable political skills

17 E.g., see Irving Bernstein, "John L. Lewis and the Voting Behavior of the CIO," *Public Opinion Quarterly*, V (1941), 233–249.

18 Cf. Key, *op. cit.*, pp. 79–80. Berelson *et al.*, *op. cit.*, pp. 37–53, report that in Republican Elmira, in 1948, not only did union members vote more Democratic than nonmembers of the same occupation, class, education, age, or religion, but also that the more pro-union workers were more Democratic, and, in an IAM-AFL local studied, the more interaction the members had with other union members, the more Democratic the vote. Also, those FDR voters who were identified working class remained most loyal to Democrats in 1948. *Ibid.*, pp. 253–273.

19 John C. Leggett, "Working-Class Consciousness, Race, and Political Choice," *American Journal of Sociology*, LXIX (1963), 171–176. Three in four of the sample belonged to a union; eight in ten of these were members of a CIO union.

in the union office and come to see political action as a necessary extension of the collective-bargaining process; (4) locally, they cultivate political influence to protect their institutional privileges—gain police support in the maintenance of picket lines; (5) in national campaigns, they articulate the national union line at a local level in informal ways, and, less often through precinct organization, see discipline in the political sphere as a normal part of trade-union loyalty; (6) all this adds up to increased political interest and activity both in and out of the union, and, when the available "friends of labor" are mainly liberal Democrats, it gives the political focus of the activists a broader "labor-liberal" flavor.[20]

STRUCTURAL ROOTS OF IDEOLOGICAL DIVERSITY: THE LIMITS OF CLASS ANALYSIS

That we find some workers who are class conscious even in a Marxian sense, that we can point to a labor vote which pro-labor politicians count on should not obscure equally important and perhaps increasingly important facts about American society. The membership of American labor organizations is only about a

[20] Harold L. Wilensky, "The Labor Vote . . ." *op. cit.*, p. 120. Cf. two sample surveys of the Detroit area—Dodge, *op. cit.*, and Arthur Kornhauser, A. J. Mayer, and H. L. Sheppard, *When Labor Votes* (New York: University Books, 1956). The latter found, for a general UAW population, what appeared in the Chicago local that I examined. Cf. two case studies which showed a positive relation between activity and acceptance of labor political effort. Arnold Rose, *Union Solidarity* (Minneapolis: University of Minnesota Press, 1952), pp. 79, 165 and J. Seidman, J. London, and B. Karsh, "Political Consciousness in a Local Union," *Public Opinion Quarterly*, XV (1951–1952), 692–702. Though popular speculation is abundant, systematic analysis of the character of labor as a political force is rare. In addition to Seidman *et al.*, Kornhauser *et al.*, and Wilensky, see F. Calkins, *The CIO and the Democratic Party* (Chicago: The University of Chicago Press, 1952); and H. E. Freeman and M. Showel, "Differential Political Influence of Voluntary Associations," *Public Opinion Quarterly*, XV (1951–1952), 703–714. The latter, on the basis of a pre-election survey in 1950 in the state of Washington using an area probability sample, concludes that business, political, and veterans' associations exert *widest* positive influence; labor and church organizations, *narrowest*. Unions, like the Catholic Church, apparently achieved high saturation of a small target; positive influence was confined to their own membership; in fact, labor's hypothetical endorsement had a negative effect on candidate preference among nonmembers.

third of all nonagricultural employees, compared with more than half in England and more than two-thirds in Sweden. American labor is conservative. Compared to European labor, it shows a low degree of class consciousness. Its leaders have become integrated into the power and status structure of a private-enterprise economy and a pressure-group polity. The mass of unorganized wage and salaried workers is similarly integrated into the mainstream of community life.

These characteristics of American labor can be explained in large part by the impact of continued economic growth on the structure of opportunity. If, on the whole, the rich were getting richer, and the poor, poorer; if occupations were becoming more manual and less skilled; if depressions were frequent and severe; if, in short, the opportunity to rise in the social and economic scale was declining while mass aspirations were rising, we might expect American labor to swing in a politically class-conscious direction. The evidence suggests just the opposite.

Occupational and income changes have brought a vast heterogeneity to the labor force. This heterogeneity is epitomized by the growing middle layers of American society—the new middle class of white-collar and professional people, the increasingly skilled upper crust of manual workers. Advanced specialization has made for finer distinctions of status and a multiplication of occupational worlds. Instead of two armies massed on an industrial battlefield—"labor" on one side, "capital" on the other—we have immense variation in interest and attitude within the ranks of each, and a consequent decline in the solidarity of each.[21] On the management side, the complexity of internal cleavages follows the increased complexity of organization—with increased bargaining over power and budget between staff advisors of specialized knowledge and power-conscious executives, between levels of authority, or on the same level of authority between rival advisors and rival supervisors. Although it is still useful to distinguish between the managers and the managed, the lines are becoming a bit blurred. On the labor side, even unionized

21 Wilbert E. Moore, "Occupational Structure and Industrial Conflict," in *Industrial Conflict*, edited by Arthur Kornhauser and others (New York: McGraw-Hill, 1954), pp. 221 ff.

27

workers divide on age, sex, seniority, and skill lines, not to mention the divisions by religion, nationality, and race. Union or nonunion, American workers display much diversity in values, beliefs, and ways of life.

Much of this diversity in the culture and structure of American life in general and the "working class" in particular has been blurred by the competing myths of the affluent worker and of the persistence of poverty. Like all myths, they contain partial truths. Let us first consider the myth of proletarian affluence, then the myth of the "Other America," uniform in its poverty culture.

The Affluent Worker and Middle-Class Culture

By world standards, many skilled workers are indeed rich, having family incomes of eight or ten thousand dollars a year.[22] But, in millions of homes, it takes two jobs and often many overtime hours (for which workers are generally eager) to put the family in the middle bracket. When it arrives, its affluence is typically unsteady. Over his lifetime, the affluent worker, like most workers, typically shifts about, moving from job to job, occupation to occupation, with periods of unemployment or retraining punctuating a cycle of ups and downs. Thus, we must be cautious when we hear that American workers are adopting middle-class styles of life or—more broadly—that, on both sides of the Iron Curtain, a culture peculiar to the working class is all but dead. The lines between upper working class and lower middle class— between the mass of foremen, craftsmen, and high-paid operatives, on the one hand and the mass of salesmen, clerks, small entrepreneurs, managers with few subordinates, semiprofessional,

[22] The median annual income of male "craftsmen, foremen, and kindred" twenty-five to sixty-four years old in the civilian labor force in 1959 was 5444 dollars, more than the 5216 dollars of "clerical and kindred workers," the 4645 dollars of "operatives and kindred," or the 3504 dollars of "laborers, except farm and mine." Comparable figures for three or four person families with two or more earners were: 7206 dollars for households headed by craftsmen and operatives combined, 5164 dollars for those headed by laborers. U.S. Bureau of the Census, *Census of Population 1960*, Final Report PC(2)–7B; "Occupation by Earnings and Education" (U.S. Department of Commerce, U.S. Government Printing Office, Washington, D.C., 1964).

semitechnical people, on the other—these lines are blurring. But much of working-class culture persists.[23]

Mass education has made at least high school available to all; manual workers, like white-collar workers, commonly want a college education for their children. But education means something different for each stratum. For his daughters, the worker less often counts on college, and for his sons, he tends to see it in strictly vocational terms. Middle-class parents, in contrast, are more egalitarian, broader in their aspirations. They expect education to pay off at once in a better job, a more enjoyable life, and skills in "getting along with other people." And, although the proportion of working-class children in college is rising, it is still lower than that in the lower middle class. Further, the type of college—community or junior college, or a mass state university —is typically both less desirable and less costly.

It is the same with housing. A satirical song by Malvina Reynolds spoofs suburbia in these phrases:

> Little boxes on the hillside,
> Little boxes made of ticky-tacky,
> Little boxes on the hillside,
> Little boxes all the same,
>
> There's a green one and a pink one
> A blue one and a yellow one,
> And they all are made out of ticky-tacky
> And they all look just the same.[24]

The idea is that suburban tract-housing is uniform and depressing, as are the people in it. Although we lack solid data on this matter, it is likely that the working-class couple, more than their middle-class counterpart, is moved to buy one of the boxes because of previous subordination to a landlord or previous experience with racial conflict in the central city. For workers, suburban homeownership is a flight to freedom; for middle strata it is

[23] The next three paragraphs rely in part on essays by G. Handel and L. Rainwater, S. M. Miller and F. Riessman in A. B. Shostak and W. Gomberg (eds.), *Blue-Collar World: Studies of the American Worker* (Englewood Cliffs, N.J.: Prentice-Hall, 1964), in part of my own observations and data.

[24] Words and music by Malvina Reynolds. Copyright © 1962 by Schroder Music Company. Used by permission.

more a routine validation of status. (For both, of course, it is mainly a search for more space and better schools for their children. And the uniformity of appearances is not confined to the suburbs.)

Differences in the quality and meaning of education and houses lead to differences in how these strata spend their money. They buy similar homes, the same automobiles, and other consumer durables; but workers spend far less for services than their middle-class colleague. The carpenter, in contrast to the bank teller, doesn't hire other craftsmen to fix up his home or car-washers and mechanics to clean and repair his car; he tends to do them himself. And as his wife confronts the family washing, she is unlikely to consult a commercial laundry or diaper service; she does it at home. For outings, the worker falls more easily into an aimless Sunday drive culminating in a park or a "drive-in" with food or film, rather than dinner in a downtown restaurant. For vacations, he is more likely to stay at home or visit relatives than to travel long distances for a planned adventure.

I believe that the differences that divide the upper working class from the lower middle class—differences in career prospects, in the quality and meaning of housing, in the uses of money and leisure—are not so great as the contrasts between the stable upper half of the working class and the depressed lower half. Unemployment rates are far higher among semiskilled operatives, unskilled laborers, and service workers than among other manual workers.[25] Their work histories are more chaotic. They face more obstacles to upward escape. They lack sophistication in shopping, are susceptible to "easy credit," and are therefore entangled in debt and victimized in the market place. The natural title for a recent study of the consumption patterns of low-income families in New York City is *The Poor Pay More*.[26] Like the lower class everywhere, they receive less of every reward modern society offers—economic security, physical safety and health, living space, and

[25] In November 1963, the unemployment rate for craftsmen, foremen, and kindred was only 3.9 per cent compared to 11.9 per cent for laborers, 7.2 per cent for operatives, 5.8 per cent for service workers (excluding private household). U.S. Department of Labor, Bureau of Labor Statistics, "Monthly Report on the Labor Force" (November 1964), p. 30.

[26] David Caplowitz, *The Poor Pay More* (New York: The Free Press of Glencoe, 1963).

opportunity for education and interesting work. The major response to this unyielding and unpredictable environment is retreat. The lower classes are more apathetic politically and more isolated socially (their ties to kin and friends are few and weak). Their leisure is more privatized (they often eat, drink, and watch television alone). Their family lives are unstable and impoverished (broken homes among some lower-class groups constitute a majority).[27] Exposed to sustained stress and lacking strong primary group support to cushion it, their rate of mental illness is startlingly higher than that of the majority of America. Divide the population into five strata by income and occupational prestige, and you will see only small differences in rates of treated psychiatric illness as you move from the top through the upper working class. Pass to the bottom fifth and the rate leaps up to almost three times that of any other stratum.[28]

My theme that the upper working class is closer to the lower middle class than either is to the poor is at first blush contradicted by some research reporting behavior and attitudes of skilled workers which is similar to those of the less skilled. Such findings usually result from weak classifications. For instance, a detailed study based on two nationwide surveys comparing "clerical, sales"; "craftsmen, foremen"; and "operatives" shows that the latter two are similar in level of organizational affiliation, types of affiliation, union membership, religious involvement, media behavior, politics, homeownership, and attitudes toward education and foreign affairs.[29] Such studies not only fail to use a control for education, they also lump stably-employed, high-income operatives with the rest to form the lowest stratum, thereby obscuring crucial differences between the two halves of the working class. Where the similarities are not a result of spurious classifica-

27 One of the best reviews of evidence is Genevieve Knupfer, "Portrait of the Underdog," in Reinhart Bendix and Seymour M. Lipset, eds., *Class, Status, and Power* (New York: The Free Press of Glencoe, 1953), pp. 255–263. Cf. Michael Harrington, *The Other America: Poverty in the United States* (New York: Macmillan, 1962).

28 August B. Hollingshead and Frederick C. Redlich, *Social Class and Mental Illness* (New York: John Wiley, 1958). The neurotic and psychotic poor rarely rest on the analyst's couch; instead, they ignore symptoms or take pills or find themselves incarcerated in custodial mental institutions.

29 Richard F. Hamilton, "The Behavior and Values of Skilled Workers," in Shostak and Gomberg, eds., *op. cit.*, pp. 42–57.

tion but are real, they are found most often in politics and in the uses of the mass media and mass entertainment—sources of cultural standardization that are powerful in every modern state.[30]

Persistent differences in structure and culture between the upper working and lower middle classes and the even greater gulf between both of these and the depressed lower class are matched by great diversity within each stratum. The point can be illustrated by the social composition of the American poor.

The Many Faces of Poverty

Most Americans consider Mississippi a national disgrace. The median annual personal income of Negroes in Jackson, Mississippi, in 1959 was only 944 dollars a year. Yet that same year, per capita income in Puerto Rico—a model of an underdeveloped area that has achieved economic success, a commonwealth whose prosperity puts it in the upper quarter of the world's nations—was 819 dollars, less than that of the mainland's most deprived urban citizens.[31]

Or consider possessions. A study of 464 families in four low-income housing projects in Manhattan, whose median annual income in 1960 was 3000 dollars, found that, in spite of their weak economic position and shaky credit rating, all but 5 per cent owned at least one television set; three in five owned a phonograph; two in five, a sewing machine; two in five, an automatic washing machine; one in four, a vacuum cleaner; and one in seven, an automobile.[32]

Plainly, American poverty is not like the grinding poverty of two-thirds of the world's population. It is poverty relative to the

[30] Harold L. Wilensky, "Mass Society and Mass Culture," *American Sociological Review,* XXIX (1964), 173–197.

[31] U.S. Bureau of the Census, *Census of Population: 1960* (Washington, D.C., 1963), pp. 26–159, reports nonwhite personal income in the Jackson Standard Metropolitan Area; Vol. 1, 53–130, reports income of persons fourteen years of age and older in Puerto Rico. The annual per capita income in India in the early sixties was about 70 dollars. Central Statistical Organization, Department of Statistics, Government of India, "Estimates of National Income 1948–1949 to 1962–1963" (February 1964), Table 1, p. 1 (counting one rupee as twenty-one cents, 339.4 rupees would make 71.27 dollars). Cf. Paul Studensky, *The Income of Nations* (Washington Square: New York University Press, 1958), pp. 228–233, esp. Table 16–3.

[32] Caplowitz, *op. cit.,* p. 37.

comfortable life of the vast majority of Americans. It is not thereby less poignant, less miserable. A minority poor, surrounded by affluence, can feel its deprivation more deeply than the majority poor of Asia, Africa, and Latin America, whose poverty is traditional. And a minority poor may be more of a drag on the conscience of the rich, as we can see when a moderately conservative president feels compelled to declare "war on poverty."

In the current debate about poverty in the midst of plenty, it is generally agreed that one-fifth to one-fourth of the population of the United States lives below a culturally and politically defined poverty line. Who are they?

If we say that an annual income of less than 3000 dollars for a family of four makes them poor, we find that about one in five of the household heads is nonwhite, one in four is a woman heading a broken home, one in three is over sixty-five. In fact, half the poor, compared to a fifth of the general population, have one or more of these three characteristics: over sixty-five, nonwhite, or female heading a household. In spite of this high incidence of poverty among the aged, women, and Negroes, however, it is important to note another concentration: a majority of all the poor, especially the chronically poor, are white, rural, Southern populations—stuck in America's underdeveloped area.[33]

Some of the poor live on welfare checks, some on pensions; some are employed, others not; some are sick, others well; some are refugees from rural poverty, others are veterans of the urban slums; some are migratory workers following the seasons and the crops, others are fixed in low-paid jobs as watchmen and housemaids. A declining fraction of the poor were part of the old immigration from southern and eastern Europe; increasing millions are their minority successors—Puerto Ricans, Mexican-Americans, and the new migrants from the southeastern United States, ranging from white mountaineers to urban Negroes.

In short, when you hear of the "working class," you must ask yourself, "Is it the underdog, down and out, going nowhere in a

[33] Committee on Education and Labor, House of Representatives, 88th Congress, Second Session, *Economic Opportunity Act of 1964* (March 1964), Part I, pp. 33–34, 38, 41. Robert J. Lampman, "The Low Income Population and Economic Growth," *Study Paper Number 12*, Joint Economic Committee of Congress, December 16, 1959.

disorganized way, or the factory worker, getting by despite some ups and downs?" When you hear of "skilled craftsmen and foremen," ask, "Are their jobs disciplined, leaving little room for discretion in pacing and timing of work, little choice of tools and techniques, or do their jobs provide much freedom?"[34] Ask, too, where did they come from and where are they going? Were they reared on a farm or not; did they follow their fathers' footsteps in a guild-like craft; move up from the bottom or down from the middle? Have their work histories been full of ups and downs, with intermittent attempts to set up a business of their own, or do they display an orderly job progression? Are they young strivers who expect steady moves to a high-income peak or men in their forties who have given up the race? Finally, when you hear of the "lower class," it helps to know whether they are the welfare poor, the aged poor, or the deserted-woman poor; whether they are militant young Negroes or apathetic old men on Skid Row.

UNSCRAMBLING THE CRITERIA FOR CLASS

The fragmentation of the working class suggested by these examples—indeed the diversity of structure and culture of every stratum—is the main reason that American sociologists have not been impressed with a Marxist framework for the analysis of political conflict in modern society. Instead, they have usually viewed classes as layers in a hierarchical system of ranks differentiated by gradual distinctions. The forms of stratification that are most prominent in American society are power and authority (the Marxist concern), occupational prestige, income and wealth, education, and descent (ethnic, racial, and often religious origin). Sociologists sometimes combine two or more of these criteria of stratification—most commonly occupation and income—and use the label "socioeconomic status." As I have shown above, much behavior and many attitudes are undoubtedly related to strata so defined; political orientations and styles of life are to some extent anchored in socioeconomic position. It is not the ideological conservatism of sociologists that has moved

34 Harold L. Wilensky, "Varieties of Work Experience," in Henry Borow, ed., *Man in a World at Work* (Boston: Houghton Mifflin, 1964), pp. 125-154.

them to adopt this view of class; on the contrary, it is the facts themselves that have forced them to a more discriminating analysis fitting the diversity of American life.

But sociologists have not, in fact, gone far enough in unscrambling the components of class, and they have sometimes abandoned the search for cleavages that count. The "end of ideology," the end of class war, is not the end of conflict. Whether or not social conflict ever had a simple economic basis, it appears that, in contemporary American life, two of the more significant factors in "class" consciousness are occupational groups and the educational institutions from which they recruit, and minority groups based on ethnicity, religion, and above all race. The influence of these groups may be somewhat softened by mobility, but they are, nevertheless, critical to an analysis of social class.

Education, Occupational Group, and Authority

That the upper strata are more class conscious than others suggests the overriding importance of education as it relates to authority, especially to the authority of expertise. Education is increasingly important as a basis of rank, as a source of authority, and as a determinant of life style. There is reason to expect this to happen in every rich country. Education is becoming the main barrier to social mobility and political power, but it is a barrier through which more and more millions pass. Further, the mass education system required by modern economies is one which trains and sorts people out for vastly varied careers and occupational groups. Thus, to insist on "occupation" as a definer of class is to insist on the importance of the content and quality of education and of the diverse tasks, work schedules, occupational groups, and work places to which various levels and kinds of education lead. Census-type "occupational strata" are accidents of measurement which obscure such variations.

The few careful empirical studies that weigh more than one aspect of social position support this view. In his analysis of *Communism, Conformity, and Civil Liberties* during the McCarthy era, the late Samuel A. Stouffer showed that education was much more powerful than occupational stratum as a predictor of the tolerance of political and personal deviance.[35] A study in France ranked eleventh occupational strata as to mean age, mean education, and four different clues to levels of living —property, auto, servant, and telephone. The only variable that consistently ranks all the white-collar strata above each of the manual and farm strata is education.[36] Wherever education and occupational group are played against general occupational stratum, they turn out to be more important as sources of a wide range of behavior.[37]

Race, Religion, Ethnicity, and Locality

Students of stratification often speak of class or class consciousness when it is more appropriate to speak of race consciousness, or the consciousness of a religious community or ethnic group sharing a common neighborhood. It is when "class," in economic terms, is combined with race, religious-ethnic origins, and locality that we find Marxist "class" consciousness in its most intense form. The Negro ghetto, the Polish-Catholic neighborhood, the craft union dominated by second- or third-generation German-American Lutherans—this is where solidarity prevails.

For instance, of three groups of Detroit Negroes hard hit by the 1957–1958 recession, fifty men displaced by an auto plant shutdown were asked, "If a bad depression were to happen again, what do you think would happen?" The modal responses were (1) Collective violence—revolution, rioting, and so on—28 per cent (". . . we would have a revolution and knock out a few of these capitalists who dog it and hog it"; "I don't see much hope for the country. These youngsters aren't going to take what we

[35] Based on a secondary analysis of Stouffer's data. Seymour M. Lipset, "Democracy and Working-Class Authoritarianism," *American Sociological Review*, XXIV (1959), 489. The occupational strata: low manual, high manual, low white collar, high white collar.

[36] Marcel Bresard, "Mobilité sociale et dimension du la famille," *Population*, V (1950), 533–566. Cf. O. D. Duncan, "Methodological Issues in the Analysis of Social Mobility," in Neil Smelser and Seymour M. Lipset, eds., *Social Structure, Mobility, and Economic Development* (Chicago: Aldine Press, 1965), in press.

[37] Harold L. Wilensky, "Varieties of Work Experience," *op. cit.*, p. 147; and "Mass Society . . . ," *op. cit.*, pp. 184–186.

took in the depression. They will tear up the country.") (2) Individual acts of violence—assault, killing, and the like—18 per
cent ("We won't have no country. There'll be fighting, stealing,
starving. No one will have no chance. Not even the rich man,")
These were high seniority semiskilled workers who had achieved
a foothold in Detroit industry and partial homeownership. An
almost identical distribution of response—about half projecting
violence—was found in two other Negro samples, one in a close-
knit Negro neighborhood with radical leadership and younger
population, half of which was unemployed (N = 32), the other in
a neighborhood chosen for comparable deprivation but without
political organization (N = 39). Most of these seventy-one Negroes
had experienced considerable recent unemployment, or the threat
of it, by virtue of low seniority position; the data suggest that the
most deprived are most prone to "violent" verbal responses.[38]
There is also some evidence that, holding income and skill constant, Polish-Americans are more militantly class conscious than
German-Americans, and Negroes are more class conscious than
either. Generally, the lower the ethnic-religious or racial status,
the more Marxist the view of class relations.[39]

At the same time, working-class militancy often reflects the
solidarity of occupational communities with an ethnic and religious base. Guild-like fraternities of Protestant printers or carpenters, third-generation Italian blue-collar neighborhoods in
Boston, metropolitan police departments dominated by Irish
Catholics, a succession of minority groups in the needle trades,
with the early Jewish and Italian garment workers giving way
to Negroes and Puerto Ricans—these are ready examples of the
convergence of occupation, minority origin, and locality.

That religious-ethnic and racial groups heavily influence the

38 D. Street and John C. Leggett, "Economic Deprivation and Extremism:
A Study of Unemployed Negroes," *American Journal of Sociology*, LXVII
(1961), 53–57, and Harold L. Wilensky and Hugh Edwards, "The Skinner: Ideo-
logical Adjustments of Downwardly Mobile Workers," *American Sociological
Review*, XXIV (1959), 215–231. The most strongly alienated men in my cur-
rent study are Negro high-school graduates on relief. Harold L. Wilensky,
"Types of Mobility and Their Measurement," in Neil Smelser and Seymour
M. Lipset, *op. cit.*

39 John C. Leggett, "Uprootedness . . . ," p. 687, and Bruno Bettelheim
and Morris Janowitz, *Special Change and Prejudice* (New York: The Free
Press of Glencoe, 1964), Chapter 2.

political behavior of their members is both an assumption of every urban politician and a finding of every major study of voting patterns. Indeed, in every presidential election from Truman to Johnson, race and religion, not class, have been the most important bases of voting blocs and voting shifts.[40]

Mobility and Class

If there is any force as powerful as minority origin as a source of the ideological diversity of the working class, it is social mobility—frequent moves between jobs, occupations, employers, and between communities, and from rural to urban areas. Some mobility involves social discontinuity—the movement between positions—whether up, down, or across—is major, sudden, unpredictable, and necessitates disruption of ties to kin and friends. The painful transformation from peasant to proletarian, farm to factory, and alien to citizen which characterized the early industrialization of America epitomizes discontinuous mobility—and, as we have seen, it can produce class consciousness and political protest. But other kinds of mobility can be orderly, predictable, and smooth, as in the gradual unfolding of a secure and stable career. A dampening of class consciousness is the most common result. In any case, high rates of mobility assure a continual shift of ambitious manual workers out of the working class and a smaller but significant downward movement of unsuccessful men from the middle.

The political and ideological effects of social mobility depend, not only on the type of mobility, but on the economic context in which it occurs. In less developed countries characterized by low per capita income, low levels of education, few ladders for mobility, and an explosion of both population and expectations, a high rate of discontinuous mobility are likely to produce social disorganization and political disruption. In these countries, the loosening of traditional ties without the immediate substitution

[40] See, for instance, Berelson et al., op. cit. Catholics among the Eisenhower Democrats of 1952 and 1956 made major shifts to President Kennedy in 1960. More than nine in ten Negro voters of 1964 lined up for President Johnson. Jews have shown almost as much uniformity in presidential voting preferences as Negroes.

of new ones provokes disaffection; nationalist and other extremist movements provide the context for the fervent expression of this disaffection.

The effect of a similarly high rate of discontinuous mobility in rich countries is more variable, although there is consensus on one line of argument. These countries are characterized by high per capita income, a high proportion of men educated beyond elementary school, a high degree of social differentiation, and therefore a large number of discrete ladders for mobility. They can sustain a large population, contain the political effects of a rise in expectations, and cushion or contain the effects of even high rates of downward mobility. The more education and income, the more urgent and widespread are great expectations; but the more differentiation, the more opportunity for their fulfillment and the more consolation prizes for those who lose out. The ladders which a man can climb are so numerous that falling behind on one or falling off another may neither cause an irrevocable loss of social position nor yield much sense of deprivation. For instance, my data show that intergenerational skidders—men whose occupations rank below their fathers—tend to marry up. Men who achieve less education than their fathers or stay on the same level (which in the United States means losing out) tend to marry women with superior education from families with occupational status higher than their own. Many skidders also marry up ethnically.[41] Other studies have reported a low correlation between income and occupational prestige; many note the high economic and occupational status of some minority groups.

Reinforcing these structural constraints on class consciousness are the cultural correlates of economic growth, particularly a success ideology which accents personal responsibility for work performance and job fate. In poor countries, which usually lack this ideology, the response to intergenerational or worklife "skidding" is externalized; it is readily channeled into collective political protest. In rich countries, the same skidding leads to self-blame, a sense of shame, and withdrawal from social contact. At the extreme, skidding and other forms of discontinuity produce

41 Harold L. Wilensky, "Types of Mobility . . . ," op. cit.

suicide—self-destruction, not societal destruction.[42] In the typical case, however, skidding is rationalized, often realistically, as a temporary setback; in American data we usually find that skidders and fluctuators are more like upwardly mobile than non-mobile men. Skidders tend to retain the values and practices of the class from which they slipped and to which they expect to return.[43] Perhaps this is the best single explanation for "working class Tories"—that third of manual workers in the United States who vote Republican, the similar proportion of the British working class who vote Conservative. Mobile workers moving in either direction, along with other workers who escape from working-class culture in spirit or practice, function to reduce working-class solidarity and social criticism from below—and thereby slow down the push toward equality.

Although the prospects of individual mobility out of the working class and the experience of falling into it from above provide a powerful force for ideological heterogeneity, the movement of *groups* may have a reverse effect. If an entire stratum, craft, or profession is declining, there is more chance of unity in misery and a collective protest—scapegoating or lashing out against symbols of oppression. The tendency is evident in the populism of family farmers facing corporate competitors or of grain-growers dependent on banks and railroads, in the anti-Semitism of obso-

[42] Comparing 103 white male suicides, age twenty to sixty and 206 men matched for race and age, Breed found that three in four of the suicides had suffered at least one form of downward mobility (intergenerational skidding, 53 per cent; recent income loss, 51 per cent; recent worklife skidding, 35 to 43 per cent depending on the base and scale used)—far more than the controls. Also, only half the suicides were working full-time just before they did away with themselves. Warren Breed, "Occupational Mobility and Suicide Among White Males," *American Sociological Review*, XXVIII (1963), 179–188. Cf. similar findings in Andrew F. Henry and James F. Short, Jr., *Suicide and Homicide* (New York: The Free Press of Glencoe, 1954); Austin L. Porterfield and Jack P. Gibbs, "Occupational Prestige and Social Mobility of Suicides in New Zealand," *American Journal of Sociology*, LXVI (1960), 147–152, confirming the original formulation in 1897 of Émile Durkheim in *Suicide* (New York: The Free Press of Glencoe, 1951).

[43] Harold L. Wilensky and H. Edwards, "The Skidder: Ideological Adjustments of Downwardly Mobile Workers," *American Sociological Review*, XXIV (1959), 215–231, and P. M. Blau, "Social Mobility and Interpersonal Relations," *American Sociological Review*, XXI (1956), 290–295. I estimate that skidders are perhaps a fifth of the working class of urban background, a tenth of all urbanites in the labor force—in time of recession, more.

lescent craftsmen, in the political extremism of small businessmen —the franchised dealer dependent on the big-business supplier, the small manufacturer dependent on one corporate customer, and the retail proprietor threatened by chain stores and discount houses.[44] Such responses are less likely and do not spread if they occur when the position of the group or stratum is stable but when the individual is threatened.

No rich country of the sixties can rule out political responses to social discontinuity until we study vanguard populations such as engineers and technicians. When these college men are displaced or thwarted, we have no reason to suppose that they will be as apathetic or personally disorganized as displaced workers in the same affluent context. Even small reverses (or threats of reverses) owing to industry cutbacks or area recessions can provoke a collective political response. An obvious research implication is to discover types of discontinuities in the lives of Goldwater activists in the mid-sixties and their counterparts in other rich countries.

The most important qualification to my consolation-prize hypothesis concerns education. If educational opportunity whets the appetite for a better life, but does not lead to job oppor-

---

[44] In my samples, as in many other studies, the "little man" who feels squeezed by both big enterprise and big labor is more prone to both extremism and scapegoating than others in the same social class. For instance, of the twenty-nine self-employed men of the middle mass who felt squeezed, 38 per cent recalled Senator Joseph McCarthy with enthusiasm—this in 1960, several years after his demise. Of the thirty-seven comparable entrepreneurs who did *not* feel squeezed, only 14 per cent were retrospective McCarthyites. Felt power squeeze is generally a better predictor of McCarthyism than blocked mobility strivings, especially among small entrepreneurs. Cf. Martin Trow, "Small Businessmen, Political Tolerance, and Support for McCarthy," *American Journal of Sociology*, LXIV (1958), 270–281; and David Rogers, "The Automobile Dealer: A Study of the Status and Ideology of the Small Businessman" (unpublished doctoral dissertation, Harvard University, 1960). On rural radicals, see Seymour M. Lipset, *Agrarian Socialism* (Berkeley: University of California Press, 1950). A French sociologist, studying 206 randomly-selected furniture-makers of the Seine Department, finds that they tend to lead solitary lives; two in five of the artisans in this declining occupation evidenced anti-Semitic sentiments. In contrast to American findings, however, the most deprived individuals within this generally obsolescent, anti-Semitic group were no more prejudiced than the least deprived. Simone Francès *Òu va L'Artisanat français?* (Paris: Centre National de la Recherche Scientifique, 1961), pp. 100–105, 121. Cf. Bruno Bettelheim and Morris Janowitz, *op. cit.*, Chapter 2 and p. 164.

tunity and income, it serves less as a compensatory reward than as a source of resentment. Thus, as their educational opportunities exceed their economic rewards and living standards, American Negroes will become more militant. Educated whites already receive roughly congruent rewards, and their political discontents are kept within manageable proportions; uneducated whites, if they are not lucky in the labor market, at least have a chance to shuck off lower ethnic or religious origins or marry up.

SUMMARY AND CONCLUSIONS

The uncritical acceptance of Marx by European scholars and activists has been matched by the avoidance or distortion of Marx by American students of stratification. Happily there is convergence on a middle ground where the great diversity of life styles and political orientations within every social class is clear to everyone at the same time that the facts of power and the clash of competing interests are not lost to view.

Class consciousness in the Marxian manner has appeared for brief periods during America's early industrialization, especially from the Civil War to World War I. It now appears as a response to discontinuous mobility among some rural migrants to our metropolitan slums, as the political stance of a few small fraternities of craftsmen and union activists who say that voting Democratic is voting the workingman's ticket and of those upper and upper-middle class families who think that voting Republican is voting against the welfare state; and as the militancy of hard-pressed minority groups, notably Negroes, in whom it is plainly more a consciousness of race than of class. In general, American labor has become integrated into a private enterprise economy and a pressure-group polity.

The social classes are slowly merging, especially in the bulging middle; standards of living of the upper working and lower middle classes are becoming similar. But some differences remain—differences in career prospects, in the quality and meaning of housing, in the uses of money and leisure. More impressive are the differences that divide the middle mass from the poor. Though the poverty of the American lower class is not the poverty of a Chinese peasant or a peon in northern Brazil, it may nonetheless put them in sharp contrast to their fellow citizens. Economic insecurity, social isolation, political apathy, family instability, mental and physical illness—these are the burdens of the remaining American poor.

Such strata—upper and lower middle, upper and lower working class—are not neat economic or occupational categories. In fact, if there is any one thing that divides them, it is educational level—increasingly a source of authority, of rank, of life style. And most important, each stratum contains within it enormous cultural and structural variation. I have discussed three powerful sources of diversity within the American working class. First is the organization of work and the nature of work experience; the separate worlds of work multiply. All rich countries display astonishing specialization by job and occupation. All develop mass-education systems whose diversity of curriculums feeds the demands of specialization.

Second is the pervasive influence of mobility. A modern population is a population on the move. For the working class, that means a large minority on the way up and out, another minority freshly down from the middle class—both sources of Tory ideology and political action. Further, the channels for mobility are multiplying as rich countries become richer. If we wish to deal with the individual's mobility experience as a source of ideology, we must bring into view all the possibilities—not merely changes in occupational status, but changes in education, income, residence, possessions, and leisure style—even the chance to escape lowly social origins by marrying up. Some of this mobility is downward, disorderly, even painful, but the pain of loss in one sphere is often offset by the pleasure of gains in another. In an environment of expanding opportunity, in the context of an ideology of success, a man who finally fails, who is blocked in every sphere, blames himself.

The third major source of diversity within the American working class is the persistent hold of religious-ethnic and racial groups. A minority man is born into this system of ranks, and he carries its mark for life, even if he later changes his religious affiliation or assimilates to the dominant white Anglo-Saxon Protestant (WASP) culture. Where skin color serves as a basis of discrimination and prejudice, the mark of minority status is, of course, permanent. For generations to come, Negroes will be a force for cleavage in the working class.

To these major sources of diversity, we must add the usual divisions by sex, age, seniority, competing crafts, and rival unions. Together, these tendencies dampen the class struggle, fragment the working class, and reduce its "class consciousness."

A slow merging of upper working and lower middle classes, a sharper distinction between both and the poorest fifth, increasing heterogeneity within each broad stratum—these trends impose limits on any "class" analysis and make Marxist categories virtually irrelevant. When we search for political attitudes that express class consciousness and then specify the groups involved and analyze their origins and prospects, the idea of class crumbles, and we are forced to search for other, more weighty forms of social differentiation. We can best look at modern society as a loose collection of overlapping communities of work, religion and ethnicity, race, class, and locality held together mainly by economic interdependence, by legal, military, and political institutions, and by the media of mass communication and entertainment. There is no class struggle here. Instead, we find a much more complicated fluid accommodation among shifting coalitions of interest groups.

This chapter draws on ideas and data in Harold L. Wilensky, "The Problems and Prospects of the Welfare State," in Harold L. Wilensky and C. N. Lebeaux, *Industrial Society and Social Welfare* (New York: The Free Press, 1965), and my *Work, Leisure, and Freedom* (New York: The Free Press, forthcoming).

3 CHANGING LIVING STANDARDS OF AMERICAN LABOR

Ewan Clague

"Standards of living—the goals we set for ourselves as consumers of goods and services and as users of leisure time, and our norms for conditions of work—have always been a dynamic economic factor in the United States."[1]

HISTORICAL IMPORTANCE OF STANDARDS OF LIVING

The current high level of consumption and standard of living of American workers reflect more than a century of industrial and economic growth, accompanied by important technological changes and changes in the characteristics of the population and social structure. A compelling desire to improve their way of life brought the first settlers to the eastern seaboard and made them and their children willing to accept the material privation of the frontiers as they pushed westward. They experienced firsthand the rising levels of living that accompanied increased productivity and sought to establish social and political systems to help them achieve these goals. Thus, recognition that the essential purpose of political action is the improvement of the level of living of citizens has been our political heritage.

Before 1860, the rural character of 80 per cent of the population, the lack of communications, the abundance of free land, and the preoccupation with land development generally made living problems and working conditions matters of local concern. However, the dominant economic thinker of this period, Henry

[1] Faith M. Williams, "Standards and Levels of Living of City-Worker Families," *Monthly Labor Review* (September 1956), 1016.

C. Carey, advanced the basic propositions that "man desires to maintain and improve his condition"; that the level of living, i.e., actual consumption, depends on the relation between capital and labor; but that "with every improvement in the quality of labour, the quantity of commodities to be divided is increased. That this increased production is attended by the power, on the part of the labourer, to retain a constantly increasing proportion of the commodities produced. He is, therefore, constantly improving in his condition."[2]

This early period saw the beginning of other ideas that have significantly affected living standards in recent years: universal free education, desirability of homeownership, and use of insurance to guarantee living standards. For example, the oldest life insurance company in continued existence in the world is the Presbyterian Ministers Fund, founded in Philadelphia in 1759. The U.S. Public Health Service was established in 1798, as the Marine Hospital Service to provide hospital care for merchant seamen. This service was financed by a twenty-cents-a-month fee from their wages—probably the first prepaid medical care in the United States.

THE INDUSTRIALIZATION PERIOD

National interest in levels and standards of living began in the mid-1860's and continued with increasing vigor thereafter. This interest grew out of the problems of living conditions caused by the rapid growth of industry, the continuous migration from farms to cities, and the immigration of workers from Europe. Between 1860 and 1900, the population increased from 31 to 76 million, with about 10 to 15 per cent of the population being foreign born. The percentage of population living in urban places doubled to 40 per cent, with the greatest increases in the large cities.

The first research and fact-finding studies of family living conditions were carried out in 1874–1875 by the Massachusetts Bureau of Labor under the direction of Carroll D. Wright. These

2 H. C. Carey, *Principles of Political Economy* (Philadelphia: Carey, Lea, & Blanchard; 1837), Vol. I, xviii, 339.

studies were concerned with the welfare of families during this period of rapid social and economic change. The study undertook to measure the welfare of the workingman's family before and after migration to the United States, to evaluate its relative welfare in the community, and to compare the levels and manners of living of workingmen's families in Massachusetts with their counterparts in Europe. Wright concluded that although, "in a majority of cases, the workingmen do not support their families by their individual earnings alone" (one-fourth to one-third of total family earnings being from children), the working classes of Massachusetts were "well fed," "well and comfortably clothed," and lived in houses that "compare most favorably with those in foreign countries and other States of the Union." He pointed out, however, the seriously inadequate housing of about one-half of the families of *unskilled* workers and the need for action on the part of the state legislature to remedy such abuses. Many of the families owned sewing machines and other labor-saving equipment, plus such items of amusement as pianos, organs, and musical instruments. More than half the families had saved money during the year.[3] However, 94 per cent of total spending went for food, shelter, fuel, and clothing, as compared with about 53 per cent today.

Edward Young, in a study of labor in Europe and America published in 1876, summarized his findings as follows:

the masses of working people throughout the country occupy comfortable homes, enjoy an abundance of good food and comfortable clothing, with opportunities for a good common-school education for their children, and possess a degree of personal independence not enjoyed on a large scale by any other laboring population on the face of the globe.[4]

He noted that a relatively high standard of living was "attested by the deep and steady current of emigration which sets toward our shores."

3 Carroll D. Wright, *Sixth Annual Report on the Statistics of Labor,* Commonwealth of Massachusetts Public Document No. 31 (Boston: 1875), Pt. IV, 221–354, 441–445.

4 Edward Young, *Labor in Europe and America* (U.S. Bureau of Statistics, Treasury, Government Printing Office, 1876), p. 820.

47

THE CONTRIBUTION OF THE IMMIGRANTS

About 90 per cent of these immigrants went into the active labor force, and it has been estimated that they constituted in excess of 25 per cent of the total labor force in the nineteenth century.[5] Although only about one-fourth of the immigrants were skilled or professional workers, they undoubtedly contributed significantly to the nation's growth by establishing new industries, passing on their skills to the native-born workers, and introducing technological improvements. The labor of the unskilled provided the necessary manpower to build the factories and the cities and to perform much of the work in the basic industries—iron and steel, textile, and mining—as well as agriculture. It is not possible to measure their total value to the growing economy, but it was undoubtedly substantial. For example, in 1876, one statistician estimated that immigrants from Germany, during the fifty-year period prior to 1870, added 2.25 billion dollars to the wealth of the nation, measured by the value of their labor.

The contribution of the immigrants to the changing standards of living and the social structure is also immeasurable. They brought with them different customs and manners of living; these were adapted to those they found and, in turn, changed existing patterns. This is perhaps most evident in patterns of food consumption in the United States, which today reflect the food habits of nations around the globe.

During the closing years of the nineteenth century, the growing trade unions did much to advance the status of all workers, but particularly of the immigrant. Using democratic processes, workers organized to bargain for higher wages and improved working conditions. The unions also established social organizations that, in addition to recreation and education, provided financial assistance to members in case of illness or death of the breadwinner.

Nationwide studies by the Federal Bureau of Labor in 1888 and 1901 revealed the influence of rising real income on levels and patterns of living. For example, expenditures for food, shelter, and clothing decreased from over 90 per cent in the 1870's

[5] Ernest Rubin, *Immigration and the Economic Growth of the United States: 1790–1914,* Conference on Research in Income and Wealth (New York: National Bureau of Economic Research, September 4–5, 1957).

to about 80 per cent of total spending, indicating a wider margin of spending for conveniences and luxuries. Studies of wages and prices revealed the relationship of productivity to high wages and low prices. The cost of subsistence as a cost of production was emphasized by economists and industrialists who were struggling with the problems of production and capital formation.

The welfare and the living standards of the workers continued to be a dominant theme in statistical research. The years before World War I were marked by advances in health and labor legislation: establishment of standards for nutrition and healthful housing, pure food and drug laws, sanitation and health regulations, women- and child-labor laws, and concerted efforts for shorter hours and factory safety regulations.

WORLD WAR I AND ITS AFTERMATH

During World War I, the impact of inflation on the standard of living became a problem of national concern. The high cost of living and the rapid increases in price levels in manufacturing and shipbuilding centers sharply reduced the purchasing power of workers who had been attracted to these centers from lower wage areas. The need for an index by which to measure the change in the prices of all goods and services that workers' families buy was evident. The Bureau of Labor Statistics conducted its third major expenditure survey, covering the years 1917–1919, and began to calculate the Consumer Price Index. This index was first published in 1921, with data back to 1913. There has been continuous study of changes in the prices of consumer goods and services since that time.

The expenditure and price data were also used to estimate the cost of different standards of living for various types of families and for different cities. The greater variety of goods and services provided in these family budgets, as compared with those provided in the standard budgets developed in 1909, attests to the substantially higher standards of living prevailing in the early 1920's. The principle that a "living wage" should provide some "comforts" was generally accepted, and rising real incomes in the 1920's enabled many families to acquire new manufactured products, such as automobiles and radios. The importance of the

49

consumer in maintaining high production levels was beginning to be recognized.

THE GREAT DEPRESSION OF THE 1930'S

In the 1930's, the rising affluence of Americans ran into world-wide depression. Emphasis shifted from higher wages to greater security. A national social-security program was adopted to protect the worker and his family from loss of income through unemployment, disability, retirement, or death. The role of the consumer in maintaining prosperity was reemphasized, and attention was focused on the need for better methods of financing consumer purchases, particularly housing and medical care.

World War II delayed the implementation of these programs, but wartime wage controls led to a demand for more "fringe benefits" in addition to cash wages and salaries. The unavailability of consumer goods during the war built up a backlog of demand, and an unprecedentedly high level of saving provided a large volume of postwar purchasing power.

STANDARDS OF LIVING IN THE 1950'S

The 1950's saw the reintroduction of the new concepts underlying wages—productivity and cost of living. Between 1950 and 1960–1961, the purchasing power of city-family income increased 22 per cent, after allowance for higher prices and personal taxes. Families consisting of wage and clerical workers showed even larger gains in real purchasing power as a result of widespread recognition of changes in consumer prices as a basis for wage increases under collective-bargaining contracts, either in formal escalator clauses or in wage-rate negotiations. There was also increased recognition of rising productivity in wage negotiations. Output per man-hour in the private economy increased about one-third during the decade. Some of this increased productivity went for more vacation and leisure time and other nonwage benefits.

The rising level of consumption and the changing manner of living during the decade reflected widespread technological changes and increased productivity in manufacturing, mining, agriculture, and marketing. Advances in the science of medicine and improved medical techniques contributed to a rising health standard. Better communications and transportation made consumers aware of a vast array of new products, from precooked and frozen dinners to color television; there was widespread and rising demand for these fruits of research.

Two postwar programs of the federal government—insured mortgages for home purchase by veterans of World War II and the Korean War and the veterans' education program—contributed to the increased level of homeownership, the movement from cities to suburban areas, and increased vocational opportunities.

Some idea of the magnitude of the increase in the standard of living prevailing in the 1950's, as compared with that of the 1920's, can be obtained by comparing the 1959 costs of "modest but adequate" budgets for self-supporting families, roughly deflated for price change, with the costs of the "minimum comfort" budgets of the early 1920's. Thus measured, living standards in the late 1950's ranged from about 55 to 85 per cent higher than those of the 1920's.

LIVING CONDITIONS IN 1960–1961

American families had reached an unprecedentedly high level of living in 1960–1961, as revealed by the pattern of spending and saving and the manner of living reported in the most recent consumer expenditure survey. Although the net purchasing power of city-family income (i.e., after adjustment for price change) had increased over the previous decade by 22 per cent, net spending for current consumption goods and services increased only 14 per cent. The margin between current consumption spending and income was used for more personal insurance, larger gifts and contributions, and higher savings.

City families spent an average of about 5,400 dollars for current annual living expenses; made gifts and contributions averaging about 300 dollars; put about 325 dollars into various life insurance and retirement funds; and, on the average, showed savings of about 175 dollars. They used only 53 per cent of their total spending for the three basic categories—food, shelter, and clothing—as compared with 57 per cent ten years before; thus, they had more left for other goods and services. They had a wide range of choice among the many kinds and qualities of consumer goods in the retail markets. Although there have been vast improvements in the growing, processing, and marketing of foods in recent years, which have greatly improved quality, variety, and availability, less than one-fourth of total spending was for food. About 10 per cent of total spending was for clothing.

HOUSING

On the average, families used about 30 per cent of their total spending for current housing expenses, including rent; homeowners' outlays for taxes, insurance, mortgage interest, and repairs; fuel, utilities, and other household operating expenses; and house furnishings and such equipment as stoves, refrigerators, washing machines, and small appliances. A little over one-half of the families owned or were buying their homes. Payments on the mortgage principal during the year represented their increased equity in these homes and were their principal saving. The houses were their major asset.

According to the 1960 Census of Housing, about three per every four renter-occupied housing units and nine per ten owner-occupied dwellings are structurally sound and have all plumbing facilities—piped hot and cold water and flush toilet and bathtub (or shower) inside the structure, for the exclusive use of the occupants of the unit. Rented dwellings, which are usually in multi-family structures, are somewhat smaller than owned dwellings, averaging 3.9 rooms as compared with 5.5 rooms. Overcrowding is a problem for some families, but 85 per cent of rented dwellings and 91 per cent of owned dwellings have one or more rooms per person. A substantial number of dwellings are new. About one-sixth of the rental units and one-third of the owned units were built in 1950 or later.

Most families have equipped their homes with a variety of house furnishings and mechanical appliances. The typical family owns rugs or other floor coverings; basic furniture for living rooms, bedrooms, and dining; a cooking stove and small cooking appliances, such as toasters and coffee makers; a mechanical refrigerator; washing machine; sewing machine; vacuum cleaner; radios; television set; and phonograph, piano, organ, or other musical instrument. Most homes have central or other installed heating, and an increasing number in the warmer areas are air-conditioned.

A NATION ON WHEELS

In the postwar years, families have been moving from the central cities into the less densely populated suburban areas, and as a result automobile ownership has increased substantially. Three-fourths of the city families are auto owners, and ownership is even higher among families living in rural areas. The extent of auto ownership varies considerably in large cities, ranging from a low of 50 per cent in the densely populated New York metropolitan area to 84 per cent in the widely spread-out Los Angeles area. The purchase and operation of these automobiles accounted for 13 per cent of total spending in 1960–1961.

CONSUMER CREDIT

American families make extensive use of credit to purchase and furnish their homes and to buy automobiles. They also use credit to improve their homes, to finance higher education for their children, and to meet large or unexpected expenses. Young families and middle-income families are the most frequent users of credit to supplement current money income and to build up an equity for the future. The paying-off of debts is sometimes referred to as "contractual saving." Borrowing to finance the purchase of homes, automobiles, and household durables enables families to acquire these goods sooner than would be possible with current earnings and to spread costs over a longer period. Borrowing also has had an important stabilizing effect on consumer demand and, hence, on the over-all level of economic activity. In 1960–1961, families had a net increase in assets over liabilities averaging about 175 dollars.

INSURANCE—GOVERNMENT AND PRIVATE

Governmental measures designed to protect the level of living of workers and their families have been greatly improved in recent years and have had a significant effect on family spending and saving. These social-welfare expenditures, which are financed by contributions from employers, employees, and self-employed persons, as well as by general tax revenue, represent about 12 per cent of the Gross National Product. They provide old-age, survivors', and disability insurance; unemployment compensation and employment service; public assistance; and a wide variety of public services, including education, health, and medical services, child welfare, and services to various groups, such as war veterans, the blind, and the disabled.

Families do not look, however, to government for all the protection that they want. They purchase private insurance of all kinds: insurance on homes, automobiles, and other personal property; health insurance and prepaid medical plans; life insurance and pensions; personal-liability insurance; and disability-income insurance. In 1960–1961, three-fourths of all city families made payments on health insurance, accounting for about one-fourth of their total medical expenses. Ninety per cent made payments amounting to about 6 per cent of their after-tax income for life insurance and public and private pension funds.

In addition, more than two-thirds of the nation's employed wage-and-salary-labor force had some form of health insurance paid for, either wholly or in part, by their employers; about three-fourths had life insurance under such arrangements; and over two-fifths had private retirement plans supplementary to social-security pension benefits.

WORKING WIVES

Wives in American families have always contributed to family income, but usually this has been done by working within the home. In recent years, employment of married women outside the home has greatly increased. About one-third of the wives are employed, with about one in ten of all wives having a year-round, full-time job. Earnings of all working wives represent about one-fifth of total family income. Those who have year-round, full-time jobs contribute about two-fifths of their family income. These working wives have thus contributed to the attainment of a higher standard of living, including acquisition of homes and better education of children, than would otherwise have been possible. The higher level of consumption made possible by their higher family income and the more limited time that they have to devote to household tasks have stimulated the development of various labor-saving devices for housekeeping and care of the family.

WORK AND LEISURE

Most workers have a forty-hour workweek. Although there has been little change in this workweek since World War II, there have been marked increases both in the prevalence and length of paid vacations provided by collective-bargaining contracts and in the number of workers eligible for such vacations. Paid holidays have also become more prevalent, increasing to an average of eight. This increased leisure has led to important changes in spending habits, particularly on vacation travel and on family activities. Participation in community activities, particularly those of religious and welfare organizations, is held in high regard by Americans, and they contribute both time and money to these activities. About 90 per cent of city families make contributions to religious and welfare organizations. These gifts amount to a little over 2 per cent of the disposable income of city families.

THE DISADVANTAGED POOR

Although most Americans have achieved a level of living that permits them to have all the essentials of living and many of the conveniences and pleasures of modern life, there are still sizable numbers of families who have not fully participated in this rising level of living. Such families include the disabled; young untrained workers; the elderly retired; members of minority groups, particularly Negroes; and the unemployed, including those who lack the skills required in modern industry and those who live in areas with little employment opportunity. Progress has been made in recent years in identifying the needs of these families and in taking steps to improve their living conditions. As mentioned earlier, there have been substantial increases in the coverage of public and private health insurance and pension plans that will contribute to higher incomes and better medical care for retired workers. Special attention is being paid by both government and private organizations to provide better housing for the elderly.

Although the average income of nonwhite families is still substantially less than that of white families, the gap has narrowed appreciably since 1939 when the median annual wage and salary income of nonwhite men was 41 per cent of that of white males; in 1960, it was 60 per cent. Incomes of nonwhite women in 1939 were 36 per cent of those of white women; in 1960, they were 50 per cent. During this time the proportion of Negroes who were employed in professional, technical, and managerial occupations about doubled, while the proportion employed as farm workers dropped from 42 to 12 per cent for Negro men, and from 16 to 4 per cent for women. Thus, the social and economic status of Negroes has risen appreciably during the past two decades.

The problem of increasing the employment opportunities of the unemployed is largely one of education, training, and retraining. American families have always recognized both the cultural and money value of an education. Studies have shown that the lifetime incomes of high school graduates are about 40 per cent higher than those of elementary school graduates, and that college graduates could expect to have a lifetime income about 70 per cent higher than that of high school graduates. The proportion of the nation's labor force completing four years of high school or more rose 70 per cent from 1940 to 1962, and the proportion completing four years of college or more, although still small (11 per cent), has nearly doubled.

THE OUTLOOK FOR THE FUTURE

In the future as in the past, maintaining and improving the level of consumption and standards of living of workers will depend on increasing employment, rising productivity, and higher real incomes. Past progress in improving living standards and working conditions has been based on increases in productivity that were consistently greater than the increases in population. This economic growth has been achieved through continuing research and advancing technology, coupled with willingness on the part of workers to work for and to accept changes. Future progress will require more attention than ever before to the education, training, and skills of the nation's labor force.

4 INCOME DISTRIBUTION OF AMERICAN LABOR

Robert J. Lampman

The typical American worker of today is remarkably affluent in comparison to his grandfather or to workers of most other countries of the world. In 1964, the median family income was 6000 dollars. In 1914, it was approximately 2500 dollars (in dollars of 1964 purchasing power). Projecting the historic rate of increase in per capita and per family income suggests that the typical worker in the next generation may expect an income of about 10,000 dollars.

Americans, who make up only 6 per cent of the world's population, produce and consume over one-third of the world's output of goods and services. Their income level is almost five or six times as high as the world's average—about twice that of Western Europe and about ten times that of Asia. This income gap has narrowed with reference to some fast-growing economies such as Japan, but, for the most part, comparative rates of growth in per capita income portend a continuing—and in some cases a widening—gap between our economic attainment and that of most other nations. Of the world's 3 billion people, only a minority live at much above subsistence levels. In this world picture, the United States stands as a mountain top—and some other nations are lesser parts of the same mountain range of high income—in a swamp of poverty and misery. The striking difference in living standards is highlighted by the fact that the average income of one of the most disadvantaged American groups, the Negroes, is above that of Frenchmen and Englishmen.

The median family income of 6000 dollars is associated with some amenities that rank with those reserved for conquerors and kings in earlier times. King Arthur and his knights of the Round Table might willingly have traded their drafty banquet halls and limited diet at Camelot for the modern houses and varied food of a Pittsburgh steelworker. And the potentates of ancient Persia would have envied the lengthened life expectancy, the reduced child mortality and morbidity, and the expanded educational opportunity which have followed the economic progress of modern times.

By any broad historical or comparative standard, the typical American worker is rich. He is rich because of the productivity of the national economy and because of the way in which the product is distributed and shared. To pursue this matter, it will help to pose and answer three questions.

1. In what form is income earned and received?
2. What degree of inequality is associated with the high average?
3. How many Americans have inadequate incomes or are what can be characterized as "poor?"

Considerable national and even international interest attends these questions. Answers to them throw light on the workings of the unique socio-political-economic system of late twentieth-century America.

IN WHAT FORM IS INCOME RECEIVED AND EARNED?

Of the total national income—which is now running at the rate of 500 billion dollars—less than one-fourth can be classified as property income. Three-fourths is payment for labor effort, including the work of farmers, managers, and professionals. In the broadest definition, most Americans are "laborers." Eighty per cent of them work for someone else; only 20 per cent (almost half of whom are of the vanishing breed of farmers) are self-employed. So it should be no surprise that the lion's share (70 per cent) of national income is in the form of "employee compensation." This share has risen with decline of self-employment and the rise of government, which now hires one out of every five employees. In the government sector there is, of course, no property income.

There is an interesting constancy to labor's income share of the total income after adjustments are made for the changing structure of the economy. Within the private sector, labor income has the same share of total income now that it had in the 1920's. However, property income has declined as a share of *personal* income because of the increasing importance of corporation taxes and of transfers. Within the employee compensation category in turn, the lion's share goes to workers other than managers and professionals: such workers in skilled, semiskilled, and unskilled occupations make up 80 per cent of employees and receive about 65 per cent of employee compensation. Within the latter group there is wide variation. An airline pilot may earn over 30,000 dollars; a migrant farm laborer, less than 1000 dollars for a year's work.

Property income in the form of profits, interest, and rent (part of which is earned by self-employed farmers, businessmen, and independent professionals) amounts to a quarter of the national income. The largest part of this is profit. Ten per cent of income is corporation profits, and a smaller share is the profits of unincorporated enterprises. Interest and rent combined amount to only 5 per cent of the national income. These forms of income from "passive ownership" total a smaller amount than is redistributed in the form of welfare-state benefits, which are also called public-income maintenance or transfer payments.

Aside from the rent of land, property income arises out of the accumulated capital invested in business enterprises and residential structures. The aggregate value of all producer wealth in the nation (excluding automobiles and other consumer durables) now approaches 2 trillion dollars and yields about 150 billion dollars of income. Personal and corporate savings add to the national business wealth at the rate of 90 billion dollars a year, thus contributing to the future productivity of labor as well as to future amounts of property income.

Property income, most notably profit, is much more unequal in its distribution than is employee compensation. It is true that certain types of property such as homes (60 per cent of American families own their own homes) and life-insurance policies are widely distributed. And it is true that 12 per cent of families own some stock in business corporations, and that millions more indirectly own business securities through insurance and bank deposits and private pension rights. However, wealth remains highly concentrated, with the top 10 per cent of families, ranked by wealth, holding over 50 per cent of the total, and the lowest one-third holding only 1 per cent. The top 1 per cent hold three-fourths of the corporate stock. Although there is validity to the characterization of the economy as a "people's capitalism" (thus there is far less wealth inequality than in England), it should not blind us to the fact most Americans still own little wealth, and most of them do not have direct title to any business wealth in the form of stocks, bonds, or equity in a farm or business. For most families, income-earning power is largely restricted to the labor power of family members and to the home they own.

There has been a stability in the over-all distribution of wealth and income which is remarkable in view of the great changes which have occurred in the economic structure and income and wealth levels. The Marxian predictions of inevitably increasing misery of the masses and of increasing concentration of wealth under capitalism have both been proved completely wrong by American experience. So far as the careful work of scholars in this field can reveal, there has been only one notable change in income inequality during this century. First documented by Simon Kuznets, this change occurred during World War II and involved a reduction in the share of income of the upper-upper income groups in favor of the upper-middle groups.[1] My own findings on the distribution of personal wealth show a moderate decline in the share of the top 2 per cent of families: from 32 per cent in 1922 to 29 per cent in 1953 and a reversal of the decline since then.[2] The 1950's were years of increasing inequality.

The trend toward equality in wealth-holding which prevailed over several decades occurred without any decline in the con-centration of business assets and as a result of a lessening in-equality in the distribution of consumer assets, including life insurance and pensions. Business assets are held today almost entirely by the top tenth of the wealth-holders, who tend, at the same time, to be the top income receivers and to be in top occupa-

---

[1] Simon Kuznets, *The Shares of Upper Income Groups in Income and Savings* (Princeton: Princeton University Press for the National Bureau of Economic Research, 1953).

[2] Robert Lampman, *The Share of Top Wealth-Holders in The National Wealth* (Princeton: Princeton University Press for the National Bureau of Economic Research, 1962).

tions—self-employed, professional, or managerial. It is, no doubt, a significant fact that, according to the Survey Research Center of the University of Michigan, the percentage of families who own stock increased from 8 per cent in 1950 to 12 per cent in 1960. This demonstrates that large numbers of people want to be and will become capitalists as their incomes and wealth holdings rise.

Aside from employee compensation and property income, there is only one other income form—transfers. These payments do not arise in the process of production, but are financed out of taxes which transfer claims on current output on some basis other than current contribution to production. These transfers, including relief or assistance and social-insurance payments such as unemployment compensation and old-age insurance, currently amount to over 6 per cent of the national income. (As we noted above, this is greater than interest and rent combined.) This percentage is sharply higher than in 1950, when it was only 3 per cent, or in 1929, when it was only 1 per cent, and indicates a coming to maturity for the U.S. version of the welfare state.

WHAT DEGREE OF INEQUALITY OBTAINS?

The inequality of the over-all income distribution has been stable in the postwar period. The top 10 per cent of income receivers (the lowest income of this group of families and single persons living alone is now about 12,000 dollars) get about 30 per cent of income, and the lowest 10 per cent, whose highest income is 2000 dollars, get 2 per cent. The median income is 6000 dollars, and the 50 per cent with incomes below that level get only 21 per cent of total income.

This particular pattern of inequality is about half of the relatively equalitarian patterns of the Netherlands and the Scandinavian countries, on the one hand, and the more unequal distributions of, say, Italy and Ceylon, on the other. It is generally believed by experts in this field that income is more unequally distributed in the lesser-developed countries than it is in the contemporary U.S. However, this comparison is difficult to make because of differences in economic and social structure and the forms that income-payment and income-sharing may take.

Characteristics of Rich and Poor

The degree of income inequality is best presented in connection with information about the characteristics of the high-income receivers and the low-income receivers. The top 10 per cent of income receivers are disproportionately headed by persons in middle-age groups, by the highly educated, by those in managerial and professional occupations, and by families having some property income, and also by families having more than one earner. One-third of married women work, and it is not uncommon to find that a family is in the upper tenth by virtue of a wife's supplementary earnings. It is interesting to note that family size shown by the income-distribution data is positively related to income level. The top 10 per cent of consumer units is 12 per cent of all persons; the lowest 10 per cent of such units only is 8 per cent of the population. The top group also includes more than its share of people from large cities and from northern and western regions of the country.

At the low end of the income scale, there is a disproportionate representation of the old and the young, the poorly educated, the low-skilled and farm occupations, the disabled, and families headed by women and nonwhites. The latter group, which makes up 10 per cent of the total population, comprised over 20 per cent of this lowest income group. Transfer income, which is by no means confined to this lowest group, is a substantial part of their total income.

As the above discussion suggests, there are some striking intergroup differences in income level. Farm incomes are about half as large as urban incomes. States in the South and in the mountain West have lower than average incomes. There is a pronounced income ladder related to the overlapping characteristics of occupation and education. Some studies have found a decidedly independent effect of education on income and have concluded that the extra cost and effort to attain advanced schooling is a good "investment," both from the individual and from the social points of view. There is also an income difference across industries, with manufacturing having relatively high wage incomes and the service industries at the low end. Women generally earn lower incomes than men, even after adjusting for the difference in part-time work. One of the most studied income differences is the white–nonwhite difference. The 20 million nonwhites—95 per cent of whom are Negroes—have incomes that are only 60 per cent as high as whites, even though their median educational attainment is 80 per cent that of whites. This income difference narrowed during World War II, but it has tended to widen since the war. Part of the difference can be explained by the educational deficiency, part by the lack of property-income, and part by regional, city-size, age, and sex differences. However, some substantial part of the income difference reflects the cumulation of past and current practices of discrimination in the provision of education and in the labor market. The 1954 ruling by the Supreme Court to end segregation in public schools and the 1964 Civil Rights Act, striking at several types of discriminatory practices in economic affairs, should work to buttress determined efforts by American Negroes to better their income levels.

HOW MANY AMERICANS ARE "POOR"?

Clearly, a good part of the income inequality shown in a survey of family money income can be explained on the grounds of differences in age and experience, education, number of members and earners in the family, and short-run variations in income owing to such things as farm or business loss. To a certain extent, therefore, the "real" inequality is overstated by the figures cited above. However, few would argue that this particular pattern of income distribution is one that reflects an ideally functioning economy. Considerable effort has already been made to modify the distribution from what it would be in the absence of government intervention. Compulsory free education, public-health programs and other transfers of services to the poor, a moderately progressive tax and transfer-payment system, and various protective measures for disadvantaged groups combine to assure opportunity and minimum incomes to the poor. Nonetheless, there exists a sizable group of Americans who have not shared the affluence of recent decades. The general public has come to the realization that there is an "invisible" or hidden poor population in the country, and that within that group are some who are alienated or withdrawn from the mainstream of community life. It has been observed that there tends to be a vicious circle of poverty, encouraging the conditions which cause or perpetuate poverty. There is the further irony that many governmental measures to promote the general welfare—and many efforts by voluntary organizations, such as labor unions—do not in fact reach the very poor. Attention has been called to the facts of poverty by dramatic protests made by Negroes who, comprising only 10 per cent of the total population, make up one-fifth of the nation's poor.

The War on Poverty

In 1964, President Lyndon B. Johnson stated the goal to eliminate poverty in the U.S. By way of a rough guidance for appraising the dimensions of the problem, he suggested a "poverty-income-line" of 3000 dollars for a family of four. By use of this guideline, which is based on a judgment that a lower income is inadequate to meet the ordinary needs of the typically situated family (still recognizing that there will be many exceptions both ways because of lesser and greater needs and because of resources other than income), it is found that 20 per cent of the American people is in poverty. This is 9.3 million families and 5 million unrelated individuals for a total of 35 million people. The median income of the families in this group was 1800 dollars. In 1947, 32 per cent of the people were below the 3000 dollar mark (measured in terms of 1962 purchasing power). This rate of reduction of poverty would leave, if carried forward to 1975, between 10 and 14 per cent of the population below the unchanging income standard. There is, presently, a considerable amount of discussion about ways in which this rate of reduction—and it is notable that the rate of reduction has tended to be slower in more recent years than in the earlier postwar years—can be speeded up. The Economic Opportunity Act of 1964 has a declaration of purpose which reads as follows:

Although the economic well-being and prosperity of the United States have progressed to a level surpassing any achieved in world history, and although these benefits are widely shared throughout the Nation, poverty continues to be the lot of a substantial number of our people. The United States can achieve its full economic and social potential as a nation only if every individual has the opportunity to contribute to the full extent of his capabilities and to participate in the workings of our society. It is, therefore, the policy of the United States to eliminate the paradox of poverty in the midst of plenty in this Nation by opening to everyone the opportunity for education and training, the opportunity to work, and the opportunity to live in decency and dignity. It is the purpose of this Act to strengthen, supplement, and coordinate efforts in furtherance of that policy.

This particular act is aimed most particularly at improving the income chances of young people—and it is important to know that one-third of the 35 million poor are children—and others who have unused employment potential. It initiates training and work-experience programs for almost half a million young people and induces "community-action" programs in numerous localities to improve education, health, and environmental standards. Additionally, there are provisions of the act which are concerned with rural areas and small business.

However, a substantial number of poor families are headed by persons—including aged, disabled, and women—who are not in the labor force. Substantial improvement in their income situation will turn on new measures in the field of income maintenance and supplementation, a field which is outside the act. Hence, the Economic Opportunity Act is best seen as one of a number of federal governmental commitments that relates to what President Johnson chose to call a national "war on poverty." Among these are the Social Security Act of 1935 and its numerous amendments, the Employment Act of 1946, the Manpower Development and Training Act of 1962, the Vocational Education Act of 1963, the major tax-reduction and reform legislation of 1964, and the Civil Rights Act of 1964. These pieces of legislation and numerous others bear on improvement of potential to earn income, enlargement of opportunity to work, and assurance of a minimum income. They provide, along with efforts of state and local governments and nonprofit agencies, a battery of measures opening up exits from poverty and closing off retreats into poverty. Combined with a growing productivity in the private economy, they offer the basis for the hope that, in the not too distant future, what is presently thought of as "poverty" will not be the necessary living standard for any families in the nation.

SUMMARY

The typical American has an income far above that of his forebears and of his contemporaries in other nations. Most of the national income arises as payment for labor effort, and only one-fourth of it can be characterized as property income. The latter form of income has declined in importance, but transfer payments have increased as a part of the income of persons. These payments, which are exemplified by unemployment compensation and social-security retirement benefits, now amount to 36 billion dollars and exceed the combined total of interest and rent. Property owner-ship and income from it remain highly concentrated, even though certain forms of property, such as homes, have become widely diffused. Income inequality is believed to be less pronounced now than before World War II and is presently of a middling degree when compared with that of other nations. High-income status within the country tends to be associated with northern and western regions, with large cities, with middle age, with high occupational status, and with educational attainment. Low income tends, on the other hand, to be identified with the inverse of the above characteristics and with nonwhite and broken families.

The rising average income and declining inequality are identified with a shrinking of the numbers of families who are below a "poverty line" of 3000 dollars income: in 1947, there were 12 million; by 1962 this number had fallen to 9.3 million. To encourage a more rapid reduction of this number, President Johnson has called for a "War on Poverty" of which the Economic Opportunity Act is seen to be an important part.

Questions of income distribution—of how to foster affluence and banish poverty—have long been of great interest to Americans. It is to be expected that they will continue to be so in the future as well.

5 THE REACTION OF AMERICAN LABOR TO TECHNOLOGICAL CHANGE

Ralph Helstein

Given the pragmatism of the American Labor Movement in this society in which less than 7 per cent of the population is engaged in agriculture, it should not be surprising to find that American labor has not only accepted industrialism, but has encouraged vast and continuing technological change. The modern labor movement has flourished and grown as industrialization and technology have constantly advanced.

Only through intensification of industrialization and vast technological change has it been possible to distribute the benefits of industry's tremendous capacity to produce among an ever-widening circle. This has been done, however, not through any redistribution of either wealth or power, but rather by creating an ever larger supply of goods and services. In this way, each group retains its relative share, but the share of each gets bigger. American labor, particularly its organized sections, can look back and say without hesitation that the last several decades have seen organized workers reach higher standards of living than ever before known by those who work with their hands. These standards are represented in housing, both rented and owned, or in the process of purchase; by the kinds of personal property in their possession such as automobiles, household appliances and furnishings. In more important ways, this higher standard of living is reflected in the number of children of industrial workers who now find it possible to attend college and who go on to advanced educational achievements. The average worker would

68

acknowledge that these standards of living have been produced by the constantly advancing technology—the higher levels of productivity that have resulted from America's increasing progress in industrialization. These are tangible gains that the American worker can see, feel, and live with. He would not willingly give them up. As a matter of fact, he would and has waged the most militant kind of struggle to get them, to keep them, and to enlarge them.

DISTRIBUTION OF THE SOCIAL PRODUCT AND THE DYNAMIC ROLE OF LABOR UNIONS

Moreover, as these standards have advanced and improved over the decades, so the institution that the worker created to advance his interests and secure his gains has become stronger, more stable and secure—the trade union. As industrialization advanced and technological change created an ever greater Gross National Product, the union has prospered: its membership has increased, its resources have grown, its influence has enlarged. As an institution, the American trade union is, on the whole, an accepted and respected part of American life. Trade unionists representing large areas of American life are active in government at federal, state and local levels. They are sought after as participants in many voluntary organizations at all levels of community life. They testify before congressional committees and administrative agencies. They are respected as lobbyists for many social and humanitarian causes at all levels of our government and society. They are advisors whose opinions carry weight with many private and public agencies. They are guests at social and public functions from the White House to city halls and from the university to private clubs. This is not to say that trade unions are not constantly under attack by certain sections of American society. Powerful forces still seek to undermine the union, to destroy and eliminate it, or, at the very least, to discredit it as an important and viable force in American affairs. Nevertheless, this brief description of its position is a reasonably accurate and fair assessment of its status at this point in the century.

69

American trade unions have become institutionalized. They have their own bureaucracy, their own customs, and mores. As is the case with other institutions in American society, the trade unions have both written and unwritten laws. Transgressors of either may well be regarded as enemies of the institution to be dealt with summarily when possible—to be ostracized or, at least, ridiculed and discredited when other methods fail. This is not said to criticize the trade union, but rather to describe its institutional character.

If the standard of living of the organized worker in America and his institutional mechanism, the trade union, have reached this high position in twentieth-century America because of the high degree of industrialization and technological change that has taken place, it should be no surprise that the developments that have made these achievements possible have been embraced.

I have not attempted any value judgments or analysis here of whether the pragmatic measure of material advancement justifies the American worker's almost loving embrace of industrialization and technological change.

THE WORKER'S ATTITUDE TOWARD MACHINES

It will be my purpose now to examine more closely the nature of this reaction—to look below the surface of acceptance and to search out the uncertainties and fears produced by an industrialized society, as well as the hatred and frustrations that have been created, and finally, to consider some of the problems that organized workers (and I speak primarily of those millions engaged in mass-production industry) presently confront, as well as problems that can be anticipated in the future.

It will be noted that just a moment ago I spoke of the American worker's "almost loving embrace of industrialization." These words were deliberately chosen: although the worker may embrace the results of the new technology, he does not embrace the role assigned to him in the factory system. It would be most accurate, perhaps, to say that in this society so affluent in many ways, the worker increasingly seeks and will jealously and rightly protect what technology makes possible in material goods, while he is repelled and angered by the price he must pay for these goods. Not in monetary terms because he probably realizes that nowhere in the world, or for that matter probably at no time in human history, could one hour's work buy as much in quantitative terms as it does today in America. The price, however, that he resents paying is what he must do to satisfy the demands that the machine makes on him. He understands that the price he must pay for the great material progress that he has been able to make because of technological change is to work at the assembly line, usually for eight hours a day, except for the regular breaks provided. During this time, he must be completely responsive to the repetitive demands of a machine whose sole function is to produce the goods which make it possible for him and tens of millions of others similarly situated to achieve a better standard of living.

The assembly line is a dehumanizing process. I believe that there is no way of making it more humane. The most that can be done—and it should be said that this is a continuing effort—is to mitigate to some degree the essentially inhumane process that work involves in a highly mechanized mass-production plant. The recognition, then, of the benefits provided by technological change can never be quite complete or absolute in the face of the depersonalization that accompanies them. This kind of ambivalence leads to deep frustrations that find their expression from time to time in strikes and industrial disputes of various kinds. For quite some time, I have thought that the drive for a shorter workweek, which finds ever stronger support among rank-and-file workers, stems as much from their hatred of the industrial process and their desire to get away from it as it does from the basic economic factors that make a reduction in work hours both desirable and inevitable.

Although I have been speaking primarily of the organized worker in mass-production industry, it should be noted that increasingly the white-collar worker doing routine operations either in competition with or paced by a machine feels and is beginning to articulate the same kind of ambivalence and frustration that I have just described for the industrial worker.

THE DISENGAGEMENT OF MAN IN A MECHANIZED WORLD

In addition to the depersonalization that occurs in the highly mechanized factory of today, an additional dimension qualifies the worker's embrace of technological change. The pressure imposed by the assembly line on the worker's humanity puts his limited participation in the affluent society into sharper focus. Technological change has raised the standard of living of two-thirds of America so substantially that today many things are possible that were undreamed-of luxuries several decades ago. To participate fully, to realize the advantages made possible by the massive technological changes that have taken place requires an educational and cultural experience for which the worker's income is still not sufficient, although higher than elsewhere in the world for comparable work. If the work process were satisfying in providing some outlet or expression of human creativity the worker's level of participation would be adequate. But when the work itself denies human dignity, satisfaction must come from elsewhere. The worker's share of the profits is still not sufficient to permit full participation in the same manner as others about him. The evidence of this denial is available to all without special effort or insight. As a matter of fact, the evidence of our technological prowess obtrudes even on those who want to avoid its recognition. Increasingly, then, the worker's embrace of technological change will be qualified by the quality of his life in the world outside the shop. This will include the nature of the city in which he lives, the quality of what he can buy, the beauty of his surroundings, and the availability to him of the benefits of technology. He embraces technology, then, for the improved standard of living that he has achieved; but he does not love it because, on the one hand, it demeans his humanity while it denies the full benefits of the promises that he finds so seductive.

THE MACHINE EASES MAN'S PHYSICAL BURDEN

How are we to comprehend the worker's basic attitude of acceptance in spite of these frustrations? To the worker there is something inevitable in the movement of industrialization. In

America it is generally regarded as progress. We in the labor movement have long since come to realize that the most difficult problems of production are capable of solution in one way or another. We believe that man's capacity to harness the forces of nature has no foreseeable limitations. We recognize that undoubtedly there will always be unsolved problems, but time and new knowledge will make it possible to overcome the existing ones, even while new ones are created or come into being. We have learned that once an idea has progressed to the point that it can be put on the drawing board, it is only a matter of time before the machine that will result is producing goods in greater volume and better quality than ever before. Given this feeling of inevitability and this sense that technological change represents progress, by the knowledge that the machine does in fact lessen the demand on the human muscle, the worker's frustrations can be handled with greater or less difficulty, depending on the individual. The labor itself is not so harsh or onerous as it once was, even though the demands of the work place are in many ways an affront to human dignity. Physical weariness and exhaustion have been replaced by emotional tension. The reduction of the amount of physical effort required becomes an important factor in creating the conditions under which the individual worker can handle the ambivalence that he feels toward the increasing industrialization of his society, which provides higher standards of living while it offends his sense of human dignity.

THE FRANKENSTEIN SYNDROME

What I have said up to now, probing below the surface of the worker's acceptance of modern technological change, has been primarily devoted to a consideration of the factors that contribute to create conflicting interests between the higher, although inadequate, standards of living provided by the machine and its demands on the individual personality and human rights. It is necessary, however, to go further and to consider not only the hatred and frustrations that exist, but also the fears and uncertainties generated by an ever advancing technology.

American labor can look back over many decades and note that as its society has become more industrialized and as technology has advanced, more jobs have been created which have, on the whole, provided more security and a better and easier life for more people. There have been periods in the past, of course, where concern that the machine would replace human beings in the work process has been real and deep. However, experience has demonstrated that because of many policies that were adopted and made possible by massive increases in productivity resulting from great technological change, more jobs resulted rather than less. The assurance that came with this experience provided a sense of certainty that the machine was not a Frankenstein that controlled man, but rather that the machine was controlled by man and would be used for his benefit. And as he looked about him, he could in many ways say that the results were good—life was better for more people.

In the last decade or so, however, we are again questioning whether, in fact, man does control the machine or is controlled by it. Has technological advance been so great that it could break away from the shackles that bound it to man's purpose? Does the new technology operate in such a way that man must follow the path the machine opens, whether it seems to make sense or not? Is the fact that the machine makes certain things possible sufficient reason for pursuing these goals, irrespective of our judgment and values? Must we watch our habitat change before our eyes while we stand by powerless to provide direction or control?

I state these questions in this broad and general way quite intentionally because it is in this context that the specific problems that cause fear and uncertainty in American labor must be considered. First, however, let me be more specific in dealing with the nature of these concerns. In this past decade, American technology has continued to make vast and important progress in the area of cybernation, which is usually called automation. By cybernation I mean that system of production in which the machine that replaced man's muscle will be controlled and guided, not by man's exercising judgment and making decisions, but by another machine—a machine which now can, does, and increasingly will be able to replace man in an ever widening circle of jobs which previously had been regarded as jobs that only human beings could do. In a great number of cases, this machine can make these decisions more quickly, more accurately, and with greater precision than man. Over the past few years, as the possibilities and potentials of cybernetics have become clearer, the demand for this type of equipment has increased. These developments represent a major technological breakthrough of such massive dimensions that it puts this technology on a level of truly revolutionary proportions. In the same period that has witnessed this revolutionary industrial development, U.S. unemployment has been rising until the official unemployment figures have averaged more than 5 per cent since 1957. It would be wrong, however, to assume that unemployment has been caused only by the developments in technology; but there is little question that it has been a contributory factor. Cybernation is clearly an important factor in our failure to create jobs as fast as they are needed if we are to have full employment, because more and more goods can be produced by fewer and fewer people.

The worker is aware of the rising levels of unemployment. He is aware of the tremendous technological change represented in the new machine. He knows that Secretary of Labor Willard Wirtz was right when he said that the worker now competes with a machine that has the educational level of high school training. His experience has taught him that the machine's educational level will continue to rise. From that experience he also knows of many other workers who have worked at the same job for many years only to be replaced by machines in some cases, or in other cases, to have their jobs eliminated completely because new and better ways have been found for doing them. Thus, he sees the threat of loss of his source of income which is implicit in the vast technological change that is setting in. He wants to think that these changes will not affect him in a harmful way, but there is a gnawing uncertainty that is beginning to undermine his security. In many cases, this leads to deep-seated fear, not only for himself, but for his children who may be entering the labor market. He knows that unemployment has hit teenagers entering the work force with the greatest severity.

75

SEARCHING FOR SECURITY
AMONG CURRENTS OF CHANGE

These fears have found expression in different ways. Among the most important has been the emphasis that the trade union now puts on provisions dealing with job security. More and more, unions have been negotiating contracts providing substantial payments for past service in the form of separation pay to employees whose jobs are eliminated. Greater emphasis has been placed on improvements in private pension plans that permit earlier retirement, with increased pension benefits over and above payments provided by the federal Social Security Act. These plans increasingly provide for vested interest so that the benefits that accumulated over a number of years of service will not be lost if the employee leaves the company's employ prior to the age of retirement. Extended vacation plans have been negotiated in many industries on the theory that they will require the employment of more people as replacements at best, but at the very least will result in fewer displacements of employees. Conscious also of the new types of demands being made by the new technology, the trade union is putting increasing emphasis on the training and retraining of workers. This is being done through both private and public training and retraining programs. And, as I have previously observed, increasing pressures have been building up for a shorter workweek. The shorter workweek has been one of America's traditional ways of dealing with problems of unemployment. In past periods, it has proved to be a successful device for alleviating many of these problems. It is only a matter of time before a workweek of less than forty hours will become standard in America.

All of these efforts: separation payments, improved pension arrangements, extended vacations, and training and retraining programs, though mitigating some of the harshness at the time of displacement, have not eliminated the uncertainty and unrest. They have not resolved the fears created by the massive changes that have occurred, since the worker understands that his opportunity to be a fully participating member of this society is dependent on his being a productive member.

These fears and uncertainties have caused industrial workers to re-examine many of their basic views toward the vast technological changes that have been occurring. I do not mean to suggest that their basic acceptance of technological advance as necessary to the maintenance and improvement of their standards of living has been shaken. It is rather a questioning of the speed at which we have been moving. A questioning of whether or not we are prepared to absorb the impact of this change. Basically the question, though unarticulated, is whether man still controls the machine.

Let me summarize the nature of the argument up to now. American labor reacts positively and with vigor to an industrial society and encourages major technological advances. It realizes that it is only through technology devoted to the purposes of man that the production of goods can reach levels high enough for man to live with decency. While recognizing these goals of industrialism, labor's acceptance of technology drives—though sincere and hopeful—remains tentative and confused. This ambivalence results from the hatreds and frustration created by the work place, from labor's inability to participate more fully in the benefits of present levels of productivity, and from the uncertainties and fears produced by massive changes that have occurred in a relatively recent period as a result of revolutionary technological breakthroughs. In spite of these concerns, however, it is my judgment that American labor will continue to support increased industrialism and technological change. Labor understands that these present problems, some of which have been with us to a greater or lesser degree for a long time, cannot be solved by turning the clock back to days which were not such good old days, in spite of the nostalgia with which some fearful ones speak of them. More people live better in America today than ever before in its history.

THE COMPLEX OF COMPLEXITIES

It is, however, important to understand that America is a very complex and involved society which, like most other societies, defies easy and simple explanation. The problems that have been produced by our highly advanced industrialism are among the most complex that we face. We are wrestling with them in many ways. We have come to understand, for example, the anachronism represented by millions living at what we define to be poverty levels—family incomes of less than 3,000 dollars per year in a highly affluent society—and we have begun slowly, hesitantly, and feebly, to attempt to deal with this question. I should note parenthetically that American labor is very much aware of the fact that hundreds of millions around the world live on incomes of less than this. We attempt to help, in many cases clumsily and ineptly, but with intelligence and skill in some cases. In all cases, we care about the question of humanity involved, whether the problem be poverty in America or elsewhere in the world. However, in our affluent nation it is not easy to change our politics to meet the demands of this highly industrialized age from that of an agrarian society which we were only a few short decades ago.

To complicate our problems even more, there is no single tradition with which to identify—there are many. There is no single American way—there are many American ways. There is no single value system—there are many. This is not a monolithic society. Majorities are necessary, and, therefore, a synthesis of diverse interests must be found. This is the framework within which American labor and, for that matter, all America must search for solutions to the problems created by these massive technological advances.

A NEW ORDER OF PROBLEMS NEEDS A
NEW GENERATION OF SOLUTIONS

Now let me finally consider some of the implications for the future and suggest what I believe will be American labor's reaction to this revolution.

First I believe America stands on the threshold of producing abundance. In all recorded history man has lived with the problems of scarcity of all kinds: food, clothing, shelter, education, communication, and transportation. Throughout very substantial sections of the world, this condition still holds true. In America, for the first time, man will soon be able to produce in such abundance that all his material needs can be met. This is a prospect of awesome dimensions. There is no previous experience on which one can draw as we search for answers to the questions posed by this development. It is a strange and disturbing paradox that as we approach the very goals for which man has searched through the ages, such frightening and disturbing questions are present. But the fact is that the problems presented by the possibility of producing in superabundance are real and frightening —but also challenging.

Second, if we produce in such abundance, what will the function of the system of wage payment be? Essentially, whether they were paid in money or in kind, wages were designed as a method of dividing up the goods then available in scarce supply. If, however, goods are no longer in scarce supply, what is the function of the wage system? If the wage system is no longer either necessary or meaningful, what will replace it? Can man devise a system of providing incomes to all as a matter of right, even though work in its traditional form will either no longer be performed, or, if it is, in ever smaller units of time?

Third, what of work? If we can produce all the necessities of life in abundance through the use of our technology, what will man's role be? Through the centuries following God's injunction on Adam that he live by the sweat of his brow, we have assumed that work consisted of physical effort for most men. Is it possible for us to redefine our concept of work? Can we accept the prospect that men may engage in creative activity because of the pleasure of achievement and the drives of accomplishment rather than because of the necessity to work in order to eat? Are we prepared to recognize that going to school should be work for which payment should be made? Can we accept the machine as the slave in this society which does the subsistential work of this age? In *The Politics* Aristotle spoke of such a development changing the relations between men when he said:

> There is only one condition on which we can imagine managers not needing subordinates, and masters not needing slaves. This condition would be that each (inanimate) instrument could do its own work, at the word of command or by intelligent anticipation, like the statues of Daedalus or the tripods made by Hephaestus, of which Homer relates that

79

> Of their own motion they entered
> the conclave of Gods on Olympus.
> as if a shuttle should weave of itself, and a plectrum should
> do its own harp-playing.[1]

The reality of our age is that "a shuttle can weave of itself and a plectrum can do its own harp-playing." Given the development of cybernation and its impact on the whole question of work, is it not a fact that man's relationship with man rather than, as it is today, with things will be of increasing importance?

Fourth, what will be the effect of our ability to produce in abundance on the nature of our communities and the manner in which we live? Will it not be possible to live in a less densely concentrated manner? Smaller communities will have all the necessary energy and machine power available so that they can be self-supporting in all respects. Advances in communications and transportation will permit us to measure distances in the half-hour rather than in the hours that we use today. Clearly the nature of our lives will change and with it, our relationship with our fellow man. In such communities, will not each of us, in important ways, come closer to making the decisions that affect our daily lives?

I know that to many, these problems will not appear real, nor will they seem practical enough to warrant further thought. I believe them to be real in America, and they must be wrestled with soon. David Sarnoff, the chief executive officer of RCA, writing, "By the End of the Twentieth Century" in *Fortune Magazine*, observed that:

> Science and technology will advance more in the next thirty-six years than in all the millennia since man's cration. By the century's end, man will have achieved a growing ascendancy over his physical being, his earth and his planetary environs.[2]

These are some of the implications of the future. They will not come on us all at once, but rather over a period of time, and we can deal with them, in accordance with the pragmatism that has been one of American labor's most useful tools, so long as we are aware of them and their implications. In their very nature,

1 *Politics* I. 4. 1253b.
2 *Fortune Magazine* 69 (May 1964), pp. 116–119.

however, we find justification for American labor's attitude toward industrialism. It is a liberating force containing the means by which the worker's frustrations and hates, as well as his fears and uncertainties, can be eliminated. This has always been the promise of a highly industrialized society and American labor will continue to strive toward assuring the conditions in which technological changes can fulfill this pledge. When it fulfills this promise, the ambivalence of American labor's attitude will disappear, and it will lovingly and unstintingly embrace that society.

In the meanwhile, American labor will continue to accept technological change, constantly pressing it into the services of man.

6 UNEMPLOYMENT IN THE UNITED STATES

Charles C. Killingsworth

The people of the United States produced more, earned more, and spent more in 1964 than in any other year in their history. By almost any measure, 1964 was a year of record prosperity. Yet unemployment averaged around 5 per cent of the labor force as it had in each of the past seven years. A dozen years ago, most U.S. economists would have defined full employment to mean unemployment of not more than 3 per cent, and that is, in fact, the rate that we achieved for an extended period early in the 1950's. Most of the other highly industrialized nations of the world today have rates of unemployment substantially lower than those that have prevailed in the United States in recent years.

Exact comparisons are difficult to make, of course, because statistical methods vary from country to country. In the United States, for example, the unemployed include those temporarily laid off from regular jobs as well as the long-term unemployed, teenagers seeking their first jobs, those seeking part-time employment, and people who are moving from one job to another. It also can be noted that not everyone who is unemployed is necessarily needy. Most short-term unemployment is covered by unemployment insurance and often, while one member of a family is unemployed, another may be working. But even so, hardly any responsible person in this country believes that we should accept a 5 per cent unemployment rate as a satisfactory state of affairs. An average rate which is that high means much higher rates for certain disadvantaged groups in our society. In recent years, young workers, old workers, low-skilled and poorly educated workers, and Negroes have had unemployment rates considerably higher than the average.

Why does the United States have such a persistently high rate of prosperity unemployment? And what can be done about it? There is general agreement in this country that these are urgent and important questions. But there is sharp disagreement about the answers. One set of answers is provided by a group of economists led by the President's Council of Economic Advisors. This group argues that the present excessive unemployment has been a result mainly of what they call "fiscal drag"—that is, a federal tax system that drains an excessive amount of purchasing power out of the economy every time we begin to approach a high level of activity. These economists argue that fiscal drag has caused a chronic deficiency of aggregate demand in the United States since 1957. This group denies that there is any evidence that shows that the nature of the unemployment problem today is any different from what it has been in past periods of lagging demand. Therefore, it concludes that the prime remedy for our excessive unemployment is to cut taxes. A big tax cut will step up private spending, and excess unemployment will "melt away," just as it did at the beginning of World War II and during the Korean War. This group concedes that such programs as manpower-retraining and area-redevelopment may be necessary to help particularly disadvantaged individuals and localities; but it argues that the problems to which these programs are addressed are no more significant or urgent today than they have been for many decades. Tax-cutting must be the "centerpiece of policy" in the attack on unemployment.

A second and different set of answers is advanced by a group composed mainly of economists who have specialized in the study of the labor market. I stand with this group, as will soon be apparent. Its view is that the massive changes in the job market since World War II are a cause of unemployment which is at least as important as lagging aggregate demand. In the postwar years, this group points out, jobs for low-skilled workers have disappeared at a faster rate than those people have died, retired, or given up looking for work. At the same time, jobs for highly skilled workers have increased more rapidly than the supply of such workers. Therefore, we argue, the unemployment problem has increasingly come to be concentrated in the low-skilled segment of the labor force. We concede that cutting taxes can increase employment and reduce unemployment a little; but hard-core unemployment will be virtually untouched by increased consumer and business spending because the patterns of increased spending simply will not be of such a nature to revive the old unskilled jobs. Continued expansion of aggregate demand will create bottlenecks in the supply of skilled workers before it substantially reduces the unemployment of low-skilled workers. Our group takes the position that, although job creation through fiscal policy is an essential part of a full employment program, it will be ineffective . . . or inflationary unless it is accompanied by massive programs to improve the capacities of the present hard-core unemployed and to provide marketable skills to the flood of young people now coming into the job market.

At the risk of some oversimplification, we can say that the first group advocates a purchasing-power approach and the second group advocates an earning-power approach. In somewhat more sophisticated terms, we can phrase the basic issues as follows: Would the expansion of the private economy to capacity operations in response to tax-cutting create only those kinds of jobs that could be satisfactorily filled from the ranks of those who are currently unemployed and those who would be drawn into the job market, and would such expansion create enough jobs of the right kinds to reduce the average rate of unemployment to tolerate levels? I will first describe why I think the earning-power remedy for excessive unemployment should be given priority. Then I will examine the views of those who favor the purchasing-power remedy.

JOB MARKET CHANGES 1950–1962

The factual basis for my own views and of those who see the problem as I do can be briefly stated by summarizing the vast changes that occurred in the U.S. job market between 1950 and 1962. (These years are selected, incidentally, simply because 1950 is the earliest year and 1962 is the most recent year for which adequate data are available.) In the twelve-year period, the total number of jobs held by workers with only eight or fewer years of education—which is roughly the bottom third of the U.S. labor force—decreased by 6.2 million. In the same period, the number of jobs held by men and women with college training—roughly the top 20 per cent of the labor force—increased by 5.3 million. Now these great changes in the nature of the jobs available could not have caused any significant changes in patterns of unemployment if the characteristics of the labor force had changed at the same rate. Whether or not there has been a lag in adaptation is a point of some controversy, however, and I want to postpone consideration of that question until I have laid before you more of the pertinent facts.

THE DECLINE OF AGRICULTURE

Let us consider where it was in the economy that the low-skilled jobs were disappearing and which factors eliminated the jobs. The largest percentage decline was in agriculture. Since World War II, we have seen the acceleration of an agricultural revolution which had its beginnings in the 1930's. Mechanization, synthetic fertilizers, chemical weed-killers, and many similar technological improvements are the source of this revolution. Back in the 1920's, the rate of improvement in agricultural productivity (as measured by output per man-hour) was only a half or a third the rate in manufacturing. Since 1947, productivity improvement in agriculture has been two or three times as rapid as in manufacturing. The demand for food and fiber has grown much more slowly than farm productivity. Hence, millions of farmers have been forced off the land and into the cities. The average educational attainment of farmers has long been lower than that of any other major group in the labor force, and few of the skills learned on the farm are useful in city jobs. Therefore, the decline of agricultural employment has substantially increased the number of poorly educated, low-skilled workers in the urban job market.

CHANGING JOB MIX IN FACTORIES

Low-skilled jobs have also been disappearing from factory production lines. Productivity improvement in manufacturing has not been much more rapid in recent years than in many prewar periods, and total employment in manufacturing has not changed very much since the early 1950's. But the composition of employment has changed quite substantially. Between 1953 and 1964, the number of production workers—mainly the blue-collar force —in American factories *decreased* by about one million; at the same time, the number of so-called nonproduction workers— mainly the white-collar force—*increased* by about a million.

This great shift in the job mix occurred during a period without a major depression or a major war, and it is unprecedented in our history. Some of this change resulted from a major shift in defense expenditures—from tanks, trucks, guns, airplanes, and other mass-produced items to missiles and complex electronic devices, requiring the employment of large numbers of highly trained scientists, engineers, and other technical personnel. But the rise in the proportion of white-collar workers has been fairly general throughout manufacturing industries. Government statisticians group our manufacturing industries into twenty-one major classifications, and all but four of these categories show substantial increases in the white-collar ratio in the postwar years. Some important nonmanufacturing industries also show substantial increases in their white-collar ratios. Examples are mining, communications, and railroads. Finally, it should be noted that in the great majority of instances where separate figures by occupational group are available, they show much greater displacement of the lowest-skilled production workers than of craftsmen, maintenance men, and similar skilled blue-collar groups.

THE IMPACT OF AUTOMATION

In my opinion, it is the great technological advances of the postwar years that have been largely responsible for this fundamental change in job mix that has surged across industry lines. The shifts in defense spending are themselves a result mainly of changes in the technology of warfare. Furthermore, many firms in nondefense industries now spend much more than they used to on research and development. The great growth of scientific knowledge in the war and postwar years has stimulated a race among firms and industries to develop new ways to put this great fund of knowledge to work. One of the most important products of postwar research and development has been the spread of what has come to be called "automation." Controversies have developed concerning such questions as whether there really is anything new about automation.

After studying the matter for a long time, I have become convinced that automation really does represent a new dimension in technological development, and that it has been one of the important factors in the changes in job mix that I have been discussing. To put the matter as simply as possible, automation has come to mean ways of performing operations automatically— that is, by machines which are able to perform jobs, and sometimes a whole series of jobs, with little or no human assistance while it is doing them. Now it is true that we have had some kinds of automatic machines for centuries, but we have made a great leap forward in the postwar years. Today we have whole families of mechanical substitutes for the human neuromuscular system—the iron hand, the electric eye, the optical scanner, and the electronic brain are examples. Consequently, the worker who can offer only his two hands and his untrained five senses in the job market finds that automatic machines have taken over a large proportion of the simple, repetitive jobs and are doing them faster, more accurately, and more cheaply than mere humans could.

But to say that automation reduces the number of low-skilled jobs is to tell only part of the story. The wonders of automation are not achieved by some kind of magic; instead, they are the product of many hours, weeks, and months of work by highly trained specialists who must design, install, program, and do all of the other things necessary to bring the automatic machine or automatic system into being and to keep it operating. Most of these specialists work in offices rather than on the production floor. Thus, one basic effect of automation is to lengthen the production process, in the sense that fewer workers are needed to oversee the physical processing of materials, but more are needed for preparatory work, such as programming. This effect is one of the major reasons for the postwar rise in the proportion of white-collar workers in manufacturing and in a number of other industries as well.

CHANGES IN CONSUMER SPENDING

It would be a mistake, though, to think that automation is the only factor in the American economy that has increased the number of jobs for highly trained people in recent years. Another major factor has been the changing pattern of consumer spending. It is a familiar fact that as a family's income goes up, the percentage of that income which it spends on basic necessities such as food and shelter goes down. The other side of the coin is that expenditures for services of various kinds go up. More is spent on health care, education, entertainment, travel, and similar services. Moreover, as the stock of automobiles, refrigerators, televisions, washing machines, and other mechanical and electrical appliances grow, there is increased need for repairmen of all kinds to keep these things running. Thus, growth patterns in employment change as a society achieves a rising standard of living. The changing patterns are clearly apparent in the postwar American economy. In 1953, for the first time in our history, total employment in service-producing industries rose above the employment in goods-producing industries, and, in the ensuing years, the margin has widened: service employment has continued to rise and goods employment has fallen year after year. Of course, some of the new jobs in service-producing industries require little skill. But the greatest growth has been in such fields as education and health care, where most jobs require many years of specialized training.

HAS ADJUSTMENT TO CHANGE LAGGED?

Up to this point, we have been dealing mainly with facts. Rational men can't disagree about facts; they can only be ignorant of them. But when it comes to deciding just what the facts mean, there is often a great deal of room for honest differences of opinion. And so it is with the facts about the great changes in the structure of the American economy in the postwar years. A large and influential group of American economists believes that these structural changes are not an important cause of our present excessive unemployment. It is now time to examine with some care the basis for their analysis and the conclusions that flow from it.

The Council of Economic Advisors has been in the forefront of those who have denied that structural changes have been an important cause of increased unemployment in recent years. Their view is that the dynamic American economy has always been undergoing structural change; that we have built-in adaptive mechanisms which prevent the development of serious labor-market imbalances; and that there is no evidence that these adaptive mechanisms have suddenly become less effective than in past years. The principal support that the Council offers for this viewpoint is the findings of an elaborate analysis of unemployment rates by industry and by occupation in the postwar years. Both the approach and the findings were summarized in late 1963 for a U.S. Senate committee by Dr. Walter W. Heller, who was the chairman of the Council at the time:

Studies of changes in the incidence of unemployment among unskilled and semi-skilled blue-collar workers—whose jobs would seem to be highly vulnerable to technological change—can provide important insights into the structural unemployment problem. One would expect an accelerated rate of technological displacement to be reflected in rising rates of unemployment for these groups—relative to total unemployment. One would also expect to find such a relative rise for workers in industries such as manufacturing, mining, and transportation where automation has so far found its widest application.

To test this possibility, we have correlated the unemployment rate in specific occupations and industries with the rate for all experienced workers in the labor force during the 1948–57 period—in other words, for the period before the main structural unemployment upsurge is alleged to have occurred. These correlations were then used to calculate what the occupational and industrial distribution of unemployment *would* have been in 1962 if the old relationships had held. If there had been a substantial increase in structural maladjustments, the actual 1962 unemployment rates for what we may call the "technologically vulnerable groups" should have been *higher* than these calculated rates. But in fact . . . a majority of the rates are *lower*. . . . And taking all of the blue-collar occupations and goods-producing industries together, we also find that the rise in actual unemployment was somewhat less than the 1948–57 experience would have suggested.[1]

POLICY CONCLUSIONS OF COUNCIL OF ECONOMIC ADVISORS

Primarily on the basis of this analysis, Dr. Heller and other economists in this group have drawn some important conclusions. Let me summarize some of them. The fundamental conclusion is, of course, that, "The problems of structural unemployment . . . have not constituted a greater cause of unemployment in recent years than in earlier periods." The present distribution of unemployment "is quite typical of all past periods of high unemployment," and there have been no recent changes in the labor market which would make the achievement of a 4 per cent unemployment rate any more difficult at present than it was in 1948 or in 1955–1957. Only after the rate has been reduced to 4 per cent will structural unemployment impose any real obstacles to further expansion of output. Therefore, "the rise in unemployment over recent years has been caused primarily by inadequate growth of aggregate demand," and the main attack on excessive unemployment should be through fiscal policy measures of the federal government.

It is the judgment of this group that the quickest, surest, and easiest way to expand aggregate demand through government action is to cut federal taxes without cutting government spending. Consumers and businesses will then spend most of the money that they otherwise would have had to pay in taxes. This added spending will raise the demand for all kinds of goods and services, making it profitable for employers to hire more people; and those newly hired will also spend more, further increasing demand. The size of the tax cut which the federal administration first proposed in 1963 was estimated at about 10 billion dollars, but the current estimate of the amount by which revenues will actually be reduced by the cut as finally enacted is about 14 billion dollars. Even on the basis of the smaller estimate of the size of the tax cut, Dr. Heller and others repeatedly stated that there

[1] Dr. Walter Heller, *Economic Report,* Appendix A (Washington, D.C.: Government Printing Office, 1964), p. 176.

was a "good prospect" that it would reduce unemployment to the 4 per cent level. Some enthusiasts have even insisted that fiscal policy measures alone, if applied vigorously enough, would be sufficient to reduce unemployment to 3 per cent.

I believe that there are serious weaknesses both in the method of analysis and in the unemployment figures on which the Council has relied; consequently, in my opinion, the effectiveness of fiscal policy alone as a remedy for the present unemployment problem in the United States has been greatly overestimated.

In the first place, I can find no basis, either in the literature on the subject or in the facts, for Dr. Heller's statement that "The main structural unemployment upsurge is alleged to have occurred" *after* 1957. In my opinion, the facts clearly show some major, unprecedented structural changes in the economy *before* 1957. For example, a sharp decline in agricultural employment began in 1948, and blue-collar employment in manufacturing started falling after 1953. Heavy investment in new kinds of automatic equipment began long before 1957 in many manufacturing industries—on the railroads, in mines, in public utilities, and in other fields. The prosperity unemployment rate was 3 per cent or less early in the 1950's; by 1957, it was at least a third higher. If I am correct in thinking that 1957 was about the midpoint of a period of rising structural unemployment, the comparison of relationships after that year with relationships before is not a valid method for testing whether structural change has contributed substantially to our present excessive unemployment.

Second, Dr. Heller's identification of the "technologically vulnerable groups" seems to have been influenced more by the availability of data than by the observed impact of technological change. It is clearly erroneous to assume that *all* blue-collar workers are "technologically vulnerable." The fact is that the recent growth patterns of our economy have greatly increased employment opportunities in certain blue-collar fields, such as repair and maintenance; and at least until quite recently, many blue-collar jobs in service-producing industries had been little affected by technological change. Thus, nothing that we know about patterns of structural change justifies lumping together all blue-collar workers, or even all unskilled and semiskilled blue-collar workers, and identifying this enormous, heterogeneous group as the "vulnerable" category.

By the same token, lumping together *all* workers in a particular division of industry, such as manufacturing, ignores the fact that recent changes in that sector have improved job opportunities for the white-collar group while worsening them for some (though not all) of the blue-collar workers.

The Heller analysis rests on two distinct kinds of data. The first is extremely broad occupational classification with no distinction as to industry, and the second is extremely broad industry classification, which makes no distinction as to the various occupations within the industry. In my judgment, these classifications are much too broad to permit any meaningful analysis of the unemployment experience of the really vulnerable groups. Such analysis requires, at a minimum, a breakdown of the unemployment rates of the major occupational groups *within* various industries; but the data simply are not available on that basis.

COUNTING AND CLASSIFYING THE UNEMPLOYED

There are additional deficiencies in the data which purport to show unemployment rates by industry or by occupation. One is that the method for assigning an unemployed worker to the appropriate occupation and industry can give misleading results. For example, consider the automobile worker who is thrown out of work by the permanent closing of the plant where he has worked for twenty years; he gets a temporary job in the shipping room of a department store during the Christmas rush and is laid off after three weeks; thereafter he is counted as an unemployed worker from retail trade, not from manufacturing. It is the most recent job that is the basis for classification, even if it has been held only briefly, and not the job on which the man has spent most of his working life.

Another deficiency grows out of our method of determining who is to be counted among the unemployed. In practice and in most cases, only those who have actively sought work in the very recent past are counted. Those who have decided, after long and fruitless seeking, that there simply are no jobs available for them and who have stopped looking are not counted as unemployed; they are considered to be "not in the labor force." There is general agreement that this method of counting has given us a large number of "hidden unemployed." These are people who are not now constantly looking for a job, but who would quickly resume their search if they thought that their chances had improved. The Council of Economic Advisors recently estimated that there are "a million or more" people in this group. It is more than likely, in my opinion, that a very large proportion of the hidden unemployed formerly worked in those occupations and industries that have been adversely affected by structural change. Yet this large group is completely excluded from consideration in the analysis on which the Council of Economic Advisors has placed such great reliance.

Let me conclude this criticism of the views of the Council of Economic Advisors by saying that I have the highest personal regard for the abilities and the integrity of the members and the staff of that Council. Their position that structural changes in the economy have not been an important factor in the recent rise in prosperity unemployment rests on sincere conviction, not expediency. And when I attack the basis for that conviction, I do so in the belief that vigorous competition between ideas is essential for the advancement of knowledge. That is the faith of the scholarly community everywhere in the free world.

THE EVIDENCE SHOWING ADJUSTMENT LAGS

Now let us return to the question that I raised earlier without answering: has the improvement in the educational attainment of the American labor force lagged behind the rapid rise in the educational requirements of jobs? Putting the question in this way implies, of course, that the amount of education that a man has had is a more fundamental determinant of his vulnerability to change and of his ability to adapt to change than membership in some very broad occupational or industrial classification. And I believe that this implication is fully justified by what we know about the impact of structural change in postwar America.

93

So, I believe that there is great significance in the fact that in the years from 1950 to 1962, the unemployment rates of poorly educated workers rose substantially, while the unemployment rates of college-trained workers decreased substantially. Although 1950 was a recession year and 1962 was a prosperous year, the average rate of unemployment was about the same in both years. In 1950, the unemployment rate for men with less than five years of education was about four times the rate for male college graduates; by 1962, the rate for the bottom group was seven times that of the top group. This comparison really understates the extent to which the difference in rates widened, because it ignores the factor of hidden unemployment.

I have made studies of hidden unemployment and have developed estimates of the distribution of this group in 1962 as compared with 1950. If we take the earlier year as our starting point, we find that there is no evidence of the development of any hidden unemployment among the college-trained group by 1962; it is most heavily concentrated among those with the least education. When this factor is taken into account, as it must be for realistic judgments, we find that the "real" unemployment rate in 1962 for the least-educated men was actually twelve times the rate for men with college degrees. I remind you that the relationship only a dozen years before was only four to one. And, of course, the redistribution of unemployment from 1950 to 1962 was not confined to the very top and very bottom groups. The worsening of unemployment rates was general among the men with limited education, and the improvement was marked even among men with only a year or so of college training. In other words, the shape of the American unemployment problem has changed greatly since 1950. There has been a growth of imbalance in the labor market, which makes it very likely that a sustained expansion of private demand would create serious shortages of various kinds of highly trained workers long before the great surplus of untrained, poorly educated workers could be substantially reduced. Even to get back to the levels of unemployment that prevailed in 1957 (taking into account both the reported and the hidden unemployment), we would have needed in 1962 an increase in jobs for the bottom third of the labor force that would have been five times as large as the biggest increase that was possible among the college-trained. I see no reason to expect such a greatly disproportionate increase in the number of low-skilled jobs as a result of the expansion of private demand.

RECENT DEVELOPMENTS

The course of events since the passage of the federal tax cut of 1964 seems to me to provide support for the conclusions that I have just expressed. There has been a large gap between promise and performance. When taxes were cut (spring, 1964), the unemployment rate was 5.4 per cent. In the first quarter of 1965, the average rate had declined to 4.8 per cent. This improvement of the magnitude of a small fraction of a percentage point is much less than what the strongest advocates of the tax cut had foreseen. Just after the tax cut was enacted, Dr. Gardner Ackley, the present chairman of the Council of Economic Advisors, had said that it was likely that the unemployment rate would be holding below 5 per cent by the end of 1964 and that it would continue down toward 4 per cent in 1965. Now, however, Dr. Ackley says that the best we can expect is an average rate of about 5 per cent for 1965 as a whole, and most analysts agree with him—except for some who expect a steady rise after mid-year. Production and employment have increased substantially since the tax cut, but the number of unemployed (according to the official method of counting) has changed very little. As more jobs have appeared, the number of job-seekers has also increased. And by mid-summer of this year, the largest crop of teenagers in our history will enter the job market. The tax cut may have substantially prolonged the life of our present business expansion, and it did create a considerable number of new jobs. But it also brought us close to some of the bottlenecks of labor supply that I spoke about above; by the end of 1964, there were widespread reports of serious shortages of many kinds of skilled workers. Far too many of our millions of unemployed simply were unable to meet the requirements of the new jobs that had been created.

THE ADMINISTRATION'S NEW EMPHASIS

It is not too soon, I believe, to conclude that the inadequacy of the purchasing-power remedy for the American unemployment problem has been demonstrated. And I think that a major shift in Administration strategy is emerging. President Johnson has recommended a reduction in excise taxes, it is true, but the size of the proposed cut is much less than the income-tax cut of 1964. The new tax cut is also much smaller than proposed increases in federal spending for education, retraining, and other programs to improve the abilities of those who are at a disadvantage in today's job market. Thus, I see the emergence of a greatly increased emphasis on the earning-power remedy for excessive unemployment. It would be a serious mistake to expect immediate and dramatic results from this new emphasis. Investment in human beings is a slow and costly process, and the difficulties are especially great when we must deal with large numbers of inadequately educated adults. Yet I venture to be hopeful about our prospects for meeting the challenge of unemployment in this way over the next few years.

Finally, I suggest that fairness requires recognition of the fact that, in some respects, our present unemployment problem is a paradoxical result of our past successes in mass education. For many years the United States has provided more years of education for a larger percentage of its population than any other country. As the educational attainment of the majority of our citizens has improved, the disadvantage of the minority who were left behind for one reason or another has increased. Our successes in mass education have also helped to stimulate the rapid changes in technology and in the patterns of consumer spending that have so greatly affected our job market. Americans have always placed a high value on education. Now we are coming to realize that adequate education for all is essential, not only for spiritual and political well-being, but also for the economic welfare of the nation.

7 ANOTHER VIEW OF UNEMPLOYMENT

Otto Eckstein

Since 1946, the achievement of full employment has been one of the main goals of economic policy in the United States. The Employment Act passed by the Congress in that year charged the federal government with promoting "conditions under which there will be afforded useful employment opportunities, including self-employment, for those able, willing, and seeking to work." This milestone legislation was a public commitment to the promotion of full employment. In the succeeding nineteen years, all administrations have abided by that commitment. And indeed, the resultant record on employment in these two decades is one that is unmatched in our history. The economy has remained free of serious depression, of the mass unemployment of the 1930's, the 1890's, or the 1870's.

Though the threat of depression is remote, unemployment has remained a major economic problem both in recession and in periods of insufficient growth. Thus, the government has launched active fiscal and manpower policies to reduce unemployment further through more jobs, better training, and more efficient matching of workers and jobs.

PROGRESS SINCE 1947

I begin with a review of postwar experience. The postwar period as a whole has seen sustained gains for the economy and for American labor. In the seventeen-year period 1947–1964, real Gross National Product was up by 83 per cent, or an annual rate of growth of 3.6 per cent; real Gross National Product per capita was up by 37 per cent, or an annual rate of improvement of 1.9

97

per cent; the purchasing power of an hour of work in the private sector increased by 54 per cent, or 2.5 per cent a year; employment increased by 22 per cent, or 1.2 per cent a year; and the fraction of gross national income received by labor increased from 65 per cent to 71 per cent, a significant gain for labor in the distribution of income.

But, over the same period, the economy did not live up to its full potential. There were four recessions, and in each of them unemployment rose by several percentage points, three times briefly into the 6 to 7 per cent range. In its fifty-third month by July 1965, the present expansion is the longest that this country has ever experienced in peacetime and could presage a major improvement of the economy with regard to the frequency and depth of recessions.

Unemployment has remained a problem even apart from recessions. Recovery from the 1958 recession was incomplete, and unemployment remained above 5 per cent until the spring of 1965. During this lengthy period, a number of observers became concerned that the economy had somehow lost its ability to achieve full employment. These fears have been based on a variety of supposedly new factors. As unemployment has moved closer to our targets this year, these fears have become abated. I shall return to them.

STATISTICAL AND STRUCTURAL DIFFERENCES

To understand the American record on unemployment, one must keep in mind the method by which these statistics are constructed. The United States bases its official national series on a monthly survey in which interviewers ask a sample of the population whether or not they were looking for a job during the survey week. If they reply in the affirmative, they are unemployed. Most other countries base their unemployment statistics on the records of the official unemployment insurance system. This means that those segments of the population who are only loosely attached to the labor force are not likely to be counted as unemployed because they are not eligible for unemployment insurance. It also means that part-time workers may be left out of figures.

A major international comparison was undertaken by the President's Committee on the Unemployment Statistics in 1962. The findings of that study are summarized in Table 7–1. It shows, for example, that in 1960 the unemployment rate in Britain, which was reported as 1.6 per cent, would have been 2.4 per cent if that country had used the American concepts and techniques of measurement. Corresponding differences exist for other countries.

TABLE 7–1. *Rate of Unemployment in 1960, as Published and after Adjustment to U.S. Definitions*[1]

COUNTRY	UNADJUSTED	ADJUSTED
United States	5.6	5.6
Canada	7.0	7.0
France	1.1	1.9
Germany (F.R.)	1.2	1.0
Great Britain	1.6	2.4
Italy	7.9	4.3
Japan	1.0	1.1
Sweden (1961)	1.2	1.5

1 "Measuring Employment and Unemployment," President's Committee to Appraise Employment and Unemployment Statistics, Superintendent of Documents, Washington, D.C., September 27, 1962, p. 220.

A comparison of actual unemployment statistics for the advanced countries in the last few years still leaves the American rates higher by 1 to 3 percentage points. Thus, the method of compiling the statistics does not account for the high American figure by itself. But it does mean that the average rate of the last seven years, which by American concepts was 5.9 per cent, would have been 3.5 to 4 per cent if we had computed our figures as France or Great Britain do.

There are also some fundamental differences between the structure of the American economy and of other economies which make for a higher rate of unemployment here. First, the percentage of the labor force in agriculture is smaller than in most other countries because of the very high productivity of American agriculture. Only 6.5 per cent of our civilian labor is needed on the farm to feed the nation and help feed the world. Unemployment rates of the agricultural labor force are usually low because under-utilization of labor does not manifest itself as open unemployment, but rather as disguised unemployment, that is, employment which keeps hands busy but producing little. Even in the United States, there is some disguised unemployment in the more backward rural parts of the country, but the extent of this disguised unemployment is probably lower than in some "fully employed" economies.

Second, the United States has a rapidly rising population. As a result, the extent of frictional unemployment, particularly that associated with the search for the first job, is higher here. Further, the United States has not experienced periods of acute labor shortage since World War II, and, as a consequence, there is very little labor-hoarding by employers. In the European countries, all of which experienced some periods of retardation of growth in the postwar period, unemployment was kept down by continuing labor-hoarding by employers afraid that they would not be able to rehire their workers. It is also much more difficult to fire a worker in many countries because of restrictions on employer action.

Further, the larger part of unemployment in the United States is of a short-run nature. Last year, for example, almost half of all unemployment was of people out of work four weeks or less. Finally, the American labor force is far less homogeneous and the American labor market of greater geographic scope and of greater range in skills than the labor markets of smaller countries, and these factors, too, make for a permanently higher average rate of unemployment.

Throughout its history, the United States has gambled on a high mobility of labor and few restrictions on hiring and firing. So far, it has been handsomely rewarded in rising productivity and living standards.

For these reasons of measurement and of economic structure, the Council of Economic Advisors has used a 4 per cent rate of unemployment as its interim target of full employment. Now that the United States has embarked on major programs of manpower development, it should be possible in the future to improve that target to less than 4 per cent.

THE DEVELOPMENT OF EXCESS UNEMPLOYMENT SINCE 1957

Since 1957, the economy has failed to live up to the 4 per cent interim target. Inadequate growth of demand kept the total private and public demand for goods and services short of the economy's capacity to produce. Total demand is provided by private consumption expenditures, private investment expenditures, net exports, and government expenditures on goods and services. In addition to its direct expenditures, the government can influence private spending by raising or lowering taxes, by changing transfer payments, and by its credit policies. Thus, the government has a large influence on the level of total demand in the economy—an influence so great that its economic policies are a major determinant of the degree of prosperity of the economy as a whole. Since the 1957–1958 recession, the level of total demand has not been large enough to fully employ the labor and capital resources of the economy. The combination of public spending- and tax-policy and our money- and credit-policies did not offset the weakening of private demands that was inevitable after the high levels of investment in the mid-1950's and the unsustainably large outlays by consumers for automobiles. Indeed, federal policies became more restrictive, culminating in the recession of 1960–1961. Since 1961, the present administration has followed a policy of stimulating private demand to move the economy back toward full potential operation. Unemployment improved from 7 to 5.5 per cent in the first year of recovery, but then remained near that level for two more years. It was in response to this continuation of unemployment that the government fashioned the 14 billion dollar tax reduction of 1964, which increased after-tax incomes and accelerated the expansion of markets, thereby reducing unemployment to 4.75 per cent within the first twelve months after its enactment.

THE PATTERN OF IMPROVEMENT OF THE LAST TWELVE MONTHS AND THE "UNEMPLOYABLE"

During the years of stubborn unemployment in excess of 5 per cent, the view was widely propounded that structural changes had occurred which made it permanently impossible to achieve the interim unemployment targets without massive new programs of manpower-development. Indeed, there was one school of thought which saw automation of such scope that work would become unnecessary and people would have to be paid their full income without working to purchase the goods produced by the automated machines without labor.

No one can foretell what the remote future holds in store. But for the present era in our economy, these theories are very much premature. Just one year of rapid expansion of demand and of markets has created the jobs for the groups whose employability had been called into question. Let me review a few figures, contrasting the employment experience of the last year of rapid expansion with the preceding trends of the recent past.

With the stimulus of the tax cut, employment rose by 1.8 million new jobs or by 2.5 per cent from June 1964 to June 1965. This is a rate of advance twice as high as the 1.2 per cent rate of annual advance during the previous four years.

Even more striking are changes in the composition of employment gains:

1. In the previous four years, employment of semiskilled operatives had risen by only 665,000, or 1.3 per cent a year. This had led many people to conclude that there were relatively fewer jobs for the semiskilled, but in the most recent twelve months, their employment shot up by 511,000, or 3.9 per cent.

2. Among unskilled nonfarm laborers, employment had actually fallen by 21,000 in the previous four years. Yet in the past year, employment for this group rose by 226,000, or 5.5 per cent.

3. Teenage employment rose by 283,000 in the last year or 1.75 times as fast as the national rate of advance.

4. Unemployment among nonwhites had deteriorated compared to whites. But in the last twelve months, nonwhite employment rose by 2.7 per cent, and their unemployment rate fell 1.5 percentage points. In addition, the new drive for equality of job opportunity under the Civil Rights Act of 1964 holds the promise for future breakthroughs for our nonwhite labor force.

5. In the previous four years, the number of individuals un-

employed for fifteen weeks or more rose a total of 23 per cent, but in the last year their numbers fell by 24 per cent, bringing long-term unemployment to its lowest level in eight years.

6. Within industries, those heavy industries that were supposedly suffering from the sharpest long-term declines made the largest employment gains. In the last twelve months, the five major metals and metal-using industries accounted for increases in employment of more than 500,000 jobs, a very large increase after eight years of relative stagnation and bringing the unemployment rate for workers in these industries down to levels previously enjoyed only during periods of full employment.

7. While the unemployment rates for males eighteen and over with less than eight years of education were falling by 1.8 percentage points from 1964 to 1965, the rate for those with four years of high school was falling by 0.7 percentage points. Thus, the least-educated improved their position substantially.

The experience of the last year demonstrates that, when overall expansion proceeds rapidly, the pattern of employment gains is especially favorable to those groups who normally suffer the highest unemployment rates, those who are the last to be hired and the first to be fired.

In an economy which has been creating over 1.5 million jobs per year since the tax cut and where disadvantaged workers have been making greater than average gains, experience has demonstrated that full employment can be attained. When the demand for labor expands, business will hire inexperienced workers when experienced workers are less readily available. Job specifications are changed and prejudices weaken when workers are less readily available.

In addition, while the quality of job opportunities demanded has risen, so has the quality of the labor force. Individuals with low education levels are concentrated in the upper-age groups. As they retire and the number of better educated young workers rises, the average education level of the labor force improves rapidly. Today's labor force is substantially better educated, with a median length of schooling of 12.2 years compared to 11.6 years in 1957.

The task of reaching full employment is far from complete.

Some 3.5 million workers were still unemployed in June 1965. The teenage unemployment rate was 14.1 per cent; the rate for nonwhites was 8.4 per cent. The over-all rate of 4.7 per cent was still 0.7 percentage points above the interim target, and that target is one which was set before we launched the manpower policies which would allow us to improve our goals. It will take continued expansionary fiscal and monetary policies to reach the 4 per cent rate, and it will take improved and expanded policies of manpower development to reach still more favorable levels.

8 THE HISTORY OF THE AMERICAN LABOR MOVEMENT WITH SPECIAL REFERENCE TO DEVELOPMENTS IN THE 1930'S

Sidney Fine

The decade of the 1930's was the most significant decade in the history of the American labor movement. During that span of years, the policy of the federal government with regard to the labor movement changed from toleration, or even hostility, to positive encouragement; the number of organized workers more than doubled. For the first time, unionism established itself in a significant way in the mass-production industries; and what had been a dispirited and demoralized labor movement became a vital and powerful force on the American scene.

WEAKNESS OF THE LABOR MOVEMENT BEFORE 1933

Throughout the history of the labor movement in the United States before the advent of the New Deal, only a small minority of American workers had seen fit to enroll in the ranks of the nation's trade unions. As of 1900, only 3 per cent of the civilian labor force (which, of course, includes many workers whom the unions made no attempt to organize) were union members. Twenty years later, the percentage of the organized had increased to twelve, but the union gains of the World War I era were largely dissipated in the early 1920's. As the decade of the 1930's opened, the approximately 3.4 million union members constituted but 6.8 per cent of the civilian labor force.

The reluctance of the American workingman to cast his lot with the labor movement is partly explained by the scarcity of labor in the United States as compared to the other factors of production. Believing that it was possible under the circumstances for him to escape from his dependent status into the class of the self-employed, the workingman saw himself, not as a permanent member of a wage-earning proletariat, but rather as an actual or at least a potential member of the middle class and thus was relatively immune to union appeals that had the solidarity of labor as their basis. The heterogeneous character of the American wage-earners, which was the product of large-scale immigration and internal minorities; the hostility of most employers to union recognition; and the obstacles placed in the path of union activity by government were additional impediments to the growth of union membership.

The law of labor relations as of 1930 recognized the right of workers to organize and to bargain collectively, but employers were, on the whole, free to interfere with this right. Reluctant to accept any encroachment on customary prerogatives, employers consequently used their superior power to discourage organization and to limit its effectiveness where it existed. The labor spy, the company union, the yellow-dog contract, discrimination against union members, and refusal to bargain were tactics resorted to by management to combat trade unionism. Not only did the state, for the most part, view these anti-union weapons permissively, but the agencies of government, and especially the courts, in effect supplemented employer efforts by using the injunction and the anti-trust laws to limit the effectiveness of the strike, the boycott, and the union picket line and even to prevent union organizers from seeking to enroll workers who had signed yellow-dog contracts. In acting as it did, government was undoubtedly reflecting a prevailing popular mistrust of the labor movement as a collectivist force, but the shape of things to come was foreshadowed by the Railway Labor Act of 1926, which restrained railway employers from interfering with the concerted activities of their employees, and the Norris–La Guardia Act of 1932, which placed severe limitations on the use of injunctions in labor disputes.

NATURE OF THE AMERICAN FEDERATION OF LABOR

As the decade of the 1930's opened, the vast majority of the workers who were union members belonged to organizations that were affiliated with the American Federation of Labor. The business type of unionism practiced by the AFL had triumphed in the late nineteenth century over a reform type of unionism which, viewing the new industrialism with alarm, looked backward to the less complex economy of an earlier era and hoped to fashion a society where every man was his own employer. Aware of the unrealistic character of reform unionism, but at the same time cognizant of the lack of class consciousness of the American worker, the leadership of the AFL espoused a brand of unionism that concerned itself not so much with the social status of the worker as with his job and the terms under which it was held.

As the method of improving the lot of the worker, the AFL placed its faith in collective bargaining and the economic power of unionism, and it rejected government assistance, independent political action, and approaches from the left as alternative means of reaching labor's goals. It viewed government as more malevolent than benevolent, and, although willing to support the enactment of protective legislation for women and children, it asked that the state neither aid nor hinder the adult male laborer and the functioning of the union of which he might be a member. It asked its members to take an interest in politics, and it came to urge them to "reward" their political friends and "punish" their political enemies, but it stood foursquare against the independent labor party as a weapon of the labor movement. Because of its appreciation of the strength of American capitalism, the middle-class psychology of the American worker, and the commitment of the American public to the concept of private property, the AFL came to repudiate socialism as the solution for the labor question, and it was a determined foe of communism from the moment that doctrine made its appearance on the American scene.

The socialists and the communists, for their part, were unable to mount a really formidable challenge to the AFL's domination of the labor movement. The Socialist Labor party, after failing to convert the AFL to socialism, set up a rival labor alliance in the 1890's, but the new labor group was hardly more than a paper organization. In the twentieth century, although a few socialists participated in the formation of the anarcho-syndicalist Industrial Workers of the World (IWW), the bulk of the trade unionists who were Socialist party members worked within the AFL, and even the unions that had socialist officers and subscribed to socialist principles, such as the International Ladies Garment Workers Union (ILGWU), functioned in about the same manner as the AFL unions that were more conservatively oriented. During most of the 1920's, Communists sought to bore from within the AFL and then, toward the end of the decade, shifted to a policy of dual unionism; but neither tactic met with any conspicuous success outside of some branches of the needle trades. The triumph of collective bargaining as the method of unionism, a unique feature of the American labor movement, and the failure of left wing and other tactics are explained, in good part, by the expanding nature of the American economy, which permitted the business type of unionism to succeed and thus discouraged the workers from seeking other means of achieving their economic goals.

Founded in 1886 by national trade unions which were disturbed at the efforts of the all-encompassing Knights of Labor to invade their jurisdiction, the AFL was committed from the start to the principles of the autonomy and the exclusive jurisdiction of its affiliated national and international unions. Each of these organizations was to be sovereign within its jurisdiction, which the AFL would seek to protect from invasion; and each was to regulate its internal affairs free from the interference of the AFL itself.

As for the type of worker whom it sought to organize, before 1930, the AFL concentrated on the organization of the skilled workers, who were embraced within craft and amalgamated craft unions, and it viewed the semiskilled and unskilled, for too long, as essentially lacking in bargaining power and hence difficult, if not impossible, to organize. Similarly, although a few industrial unions, such as the United Mine Workers (UMW), were affiliated with the AFL, the Federation favored organization by trades rather than by industries, and as of 1930, the great mass-production industries, notably the steel and automobile industries, were almost entirely without organization. The bulk of the AFL membership at that time was concentrated in the building trades, printing, transportation and communication, and coal mining. Less than 15 per cent of the Federation's members had jobs in the manufacturing sector of the economy, and less than 20 per cent were enrolled in industrial unions.

On the defensive throughout the prosperous 1920's and severely challenged by employer tactics designed to block independent unionism, the AFL, as one labor historian has observed, abandoned "militancy" for "respectability."[1] It sought to improve its position and increase its membership, not by vigorous organizing drives nor—except for the railway unions and eventually the UMW—by seeking government assistance, but rather by union-management cooperation and by attempting to convince employers and the public of its respectability and patriotism. When the depression of the Hoover years swelled the ranks of the unemployed to an unprecedented 25 per cent of the civilian labor force and reduced the ranks of the unionized by almost 470,000, the AFL was initially reluctant to abandon old ideas and strike out along new paths. Before Roosevelt became president, it did not abandon its position regarding the virtues of craft as compared to industrial unionism, and it was only toward the close of Hoover's term that it gave some evidence that it was prepared to alter its views with respect to the role of government in the sphere of industrial relations. It was FDR's New Deal that was to revitalize and transform the labor movement and was to produce a profound change in its composition and in many of its basic principles.

THE NEW DEAL VIEW OF LABOR

The theory of the New Deal with regard to labor was that it was receiving an inadequate share of the national income, or that at least the purchasing power of workers was inadequate to sustain prosperity, and that the bargaining power of organized labor was considerably less than that of management. It sought to cope

[1] Irving Bernstein, *The Lean Years: A History of the American Worker, 1920–1933* (Boston: Houghton Mifflin, 1960), p. 97.

with these problems by legislation designed to raise the standards of labor throughout the economy, particularly among the less fortunate members of the labor force, and to increase the strength of organized labor so that the unionized workers could improve their economic position by their own efforts. The executive branch of the government was primarily responsible for the New Deal legislation with regard to labor standards, but neither President Roosevelt nor Secretary of Labor Frances Perkins, at least during the early years of the New Deal, was especially interested in the promotion of unionism. It fell to Congress, and particularly to Senator Robert F. Wagner of New York, to initiate the legislation designed to encourage labor organization and collective bargaining.

THE NEW DEAL AND LABOR STANDARDS

The objectives of the New Deal with regard to labor standards were to spread the work by reducing the hours of labor, to increase purchasing power by raising wages and increasing employment, and to reduce child labor. The initial effort of the New Deal to secure these goals was embodied in the National Industrial Recovery Act (NIRA) of 1933. The statute permitted trade or industrial associations to draw up codes of fair competition whose provisions were to become "the standards of fair competition" for the industry or trade concerned when the codes had been approved by the president. Each code had to specify that employers were to comply with the maximum hours of work, the minimum wages, and other conditions of employment that might be approved or prescribed by the president. Although it was a questionable experiment insofar as the general control of the economy was concerned, the NIRA, the first statute in American history to provide for the regulation of working conditions on a general basis, did lift the prevailing level of labor standards throughout the nation. Definite progress was made in curbing child labor, sweatshop conditions were alleviated, a decided impetus was given to the shorter hours movement, and unusually low wages were raised.

The New Deal did not abandon its efforts to ameliorate working conditions when the NIRA was declared unconstitutional in May 1935. In 1936, Congress enacted the Walsh-Healey Public Contracts Act, which specified minimum labor standards to be observed by government contractors. More general, although far from complete, coverage was not provided until the enactment of the Fair Labor Standards Act of 1938. The statute provided for a minimum wage that was to rise to 40 cents per hour by October 1945 (the legal minimum has been raised several times since and now stands at $1.15–$1.25), a basic workweek that was to be reduced to forty hours by October 1940, a time-and-a-half rate for hours worked above the maximum, and the abolition of child labor under sixteen years of age and between sixteen and eighteen years in hazardous occupations. The Fair Labor Standards Act has made the forty-hour week the standard workweek in America, has raised the wages of the most poorly paid workers, and perhaps has had a ballooning effect on wages above the minimum, and has wiped out child labor in almost all industries.

The New Deal not only sought to raise prevailing labor standards, but it was also responsible for innovating legislation in the area of social security which although not confined to the nation's toilers was of particular importance to them. The Social Security Act of 1935, the New Deal's response to the widespread feeling of economic insecurity produced by the great depression, provided for a federal system of old-age insurance; a cooperative federal-state system of unemployment insurance; and federal grants to the states for the needy aged over sixty-five, for the blind, for dependent children, and for a variety of public-health services. Although the coverage provided by the statute and the size of the benefits paid under it left much to be desired, the important fact was that the principle of federal responsibility for social security had been accepted and a foundation laid on which subsequent congresses and the labor movement itself have been able to build. Not only did Congress in later years widen the coverage and increase the benefits initially provided by the statute, but through collective bargaining, many unions have been able to make provision for management to supplement what the workers receive from the government in the form of old-age pensions and unemployment insurance.

111

SECTION 7(a) AND ITS EFFECT

Organized labor had relatively little to do with the framing and enactment of the New Deal legislation designed to improve labor standards and to enhance the security of the workingman, but in a historic reversal of policy, the AFL played a major role in the enactment of New Deal statutes that sought to protect the right of organization and collective bargaining from employer interference, for the first time in American history on a general basis. The NIRA was the initial effort of the New Deal to protect the self-organization of workers. Since the statute encouraged associative action by business groups, in order to secure the cooperation of organized labor and to balance the concessions to organized business, the framers of the law required in Section 7 (a) of the statute that every code provide that employees were to have "the right to organize and bargain collectively through representatives of their own choosing" and were to be free from "the interference, restraint, or coercion" of employers in designating their representatives, in self-organization, or in "other concerted activities for the purpose of collective bargaining." Finally, neither an employee nor a person seeking employment could be required as a condition of employment to join a company union or to refrain from joining or aiding a labor organization of his own choice.

Unfortunately, Section 7(a) raised more questions than it answered. It did not indicate how representatives were to be selected nor whether the representatives of the majority of employees were to bargain for all the employees in a particular bargaining unit or only for those who had selected them. It did not specifically obligate employers to deal with employee representatives, did not appear to have prohibited individual bargaining or company unions per se, and did not define the particular employer tactics that constituted "interference, restraint, or coercion." Most important of all, no machinery was provided for the section's enforcement. Government labor boards created by the President answered most of the questions posed by Section 7(a) and, in the process, defined the content of collective bargaining, but because of the lack of significant penalties attaching to noncompliance, employers defied the rulings of these boards with virtual impunity.

Whatever its defects, Section 7(a) provided at least some encouragement to unionization, and such organizations as the UMW and the unions in the garment trades capitalized on the opportunity and expanded their membership substantially. The AFL, however, still not convinced that the unskilled could be successfully organized, lacked the zeal, the creative leadership, and the will to organize the unorganized on any large scale; and it proved itself unable to deal realistically with the need for industrial unionism in the mass-production industries. It did, to be sure, charter a substantial number of national labor unions (plant unions) in such previously unorganized sectors of the economy as the automobile and rubber industries; but the craft unions protested the inclusion in these unions of the skilled workers over whom they claimed jurisdiction, even though they had failed to organize these workers themselves. As the experience of the United Automobile Workers (UAW) was to demonstrate, moreover, national labor unionists had to reckon with the probability that when the national labor unions in any industry were joined together to form a new international union, the AFL would insist that the skilled workers whom they had enrolled be transferred to their appropriate craft unions.

In sum, union membership as a percentage of the civilian labor force inched upward between 1933 and 1935 from 5.8 to 6.9, which represented a membership increase of only 686,000 (from 2,973,000 to 3,659,300). These membership gains were certainly not as impressive as they might have been, considering the opportunity presented by Section 7(a), but the NIRA experience was nevertheless of momentous significance for the future of the labor movement. The content of the legislation to replace the defunct Section 7(a) was, for one thing, significantly influenced by the principles formulated by the government labor boards created during the NIRA period. It had been demonstrated, furthermore, that not only government support but also union militancy and daring were required if organization were to be brought to the unorganized. Finally, the unions that were to spearhead the great organizing drives after 1935 were precisely those unions like the UMW that had taken advantage of Section 7(a), and a beginning —however feeble—had been made in the organization of the mass-production industries.

The failure of the AFL to resolve the problem of industrial unionism to the satisfaction of the minority of industrial unionists in its midst led to civil war in the labor movement. Unable to secure an endorsement of industrial unionism at the 1935 AFL convention, the industrial unionists in the organization, led by John L. Lewis, created a Committee for Industrial Organization to promote the cause of industrial unionism within the AFL. In an action that was not authorized by the Federation's constitution, the AFL Executive Council, in September 1936, suspended the ten unions affiliated with the CIO. When efforts to effect a reconciliation failed, the AFL in 1938 expelled the CIO unions, and they thereupon formed themselves into the Congress of Industrial Organizations.

THE WAGNER ACT AND ITS EFFECT

The task of union organization had in the meantime been facilitated by the enactment in July 1935 of the National Labor Relations or Wagner Act, a statute that went considerably beyond Section 7(a) in the protection it afforded to unionization and collective bargaining. Unlike Section 7(a), it not only asserted the right of employees to organize and to bargain collectively through their chosen representatives, but it also specifically defined the unfair practices that constituted interference with this right. It was henceforth to be an "unfair labor practice" for an employer: (1) to "interfere with, restrain, or coerce" employees in the exercise of their right to organize and to bargain; (2) to dominate or interfere with a labor organization or to contribute to its support; (3) to discriminate against employees for the purpose of encouraging or discouraging membership in a labor organization; (4) to discriminate against an employee for filing charges or giving testimony under the act; and (5) to refuse to bargain with employee representatives.

In contrast to Section 7(a), the Wagner Act provided machinery for its enforcement, and it supplied the answers to the questions regarding representation posed by the earlier measure. It established a National Labor Relations Board (NLRB) to carry out the terms of the statute and authorized it to issue orders requiring the cessation by employers of unfair labor practices and to appeal to the federal circuit courts for the enforcement of these orders. It accepted the principle of majority rule in the designation of employee representatives (rather than proportional representation or some other form of collective-bargaining pluralism) and thus resolved the most contentious question that had arisen under Section 7 (a). It authorized the board to hold elections to determine whom the employees wished to represent them and lodged in the NLRB the power to determine the appropriate unit for collective-bargaining purposes.

By disestablishing illegally constituted company unions, reinstating, with back pay, workers against whom discrimination had been practiced, ordering employers to bargain, holding elections to determine employee representatives, and insisting that labor agreements take the form of signed contracts rather than unilateral statements of policy by employers, the NLRB protected the right of employees to organize and to bargain and helped to create an atmosphere conducive to union growth. The union cause was further aided by the hearings beginning in 1936 of the Senate's La Follette Committee, which exposed the variety of tactics resorted to by employers to combat unionism, and by Supreme Court decisions after 1937 that took a tolerant view of such union weapons as picketing and that severely limited the application of the anti-trust acts to labor unions.

Whether the spectacular union-membership gains of the latter portion of the 1930's could have been made and maintained without the protection afforded by the Wagner Act is doubtful. But the Wagner Act and the NLRB did more than encourage union growth. The board instructed unions and management that they must bargain, although not necessarily agree, about such matters as bonuses, paid holidays, and, at a later time, pension funds, and in effect, it threw its support in the 1930's to industrial rather than craft unionism by deciding in cases that were before it that the plant and sometimes the company or even the industry were the appropriate units for collective-bargaining purposes. The NLRB thus played a part in the bargaining process and in fixing jurisdictional boundaries that was altogether inconsistent with the concept of exclusive jurisdiction and with the pre-1930 views of the labor movement regarding the proper role of government in the sphere of labor–management relations.

MEMBERSHIP GAINS OF AFL AND CIO

It was not until April 1937, when the Supreme Court declared the statute constitutional, that the employers accepted the fact that the National Labor Relations Act however much they still disapproved of it as a one-sided measure was the law of the land. It was also in 1937, the *annus mirabilis* of the American labor movement, that the CIO, brilliantly led by John L. Lewis, then enjoying his finest hour, made a dramatic and crucial breakthrough in the organization of the mass-production industries. In the first four months of the year, the UAW, a CIO affiliate, used the tactic of the sit-down strike to bring General Motors and Chrysler Corporation to terms, and the United States Steel Company surrendered without a fight to the CIO's Steelworkers Organizing Committee, which had been conducting a precedent-making large-scale and well-financed organizing drive in the steel industry. The CIO tide in the 1930's also swept over the rubber industry, the electrical and radio manufacturing industries, and a segment of the maritime trades; but less success attended the CIO campaigns in the textile industry, where employers in the South and a large number of middle- and small-sized firms worried about their costs, offered stern resistance, and in the petroleum industry, where the liberal wage policy of management was a deterrent to union success.

The triumphs of the CIO stimulated the AFL and its affiliates to provide the money and the organizers to launch major organizing campaigns of their own, and, in the process, the distinctions between craft and industrial unionism that had caused so much discord were conveniently ignored. The Carpenters entrenched themselves in a portion of the lumber industry; and the building trades as a whole expanded into such new areas as heavy and highway construction; the Teamsters tripled their membership between 1936 and 1941; and the Machinists and the Electrical Workers successfully invaded the mass-production industries. By 1940, union membership, which had stood at a little more than 3.6 million in 1935, had zoomed to over 8 million, and the unionized percentage of the civilian labor force had risen from 6.9 to 14.6. Because of the difficulty of estimating the actual as distinguished from the claimed membership of the CIO unions, it is possible that the 1940 membership figures are somewhat inflated, but, at the very minimum, the number of unionists increased by more than 3 million in the second half of the 1930's despite the fact that the unemployment rate during these years never fell below 14 per cent of the civilian labor force. The CIO claimed, in 1940, a membership approximately equal to that of the AFL, but there is little doubt that the Federation, which had better withstood the shock of the recession of 1937–1938 than its rival, was numerically the stronger of the two organizations.

The most significant union membership gains in the latter half of the 1930's came in the manufacturing sector of the economy. Slightly more than 34 per cent of the wage and salaried workers in manufacturing were organized in 1940, as compared to less than 9 per cent in 1930 and a little over 13 per cent in 1935. Remarkable progress was also made in the areas of transportation, communication, and public utilities, where the percentage of the organized increased from 23.4 in 1930, and 26.4 in 1935, to 48.2 in 1940. Less spectacular but solid gains were achieved in sectors of the economy where unionism was already strong, but despite the successful organization of railway clerks, communication workers, and newspaper reporters, unionism was woefully weak in the growing white-collar sector of the economy. Geographically speaking, union strength in 1940 was concentrated in the Middle Atlantic and East Northcentral states and was least in evidence in the South.

DIFFERENCES BETWEEN THE AFL AND THE CIO

The distinction between the AFL and CIO with regard to industrial unionism tended to be blurred as the AFL reached out for the semiskilled factory worker, but there were other differences between the two rivals. Aware that it had been greatly assisted by the legislation of a friendly administration, the CIO was more inclined than the AFL to favor the intervention of government in the economy, and it was far more politically-oriented than the Federation. Proponents of what became the Fair Labor Standards Act thus drew support from the CIO but not the AFL, and Labor's Nonpartisan League, set up in 1936 to ensure Roosevelt's re-election, was essentially a CIO organization. The AFL did not become so politically active as the CIO until the close of World War II; but despite its official position, it had ceased to be neutral politically since 1936 and, like its rival, had been giving its support mostly to the Democratic party.

Whereas many of the unions affiliated with the AFL in the pre-New Deal era either excluded Negroes from membership or placed them in segregated locals, the CIO unions, particularly at the national level, gave Negroes full membership rights on a nonsegregated basis. At its 1936 convention, the AFL did pass a resolution calling on its member organizations to end discriminatory practices, but it could not force its autonomous affiliates to modify their discriminatory policies, and the progress that was made in most unions did not satisfy the proponents of equal rights.

Unlike the AFL, John L. Lewis, anxious to take advantage of their experience and confident that he could control them, knowingly employed Communists in the organizing drives of the CIO. Since Communism was then in its united front phase, American Communists enthusiastically lent their support to the CIO cause and infiltrated many of the CIO unions, eventually gaining control, at the very least, of unions with 25 per cent of the CIO membership. Whereas Communism was a problem for the CIO, corruption was more a problem for the AFL. The CIO expelled its Communist-controlled unions in 1949 and 1950, and the AFL, in the early 1950's, began taking more forthright action to deal with the corruption that plagued a few of its affiliates, thus removing two of the obstacles that stood in the way of the merger of the two organizations, which was accomplished in 1955. The emergence of new leadership in the AFL and CIO, the lessening of differences in their policies, the belief of both groups that they were politically on the defensive, their successful cooperation in the International Confederation of Free Trade Unions and in various foreign-policy programs, and the desire of the affiliates of the two organizations to protect their memberships against raids from their rivals were other factors that led to the unification of the labor movement.

RECENT PROBLEMS OF THE LABOR MOVEMENT

At the time that the AFL-CIO merger was accomplished, the labor movement no longer enjoyed the degree of public support that had been accorded it at the height of the New Deal. The emergence of a powerful labor movement in the 1930's led to the demands in some circles that labor unions, like corporations, must be regulated in the public interest and that restrictions must be placed on union behavior. Five states adopted statutes of the Wagner Act type in 1937, but the legislatures of many more states balked at the passage of such legislation. In 1939, four states adopted laws that struck at the "unfair" labor practices of unions as well as management, and in the years to come additional states were to adopt regulatory laws of the restrictive type. The federal government fell into line with the enactment in 1947 of the Taft-Hartley Act, a statute which also gave the President the power to delay strikes that threatened the national welfare. Twelve years later, the Labor Management Reporting and Disclosure Act, for the first time in American history, authorized significant federal intervention in the internal affairs of labor unions.

Not only did the labor movement find itself subjected, after 1947, to government controls of which it disapproved, but it has also been troubled in recent years by the failure of union membership to grow at a faster rate. Union membership soared during the defense and war periods, the total reaching 13,379,000 in 1945, which constituted about 25 per cent of the civilian labor force. Such gains as were made, however, came largely in areas of the economy where unions were already well established at the end of the 1930's. Between 1945 and 1953, union membership expressed as a percentage of the labor force increased slightly, but since the end of the Korean War, the percentage of those organized has actually decreased somewhat. Employment has been receding in such heavily unionized sectors of the economy as manufacturing, mining, and transportation, but has been growing in the much less well-organized white-collar occupations; women, less likely to join unions than men, have been entering the labor force in increasing numbers; and industry has been moving to the South and the smaller towns, where unionism is weaker than in the rest of the country. Whether the union forces will be able to develop strength in areas of the economy where unionism has been weak to offset losses in areas where it has been strong is a question of transcendent importance to the future of the American labor movement.

9 FORCES AFFECTING THE GROWTH OF THE AMERICAN LABOR MOVEMENT

Irving Bernstein

My topic is complicated, subtle, and is the subject of controversy in the United States. There are several reasons for this, and I think it important that you understand them before I move into the substance of the discussion.

The first is that the trade union in the American environment, as a penetrating student of this question, Robert F. Hoxie, observed, is "one of the most complex, diffuse, and protean of modern social phenomena."[1] It is, therefore, impossible to interpret the labor movement or to explain its growth or decline with a single theory. Rather, one must develop, as Hoxie put it, a "pluralistic" system of explanation.

Second, although American statistics in many areas are very good, we have serious inadequacies in our measures of trade-union membership. There is, for example, disagreement over how a "member" should be defined and even over the definition of a "union." Many of our labor organizations call themselves "internationals" and report their membership in Canada, Puerto Rico, and the Canal Zone, as well as in the United States. We have no consistent statistical series going back over many years and cannot make exact historical comparisons. Fortunately, the statistics are now getting better, but they still leave much to be desired.

For these reasons, there is considerable room for disagreement in interpretation, and scholars who have studied this topic have often reached differing conclusions. Thus, you must understand

[1] Robert F. Hoxie, *Trade Unionism in the United States* (New York: Appleton-Century, 1921), p. 1.

that the interpretations that I shall offer are not universally accepted; they are, rather, my own views.

With this caution out of the way, I should like to set out the three subjects that I intend to cover: (1) the size and distribution of the American labor movement in the 1960's; (2) an explanation of how this contemporary labor movement grew into its present size and shape; and (3) a suggestion of the problems that the American labor movement will probably face in the future, if it is to continue to play a significant role in American society.

SIZE AND SHAPE OF THE LABOR MOVEMENT

In 1962, the latest year for which the Bureau of Labor Statistics has made a count, there were 16,958,000 dues-paying union members in the United States. This statistic excludes the following categories: members who paid less than full dues because they were unemployed, retired, or on strike; employees in units for which unions bargained collectively who were not themselves members; members of associations which were not classed as unions, but which have bargaining functions; and dues-paying members of American unions who lived in other countries. This figure—just under 17 million members in 1962—constituted 23.1 per cent of the 71.9 million persons in the civilian labor force and 29.7 per cent of the 55.8 million people who were employed outside agriculture. In comparison with other industrialized democratic countries, union organization of the labor force is relatively low in the United States.

The organized workers in 1962 were members of 181 national and international unions which had about 60,000 local unions affiliated to them. In addition, there were some 1,300 local unions which had no affiliation with a national organization. The great majority of both national unions and members were associated with the central labor federation—the AFL-CIO.

CONCENTRATION OF MEMBERSHIP

Like American industry, membership in U.S. unions is concentrated. About 80 per cent is in forty-four national unions, each of which has at least 100,000 members. The six largest unions in 1962 each had over 700,000 members: the Teamsters—1,457,000; the United Automobile Workers (UAW)—1,074,000; the Steelworkers—879,000; the Machinists—868,000; the Electrical Workers—793,000; and the Carpenters—739,000.

The membership of American unions is also concentrated in those industries which employ a high proportion of manual workers, notably manufacturing, mining, construction, and transportation. In 1962, 76.2 per cent of union membership was found in these branches of industry. The six largest unions just mentioned, for example, are all predominantly manual worker organizations. Yet, in 1962, only 40.2 per cent of the people employed outside agriculture worked in manufacturing, mining, construction, and transportation. Thus, the American labor movement is predominantly blue-collar rather than white-collar. This is not only characteristic of the membership, but it is also the case with its leadership, its traditions, and its outlook. Of the almost 17 million members of American unions in 1962, only 2,285,000 were white-collar workers, but composed 13 per cent of union membership. These were hardly more than one-tenth of some 22 million white-collar people at work in the United States.

As one might expect from this heavy concentration in manual work, the American labor movement is overwhelmingly male. In 1962, 3.3 million union members were women, only about one-sixth of the membership. Yet, in that year, one-third of the people at work in the United States were females. They were employed primarily in those industries that unions had not penetrated significantly—trade, finance and insurance, the services, and government.

This, then, is a sketch, largely statistical, of the size and significant distribution of the American labor movement. But before we can move to a discussion of the factors that affect its growth, I must give you some notion historically of how it reached its present state. For this purpose I shall use figures of both the actual membership in American unions and that membership expressed as a percentage of the civilian labor force. The latter suggest the extent of penetration of unionization into American industry at any given moment of time. I shall seek to break the years since the late nineteenth century into short spans of time that have historic significance. It is necessary to start with 1897 because this is the first year for which we have a statistic.

HISTORICAL GROWTH

In 1897, there were fewer than 450,000 union members in the United States, probably less than 2 per cent of the labor force. In the years following, at the turn of the century, the nation fought the Spanish-American War and enjoyed rising economic activity. Union membership by 1904 had spurted upward to over 2 million, more than 6 per cent of the labor force.

In the succeeding decade, a period of peace and relative prosperity, membership moved modestly forward to 2.7 million in 1914, but still remained below 7 per cent of the labor force.

During World War I and the immediate postwar period, a time of high employment and price inflation, membership soared. By 1920, union membership was over 5 million, which was 12 per cent of the labor force.

In the twenties, the unions lost ground—severely in the depression years 1920–1922, and more slowly in the more prosperous times of 1923–1929. By 1929, membership had fallen to just under 3.5 million, or 7 per cent of the labor force.

This decay continued during the worst years of the Great Depression, from the stock market crash of 1929 to the inauguration of Franklin Roosevelt's New Deal in 1933. By 1933, membership was under 3 million and the organized sector of the labor force was less than 6 per cent, lower than the figure for 1904.

Between 1933 and 1947, the American labor movement enjoyed sustained and even spectacular growth and took the essential form we have already seen. In the part of this period that preceded World II, there was a modest economic recovery from the worst years of the depression; and the government encouraged unionization, particularly with the passage of the National Labor Relations Act in 1935. During and immediately following the war, employment was at an unusually high level and prices rose sharply. By 1947, over 14 million American workers had become union members, and they were more than 23 per cent of the labor force.

In the period 1947 to 1956, union membership continued to

rise, but at a slower rate. This was, with secondary exceptions, a time of high employment, sustained in part by the Korean War. By 1956, membership in the U.S. was 17.4 million and represented 25 per cent of the labor force.

Between 1957 and 1961, the nation sustained two recessions and the level of unemployment was always at least 5 per cent. By 1961, membership had fallen to 16.7 million, 23 per cent of the labor force.

Since 1961, of course, there are no national statistics except for the year 1962. There can be little doubt, however, that the earlier decline was reversed as economic activity rose. The probability is that union membership has been increasing in the past four years at a modest rate. It is more doubtful that unions have increased their share of the labor force because the latter has grown at a very rapid rate owing to the entry of large numbers of young people born during and immediately following World War II, when the American birth rate shot upward.

BASES OF UNION GROWTH

This historical background now gives us some basis for determining the forces that shape union growth in the United States. But before we do so, it is important to make a general observation: historically considered, unions have faced more difficulty in gaining acceptance in the United States than in almost any other nation. Some of the reasons for this will become evident as we analyze the causes of union growth.

The statistical and historical facts that I have presented suggest two quite different patterns in the development of the American labor movement. One is long term, or, as the economists say, secular: over a long period of time union membership tends to get bigger. In 1897, there were fewer than 500,000 members; by 1962, their number had reached nearly 17 million. The other is short term: in certain periods, sometimes as brief as two or three years, membership either spurts upward, advances slowly, shows no change, or declines. In the face of this diversity it is important to search for "plural" explanations rather than for a single theory of causation.

SECULAR FORCES

Let us turn first to an explanation of the long-term thrust upward. Why is it that American workers have joined unions in growing numbers in the long run? Here it seems that there have been four secular forces that have worked to increase the size of the labor movement.

The first and most obvious has been the gradual expansion of the labor force, which is closely related to the volume of employment over the long run. In 1900, there were only 29 million persons in the civilian labor force; today their number approaches 75 million. The rate of growth, which is largely determined by the birth rate of a generation earlier, is quite steady, and the size of the labor force does not decline. Thus, the union potential for organization slowly becomes larger. Even if nothing else were at work, one would expect the labor movement to expand at this slow rate.

The second long-run force has been the growing acceptability of unionism in American society. The worker's attitude toward the union tends to be shaped by the attitudes of the people he meets in his day-to-day life—his employer, his fellow workers, his relatives, friends, and neighbors. If they are hostile to the union, he is likely to be; if they are friendly, he will usually be too. Over a long period of time and for a variety of reasons, hostility has given way to friendliness. Though there have been ups and downs in this process and there are variations between towns, by and large, communities were far more ready to accept unions and collective bargaining in 1964 than they were in 1900. In the law, in the shop, and in the community, trade unionism has won increased respectability, has become a more familiar institution on the American landscape.

The third factor has been the growing homogeneity of the American labor force. Here it is important to remember that, excepting a small number of Indians, all Americans come from immigrant stock, mainly from Europe, but also from Africa, Latin America, and Asia. These immigrant groups brought with them their old country languages, customs, religions, and living habits. For at least one generation and sometimes for more, they felt more comfortable in their own groups; they tended to live together, to preserve their own languages, and so on. Obviously, it was easier to organize workers who were socially homogeneous, say in England or Sweden, than to unionize so divided a working class as we have had in the United States.

In the past—and occasionally even now—anti-union employers found it possible to pit one immigrant group against another, or Negroes against Caucasians, or Latin Americans or Asians against either. Time has tended to blunt some of these differences. During and shortly after World War I, restrictive laws slowed down immigration to the United States; and education, laws, institutions, travel, and the mass media have tended to integrate immigrant groups into American society. Unions have been among the principal beneficiaries of this integration process. To use an illustration: the AFL was unable to unionize the steel industry in 1919, in part, because many, perhaps most, of the workers did not speak English; in 1936–1941, however, the CIO succeeded in organizing steel partly because the workers could now be reached in the English language.

The significant groups that presently remain to be integrated into American society are the Negroes in most parts of the country, the Puerto Ricans in New York City, and the Mexican-Americans in the Southwest and in California. As this process goes on, one would expect union membership to be fed from these groups.

The fourth secular force stimulating union growth has been the extension of collective-bargaining agreements imposing some form of union security, of which the "union shop" is presently the most widespread. Here the worker must join the union as a condition of employment within thirty days of his date of hire. As the number of collective-bargaining agreements with the union shop has expanded, the number of workers who have been required to join the union automatically has also grown.

WAR AND SOCIAL UNREST

The short-term growth of unions is closely related to two factors—war and social unrest stemming from major depressions. In the span of time beginning in 1897, there have been five periods of rapid union expansion—1897 to 1903, 1917 to 1920, 1934 to 1938, 1942 to 1944, and 1951. Each of these five is related to either a war or to social discontent or both. At the turn of the century, the United States emerged from the deep depression of the nineties which ended with the Spanish-American War. The years 1917 to 1920 reflected World War I and post-Armistice conditions. The period 1934 to 1938 witnessed the expansion set off by the profound social disturbances of the Great Depression. World War II left its imprint on union growth from 1942 to 1944. Similarly, the Korean War influenced the development of membership in 1951. In summary, we find three periods of the five related to wars, one to social upheaval alone, and one to both factors.

One may inquire why it is that war and social unrest should lead to rapid union expansion. Here again it is necessary to rely on Hoxie's idea of "pluralism." And there are quite different causes for growth in each case. Let us start with the factors that affect union growth in wartime, of which, it seems to me, five are worth noting.

The first is the obvious one that during a war the business cycle turns sharply upward, carrying high employment with it. But even more important in the present context is the inevitable rise in the cost of living that accompanies wars. It seems safe to generalize that a very sharp increase in consumer prices is accompanied by a similar increase in union membership. This was the case during both world wars and the Korean War. During the Spanish-American War, however, the rise in prices ran behind union expansion, suggesting that the latter was primarily the result of social unrest. The reason for this relationship between prices and membership is that the mounting cost of living depreciates real wages, causing workers to join labor organizations in the hope of lifting their money wages.

The second cause of growth in wartime has been the enlarged role of the government in the economy, both as direct employer and, indirectly, as the principal consumer of the product of private industry. That is, unions find organization easier to achieve when they deal with the government or with an employer who relies primarily or totally on sales to the government. The railway unions, for example, first won general recognition for the nonoperating crafts during the World War I period of federal control of the railroads and promptly lost it after the war when the railroads were returned to private control. The shipbuilding industry was unionized during both world wars; and the aircraft industry, during World War II. The pressures of war, as will be emphasized shortly, induce the government to seek union support for the war effort and cause the government to influence employers dependent on it to avoid hostility to unions.

Third, the necessity to achieve unity in prosecuting a war enhances the political power of organized labor. This rests on the need of a democratic government to enlist all the important elements in society in the common effort. Churchill, for example, at once invited the Labour party to participate in the wartime coalition government when he took power in the dark days of 1940. Less dramatically, the administration of Woodrow Wilson, Franklin D. Roosevelt, and Harry S. Truman offered the unions a voice in matters of direct interest to them during the three most recent wars in which this country engaged. Labor had representation on the National War Labor Boards of World Wars I and II and on the National Wage Stabilization Board during the Korean conflict, all agencies concerned with the settlement of labor disputes as well as with regulating wages. During wartime, unions increase their prestige, respectability, and acceptability to both workers and employers.

The fourth factor is the breakdown of employer hostility to unions during wars. This has been noted for the firm dependent on government contracts. The employer with a private market has similar, though less severe, pressures. He must operate in an economy of scarcities; he risks the charge of inciting a strike; his workers can easily find other jobs if they quit; and he finds it simple to grant higher wages by raising the prices of his products.

Finally, wars are accompanied by social tensions and dislocations, and workers need means to express their discontent. Unionism provides a vehicle for this purpose.

The forces that spur union growth in a period of social unrest are of a different character. They arise only in the wake of a depression so severe as to call into question the very foundations of society. Secondary business downturns, such as those of 1907, 1920, and 1937, do not produce this effect. In the period we have been discussing, there have been only two very severe depressions —the collapse that began in 1893 and the Great Depression that started in 1929. In both cases, the great expansion of the labor movement commenced four years after the onset of hard times— in 1897 and in 1933. That is, unions declined with the economy and swung up as the economic system began to recover. What, then, were these depression-born forces that caused union ranks to expand so markedly?

The first factor is, of course, labor unrest. A severe and prolonged depression imposes heavy burdens on workers and their families. This causes them to develop sharp grievances against the existing social order. They are, therefore, more willing to join protest organizations, either political or economic. In the American environment, they are more likely to choose the latter, the trade unions.

The second cause is the decline in the standing of the employer during a depression. As a great slump draws to its close, the community is inclined to discredit the businessman. The economic system for which he speaks has just shown its ineffectiveness. If he voices hostility to unions, few listen.

These two factors combined permit the third, intervention by the government to protect the right of workers to organize and bargain collectively. At the turn of the century, Congress passed a law to protect union organization on the railroads and authorized an exhaustive investigation of labor relations that led to a condemnation of anti-union practices by employers. There was also a good deal of state legislation that sought the same ends. During the 1930's, both the federal and state governments enacted laws to protect the right of workers to organize into unions of their own choosing, the most important being the National Labor Relations Act of 1935.

OUTLOOK FOR THE FUTURE

With this basis in history and causation, we shall now examine the current problem of growth in the American labor movement. This is a question which has disturbed many trade-union leaders in the United States in recent years and has been the subject of much examination by students of labor.

It may be helpful to remind you of certain facts that were brought out earlier but which have a special significance in the present context. The first is that membership in American unions is highly concentrated in industries and occupations that employ manual, blue-collar workers. The second is that this membership is predominantly of the male sex. Finally, the peak year for trade-union membership was 1956, when there were 17.4 million unionists, who constituted 25 per cent of the labor force. In the following period, at least until 1962, the latest year for which data are available, there was a decline in both actual membership and penetration of the labor force.

In assessing the significance of these facts, one must note the year 1956 as a turning point. One event that occurred in that year is merely symbolic, but does call attention to a pervasive long-term tendency in American society with which the unions must reckon. In 1956, the number of nonmanual white-collar workers exceeded the number of manual or blue-collar workers for the first time in the history of the United States. In all advanced industrial societies, of course, there is a shift away from physical to overhead labor. This is a continuing tendency everywhere, and one that has gone on in the United States slowly for more than a century. Its current significance is that over half the people who work in the United States now perform nonmanual operations, and their proportion of the labor force will almost certainly rise in the future.

The other point to be made about the year 1956 is that it marked the end of an economic phase from the standpoint of employment. Between 1941 and 1956, American workers, except during a handful of years, enjoyed full employment. Since 1956, they have had to face continuous and quite severe unemployment and underemployment. And much of this recent joblessness has concentrated in the industries with a high manual-worker content, such as railroads, coal mining, and heavy manufacturing.

Thus, for almost a decade the American labor movement has been frustrated by these two powerful tendencies which were not of its making—the shift in employment into industries and occupations that were weakly organized and unemployment in the industries that were strongly unionized. The solutions—organization of white-collar workers and the stimulation of full employment—are easier to perceive than to achieve. In the last two or three years, doubtless some gains have been made toward both these goals, but there remains a great distance to go.

Although this is not the place to comment on the problem of increasing employment in the United States, a few of the very recent organizational developments may be worth noting. Insofar as trade unions are involved, the advances seem to have concentrated thus far in public employment (federal, state, and local), in trade, and in the services. But another interesting development, particularly in government, has been the growth of independent associations of public employees, some of which engage directly in collective bargaining and others of which have functions related to bargaining.

As one surveys American labor organizations at the present time, one has the sense of a transitional phase in their growth, a feeling that we may soon witness a significant extension of organization to the very large and growing nonmanual and substantially female sector of the labor force. If this takes place, it will in turn raise an important structural issue: whether the AFL-CIO, with its strong manual traditions, will be able to accommodate itself to white-collar organizations or whether the United States shall ultimately find itself with two federations of labor, one for manual workers and the other for nonmanual, as in Sweden.

10 THE PHILOSOPHY OF THE AMERICAN LABOR MOVEMENT

Philip Taft

GENERAL CHARACTERISTICS

In general, the American labor movement resembles those of other countries. It is made up of local, regional, national, and international (the latter are the members and locals in Canada) units. To some extent, the labor organizations of democratic countries carry on the same general activities. They negotiate agreements with employers, withdraw their services when they are unable to reach a satisfactory settlement, boycott unfair products, and provide beneficiary or fraternal and protective benefits. American labor has also developed special characteristics which are weak or absent in labor organizations outside the United States and Canada.

Aside from the few small fringe groups which espouse a variety of socialist or communist doctrines, the American labor movement is made up of the large number of trade and labor unions affiliated with the AFL-CIO and the unaffiliated unions which resemble the others in structure and outlook, the most important of which are the Teamsters Union and the United Mine Workers of America. Units of the Teamsters and Miners unions still maintain fairly close relations with many locals and regional groupings of the AFL-CIO, and they often cooperate with one another on political and economic matters.

The American labor movement is predominantly a movement of trade and labor unions headed by men who originally come from the shops, the mines, the transportation systems, and, in a few instances, the offices. Although many of the leaders have become well-educated, possess administrative talent, and ability to express themselves in speech and writing, only a minority are much concerned with the theories governing their activities, or even with the precise destination to which they are moving, except that it should be forward. Most labor leaders are not likely to be too much concerned with the philosophy of the organizations or with their ultimate purposes. As they seek higher wages, improved working conditions, and a greater voice in the regulation of conditions on the job, leaders of unions and their members do not normally feel the need to base their demands on philosophical foundations. The answer to the demand for higher wages is likely to be a simple one. It may be based on a desire to attain an improved standard of living, the employer's ability to pay, the right of workers to share in the growing productivity of the economy, and sometimes a slightly more sophisticated view of the relations between spending and employment.

ABSENCE OF INVOLVED PHILOSOPHY

The absence of an involved philosophy or even of a long-term program is no accident. It arises mainly out of the special conditions which existed in the United States. Industrial workers gained the right to vote early in the history of the country. Certainly, the great majority did not require special organizations to gain full civil rights. The opportunities for improvement that existed in an economically expanding nation with a limited supply of labor also influenced the outlook and expectations of American workers. In many instances compelled to bid for a small pool of labor, entrepreneurs were forced to offer higher returns. The existence of large reserves of raw materials and land for the production of food and fibers provided American businessmen with great opportunities.

The expansion of the economy provided the means for long-run raises of labor's real income. The rates of increase were uneven, and were influenced by cyclical and long-term forces, but the general movement of wages over time was upward. Thus, workers in the United States found that the possibility to improve the standard of living was no idle dream.

Experience demonstrated the possibility of labor progressing within the framework of the existing social and economic structure and lessened the appeal of doctrines that sought to demonstrate that, in a free-enterprise system, the position of labor inevitably deteriorates. As time has long demonstrated that the possibilities for improving the living and working conditions within the social and economic framework of the United States exist, the theories stressing the necessity for a displacement of the existing system by some form of collectivism were never without sponsors. Some of these views assumed the inability of a private-enterprise economy to grow over time and to provide labor with a rising standard of living. Others emphasized equality as an ideal and attributed a wide variety of evils to the unequal distribution of wealth and income. Based on ethical, political, or economic principles, every variety of anarchism, communism, socialism, and syndicalism has had followers in the United States and has been presented to American workers as a panacea for all their ills. The sponsors of these views also differed among themselves in the means that they suggested to achieve their goals. Some stressed education or political action; others, the use of economic weapons such as strikes and sabotage, and even the revolutionary overthrow of the existing government. It is important to recognize that no legal barriers to the presentation of heterodox views normally existed, although more severe scrutiny and even repression might take place during a war with a foreign power or during periods of widespread fear.

COLLECTIVIST THEORIES

One should note that almost simultaneous with the formation of the first traditional type of labor organizations, collectivist theories were offered to the workers of the country as a means for rapid and certain solutions to the social and economic problems of developing industrialism. The influence of such ideas has fluctuated over time as has the strength of the moderate and traditional unions. The growth of some evil or injustice, the spread of unemployment would tend to swell the ranks of the believers in the necessity for more fundamental reform. Yet, while reform and revolutionary movements with collectivist aspirations have appeared and reappeared, sometimes only as a small group espousing a strange doctrine and at other times with thousands of earnest devotees, none of them was able to build an effective counter-weight or alternative to the American trade and labor unions with their limited goals and achievable aspirations.

The failure of American labor to accept the programs for reorganizing the economy on what their sponsors regarded as a more rational basis has often been attributed to guile or conspiracy by reactionary forces which diverted the natural inclinations of the workers of the United States and Canada from their true course. However, a glance at the past will show that no matter how unusual these ideas might have appeared, their profession did not normally arouse reprisals. It is true that advocacy of the overthrow of the government by force or propaganda by the deed, which called for the use of explosives and assassination as means for calling attention to social injustice, was outlawed.

On the other hand, workers organized in trade and labor unions for the promotion of better wages and working conditions faced bitter opposition from the beginning of their existence in the United States. The conspiracy laws were applied in the early nineteenth century to the fledgling unions at the same time that Thomas Skidmore was able to propagate his doctrine of land nationalization without restraint. Skidmore's exposition was protected by the First Amendment to the Constitution guaranteeing the right of freedom of speech; at the same time, the organized shoemakers were being tried for conspiring to raise wages. It is an interesting and often ignored fact that in the United States, the greatest opposition has not been directed against exponents of heterodox ideas, but against workers organizing to improve the terms of employment. From the great railroad riots of 1877 to the most recent fracas on the picket line, the resistance to labor is greatest when it seeks by organization to affect the terms of employment. For example, the violence and riots of 1877 began in every instance by efforts to introduce changes in wages or working conditions. Having taken several wage cuts during the depressed times of the early 1870's, the railroad workers revolted when the companies again sought to pare their pay checks or to change the rules to increase responsibility or work. It is true that before the rioting was over, the worker–

demonstrators were joined by rowdies and toughs—Marx's *lumpenproletariat*—always on the prowl for disorder to be converted into an occasion for looting.

One need not stop at the railroad strikes to show that the bitterest conflicts between labor and management have been over the terms of employment. What was the issue in dispute in the Homestead strike of 1892, or the Pullman strike two years later? Both of these episodes followed attempts by the employer to cut wages; in Homestead, Pennsylvania, the Steelworkers Union of the time revolted; and in the Pullman shops, the unorganized workers rejected a wage cut. Although the strike in Pullman, Illinois, was greatly enlarged by the refusal of railroad men, led by the newly formed American Railway Union, to handle Pullman cars, the fact remains that the controversy could have been ended by the company's rescinding its wage reduction, and once the strike had spread to the railroad workers, by agreeing to reemploy the sympathy strikers without discrimination or penalty.

These episodes do not exhaust the struggle for union recognition and the right to bargain collectively. The bitter coal strikes in West Virginia in 1911, 1912, and 1919, culminating in armed conflict, and the Ludlow tragedy in Colorado were the result of a demand for union recognition as were the steel strikes in 1919 and the Little Steel strike in 1937. Had the Little Steel firms agreed to sign an agreement with the Steelworkers Organizing Committee granting the latter a limited kind of recognition, the strike would not have been called. It needs to be repeated that the bitterest resisance by employers in the United States has always been, and is today in a few places, to union organization which seeks to influence the terms of employment. In their resistance in the past, frequently employers had the support of local governments and the courts. Let it be noted that the American worker did not gain the right to organize as a gift from an enlightened employing class. As a matter of fact, for many decades employers in a number of industries used many stratagems—armed guards, private police and spies—to frustrate the organizing efforts of their workers. In many instances after the employees of given concerns had established a union, the employers would refuse to deal with it. Only after numerous struggles and countless sacrifices did the American workers establish unions in their crafts and callings.

A SIMPLE PHILOSOPHY

The philosophy of American labor is quite simple, but it is not static. A movement that is essentially made up of toilers in the shop and office is not likely to indulge in long-drawn speculation on where it is going. The American labor leader and his followers are not so much concerned about the destiny of the movement as they are with the belief that the next year should be a better one than the present. If one can describe such a simple outlook as a philosophy, one would say that it is a hope, supported by bargaining power, that the future will be better than the past. Some might regard such a simple view as superficial and narrow, but, thus far, it has been founded on a correct appraisal of the potentiality of the American economy. There is a tendency for men of imagination and learning to downgrade the aspiration for a better material life for those who work, but is that not the aim of every reform and revolutionary system that has been offered to mankind by the seers and philosophers of the past? Is success a sin? Is not the desire to abolish want—to lift the age-long burdens from the back of man—the moral driving force of every movement to regenerate mankind?

From the beginning, American organized labor was aware that many problems facing the worker could not be solved at the place of employment. Education, child labor, the conditions of work of women employees, immigration, and a variety of questions ranging from the sanitary standards at the work place to the voting rights of citizens can only be answered by government.

Union leaders of the past and present have understood that the government can influence, if not determine, the well-being of the working population. The differences that have arisen over political action, if one excludes a small number of anarchists and syndicalists, have been over the type of politics that the labor movement was to promote, and the extent and kind of program that the labor movement would endorse. In fact, one of the reasons that the AFL was launched in the middle 1880's was to help establish the state federations of labor as the political arm of the labor movement.

POLITICAL ACTION

Both foreign and domestic observers have tended to confuse the promotion of a labor party with political action. The tactics used by American workers go back to the first political efforts by organized workingmen in the United States in the 1830's. Reliance on pressure politics instead of a special party of labor made sense in terms of the political structure of the United States. Political parties were not centrally controlled, and the local parties would respond to pressure for enactment of measures. In other words, politicians in the United States were more concerned with gaining the support of their local constituents than with carrying out the program devised by the central party organization.

The unionists of the early years were aware of the importance of gaining support in the state legislatures where many questions affecting the welfare of the worker were decided. The first state-wide labor-political group for lobbying at the state capitol was established in New York in 1865, twenty years before the founding of the AFL, and its purpose was to seek legislation favorable to the men and women who work.

It is true that the AFL sought to avoid dependence on government for reforms of working and living conditions, but it always recognized the importance of government and the need for influencing its decisions. The leaders of the time reflected the general view that the activities of government should be restricted more narrowly than at present. Many, including Gompers, were even afraid that unemployment insurance might become a means of enslaving the wage-earner. In part, these attitudes reflected philosophy and, in part, they were a conclusion based on experience. Labor organizations initially developed in a society generally hostile to their activities. The application of the conspiracy laws, the restrictions on striking and picketing, the use of the power of government to break strikes and limit the use of the boycott created the belief that the role of government should be limited.

Under the doctrines espoused by the United States Supreme Court prior to the mid-1930's, the government's role in labor disputes could at best, from the point of view of labor, be described as one of neutrality. Outside of the railroads, the government had no power to intervene, and employers could legally demand that they be protected against harassment and violence, even in cases where the employer refused to recognize the union chosen by his employees to represent them. There were a few instances in the railroad industry, and in the anthracite coal strike of 1902, where government pressure compelled negotiations. In general, however, governmental power meant the protection of property during labor disputes. Despite the fear of government and the desire to avoid dependence on it, the leaders of labor made constant and vigorous efforts to affect legislation in the state legislatures and in Congress.

The laws sought can be divided into three groups. There were first the rules and regulations needed by specific bodies of workers to protect them against some danger or special condition. Laws setting up safety requirements on building construction, sanitary standards in barber shops, apprentice rules in some of the crafts, and the prohibition of certain chemicals and materials were a few of the laws designed for the protection of special groups who might not succeed without the support of the general movement. Laws protecting the payment of wages, requiring that they be made periodically; laws prescribing days of rest, general inspection of premises; laws for protection against wage loss arising out of industrial injury and unemployment; and holiday-closing are examples of the kind of laws that affected all labor. A third type of law supported by labor was designed to help the worker as a citizen. Such laws dealt with the financing of education, immigration, public power, the rights of the individual and similar issues. Because political leaders tended to respond to economic, ethnic, and social influences in their districts, it was possible to gain sympathetic consideration from the legislator for demands and needs of his constituents, even for bills that might be opposed by the central organization of the party to which the legislator belonged. The large body of labor and welfare laws which have been enacted in state legislatures and in Congress testifies to the effectiveness of this method.

Labor's political tactics were based on the philosophical assumption that the worker was a free citizen and not a member of a special class, and that redress of grievances was possible within the framework of American political life.

THE AMERICAN ECONOMY AND LABOR

American labor's philosophy has been based on the view that the American economy possesses possibilities for continuing growth, out of which can come the rise in real wages which American workers and their leaders believe is possible and just. This view was summarized by Samuel Gompers as "more and more," a view derided by the socialists and others who publicly wondered whether at some point the entire product would not be exhausted and no increase in real wages would be possible. What the doctrine of "more and more" clearly implied was that a free-enterprise economy possesses sufficient dynamism so that total and per capita production are continually increasing. Instead of a belief in the increasing misery of labor under a developing industrialism, the workers' leaders in the United States envisaged the possibility of continuing growth.

As free men with the right to influence not only the conditions of work, but also the distribution of the national product and income, they regarded an expanding economy as a means for greater capital accumulation or for the building of a great military plant, as well as a source for the enrichment of the life of the worker by raising his real wages. The American labor movement has at no time cried out against accumulation or investment. It has recognized that only by raising investment can the economy supply the labor force with the most modern tools and equipment. It has, however, refused to acquiesce in a policy which would deprive the present generation of all of the fruits of progress on the theory that greater productivity will be created for the future. The view coincides with the general outlook of the American labor movement in other matters. The union is the guardian at the plant and on the industrial level so that, in the quest for efficiency, the needs of the worker will not be lost, and the labor movement reflects the same attitude with regard to the use of the gains from rising efficiency. The workers' needs as consumer must be considered here and now.

While stressing improvements in the place of employment, American labor has always been aware of the need for aiding those outside the protection of the union agreement. The organization drives to recruit the unorganized, the assistance rendered to those on strike, and the aid given to those who belong to other crafts and callings so that they would be able to maintain viable organizations of their own were always given. On the legislative level, the American labor movement has sought laws for the benefit of all workers, not only for those who are organized. In fact, the concern of American labor has frequently gone beyond the boundaries of the country. It has supported the labor movements of other countries, and it has tried to influence government policy to support the countries where democratic labor movements flourish.

CHANGES IN TACTICS

While the American labor movement continues to rely on its own efforts for the development of codes of rules in the plant and has developed a system of employer-financed benefits which includes old-age pensions, supplementary unemployment insurance, hospitalization and offsets to wage-loss arising out of non-occupational accidents and illness, it has realized that the role and significance of government activities has drastically changed. A labor movement of 18 million has not regarded its views as immutable dogmas. Influenced by the experiences of the great depression of the 1930's and the recruiting of millions of semiskilled workers into its ranks, it has increasingly accepted and, in fact, called for a more active government role to support programs of low-cost housing, education, and monetary and fiscal policies conducive to high employment and a prosperous economy. With the importance of the government in labor relations and in the operation of social-insurance systems, the labor movement has given over more time to government policy and elections. However, it has refused to enter into formal political alliance with either party, and it has formally continued its nonpartisan policy of supporting friends and opposing enemies.

11 THE RISE OF INDUSTRIAL UNIONISM

Jack Barbash

DEFINITION

Industrial unionism means *inclusive* unionism. An industrial union admits and bargains for all or almost all classes of workers in a given industry or plant. It is a union of the skilled and unskilled. This inclusiveness of industrial unionism is in contrast to the *exclusiveness* of the so-called craft unions. Craft unions limit their members to a specific craft or trade. They are unions of skilled workers.

In practice, the lines between industrial and craft unionism are not so finely drawn now. Most industrial unions are multi-industry unions. Witness, for example, the United Automobile Workers in automobiles, agricultural implements, aircraft, and space. There are very few (if any) pure craft unions—perhaps the Patternmakers is one of these few. Most craft unions are really multi-craft or trade unions, like the Carpenters with membership among "carpenters and joiners, railroad carpenters, bench hands, stairbuilders, millwrights," and twenty-five additional "trades." Moreover, an "industrial" national union may divide its members into craft locals. And in the same way, a predominantly "craft" national union may have "industrial" locals.

EVOLUTION

Unions first appeared in the United States and Britain in the early 1800's and were craftsmen's unions. Inclusive movements of workers emerged later, more as concerted expressions of protest

143

against the economic injustices of the emerging industrial revolution than as unions concerned over wages and hours. Robert Owen's Grand Consolidated Trades Union in England (1834) which sought to combine all workers into "one big union," and the Noble Order of the Knights of Labor (1869–1890's for practical purposes) in the United States, with its slogan of "an injury to one is the concern of all," were the most significant examples of these embryonic but short-lived experiments in inclusive unionism.

Between the end of the Civil War and the onset of the Depression (1929), craft unionism represented the prevailing structural form. Craft unionism survived because it was dealing with relatively small and therefore weaker employers, because bonds among workers are always strong, and finally because the craft unions pursued limited economic goals. The victory of craft unionism was marked somewhere in the late 1880's or early 1890's by the replacement of the Knights with the American Federation of Labor as the principal labor federation in the United States.

Industrial unionism had its isolated enclaves in the United Mine Workers in coal mining, in the Brewery Workers, and in the "needle" trades in women's and men's clothing. But for most of their existence prior to the 1930's, these unions were never above subsistence and more continually under attack from employers, or, as in the case of the Brewery Workers, under siege from rival craft unions.

The AFL was not entirely unresponsive to the pressures for industrial unionism. It established departments in the construction industry (1908), the metal trades (1908), and the railroad shop crafts (1909) to provide internal machinery for craft union collaboration in jurisdictional and collective-bargaining problems. Samuel Gompers, the AFL's first president, pushed for mergers of kindred craft unions with some minor successes. The AFL rejected affiliation from national unions with unduly restricted jurisdictions. The UMW was specifically exonerated from the jurisdictional claims of craft unions in the Scranton Declaration at the AFL's 1901 convention.

For brief periods, anti-AFL movements favoring industrial unionism flashed across the horizon. Eugene V. Debs' American

Railway Union (1894) called a sympathetic walkout of Chicago railroad workers in support of its strike against the Pullman Company, but neither the strike nor the organization could survive the onslaught of federal troops and federal injunctions. The Western Federation of Miners (nonferrous metal mining) was instrumental along with a group of socialists in creating the Industrial Workers of the World (1905) with an avowedly socialist-syndicalist orientation. The IWW (or the Wobblies) engaged in sensational organizing adventures among casual farm laborers and other unskilled workers. A combination of intense factionalism, government suppression, and conflicting temperaments acted to eliminate the IWW as a significant force by the end of World War I.

During World War I, union membership and influence rose to unprecedented heights, raising hopes that this strength could be extended into the postwar period. The most important mass-production effort in this direction was a titanic conflict between the powerful steel industry and a combine of twenty-four AFL craft unions with jurisdiction in the industry. The steel strike (1919–1920) was crushed after three and a half months, but not before 367,000 workers had walked out. In 1921–1922, 45,000 packinghouse workers in thirteen cities struck for two and a half months under the reluctant leadership of the Amalgamated Meat Cutters.

Post-World War I Decline

In the middle 1920's, the AFL appealed to the leaders of industry directly to agree to the organization of their employees voluntarily and collaboratively. The AFL worked out a philosophy on the role of the trade union as a partner in industry rather than as an antagonist. Although it found a few willing listeners, including Owen D. Young and Herbert Hoover, this appeal to reason never materialized into union organization.

By 1932, organizing the mass-production workers looked hopeless. Professor George Barnett, president of the American Economic Association and a distinguished labor economist, speaking in December 1932, just after Roosevelt's election, doubted that the American labor movement could "so revolutionize itself . . .

within the next decade" to adjust itself to the "technological revolution."[1] The AFL leaders conceded that they had not been able to make headway in the mass-production industries, but neither had their radical critics like the socialists and the IWW done any better despite their "correct revolutionary spirit."[2] John P. Frey a leading craft-union spokesman said, that

> the tremendous handicaps; the revolutionary industrial changes which the American trade-union movement has been compelled to face in recent years, particularly since 1914, [the] enormous displacement of labor in the manufacturing industry, [the] replacement of American workers by those from central and southern Europe, the judicial doctrine . . . which has held that practically all trade-union activities to which employers objected, were, in reality, criminal conspiracies, particularly the yellow-dog contract [were the main obstacles to progress.][3]

The central problem, then, of the labor movement on the eve of its rebirth during the New Deal was that power was lacking precisely in the most dynamic sectors of the American mass-production-oriented economy. Conceding the great handicaps in the way of union growth in heavy industry, there were, nevertheless, grounds for doubt that the AFL leadership was even constructively concerned about the problem, to say nothing of doing something about it. Prof. Selig Perlman, no harsh critic of the AFL, had observed in 1928,

> The psychology of a big majority of leaders today [is] a curious blending of "defeatism" with complacency. Every union leader admits that the organization of labor must be expanded into the basic industry. . . . But at the first encounter with the difficulties of the task—difficulties which are admittedly enormous, made up as they are of the employers' active opposition and of the inertia on the workers' part begotten by the Coolidge prosperity and by "welfare capitalism,"—or in many cases even before such an active encounter, union officers and organizers lose their hearts for the task, and rarely proceed beyond ex-

[1] George Barnett, "American Trade Unionism and Social Insurance," *American Economic Review* (March 1933), p. 6.

[2] James Hatch, *International Molders Journal* (May 1932), p. 27.

[3] John P. Frey, "The Federation of Labor: A Defense," *International Molders Journal* (August 1932), pp. 461 ff.

pressions of good intentions. Thereupon having gone through the motions of organizing in new fields, and thus eased their organizer's conscience,—the same leaders settle down to a smug survey of the well-oiled machinery of their little organizations which suggests at least a suspicion that these leaders might not entirely welcome too many members, whose alignment in the politics of the union would at best be uncertain.[4]

Rebirth and Resurgence

Franklin D. Roosevelt was elected President of the United States in 1932, assuming office in March 1933. As late as June 1933, the *United Mine Workers Journal* could say, "No one seems to know anything about what policies Roosevelt will adopt in dealing with the ills of the republic."[5] One month later, the same journal proclaimed "a tidal wave of enthusiasm [sweeping] coal areas, as miners by the thousands join the UMWA."[6] The International Ladies Garment Workers Union described "a tide of eager hopefulness rising actually by the hour under the impact of the New Deal."[7]

What Roosevelt's New Deal did was to generate a climate of hopefulness for all of the people by the forceful manner in which he put government power to work in confronting the problem of economic collapse. For the labor movement specifically, the New Deal was Section 7(a) of the National Industrial Recovery Act. It restored hope. The NIRA was a wholesale plan for the economic self-government of American industry and a system of relief and public works to create employment. Section 7(a) established the right of employees "to organize and bargain collectively through representatives of their own choosing . . . free from the interference, restraint, or coercion of employers of labor." Section 7(a) brought about, in the words of a contemporary scholar, "an organizing fever . . . through the ranks

4 Selig Perlman, *Theory of the Labor Movement* (New York: Macmillan, 1928), p. 232.

5 "The Old Order Changeth, The New Day Is at Hand, Labor Is Being Emancipated," *United Mine Workers Journal* (June 1, 1933), p. 6.

6 *Ibid.* (July 1, 1933).

7 International Ladies Garment Workers Union, *Proceedings* (1934), p. 8.

of American labor recalling in scope and intensity the greatest labor organizing periods of the past."[8]

Section 7(a) was only indifferently enforced, but its impact went beyond whether employers complied fully or not. First, it put the stamp of government approval on union organization—or so the union organizers proclaimed. Second, it provided an indispensable testing ground for a subsequent piece of legislation that was ultimately to provide even greater leverage for industrial union organizing—namely the Wagner Act, or, more formally, the National Labor Relations Act.

IMPACT OF LAWS FAVORING UNIONS

The big union push in the mass-production industries occurred after the Wagner Act's passage (1935) and constitutionality (1937). But between 1933 and 1937, deep union roots were meanwhile being sunk in every major industrial area and in every mass-production and mass-employment industry. President William Green of the AFL reported to the 1933 convention, "a sight that even the old, tried veterans of our movement never saw before. ... The workers are marching, organizing, keeping step, coming with us into the great American Federation of Labor."[9] In 1934, convulsive upheavals of general strike proportions erupted in San Francisco, Toledo, Minneapolis, and the textile industry. By 1935, industrial-union footholds were being established in the former anti-union citadels of every mass-production industry, either by recapture of old power—as in coal and clothing—or in new inroads—as in steel, automobiles, rubber, glass, electrical manufacturing, etc.

The National Industrial Recovery Act including Section 7(a) was held unconstitutional in 1935 and that year, despite some misgivings, Roosevelt supported and secured the enactment of the Wagner Act. The Wagner Act transformed industrial unionism from an ideological issue into a practical issue of union policy and action. The Wagner Act made industrial unionism practical because it created the essential preconditions of industrial union-

8 Lewis Lorwin in Leverett Lyon *et al., The National Recovery Administration* (Washington, D.C.: Brookings Institute, 1935), p. 489.

9 American Federation of Labor, *Proceedings* (1933), p. 8.

ism by protecting the right of workers (1) to form unions and (2) to bargain collectively through representatives of their "own choosing," free from—and this is the important fact—employer coercion and interference. Moreover, learning from 7(a) experience, the Wagner Act set up an effective agency—the National Labor Relations Board—to enforce these rights to union association and to collective bargaining. Now, to be sure, workers had been legally free to join unions and to bargain collectively for almost a century; but as a distinguished scholar and practitioner, William M. Leiserson, was to observe in 1938, "The law [also] recognized the equal freedom of the employers to destroy labor organizations and to deny the right of employees to join trade unions."[10] The Wagner Act rendered illegal the employer's right to destroy labor organizations.

CRAFT AND INDUSTRIAL UNIONISM

The issue of industrial unionism—now a realizable goal—erupted full blast at the AFL's 1935 convention. The protagonists for the industrial unionists were headed by John L. Lewis of the Miners; and the craft unionists were led on the floor by AFL vice president Matthew Woll and by John P. Frey, president of the Metal Trades Department—but William Hutcheson of the Carpenters and Arthur Wharton of the Machinists were probably the principals. The industrial unionists asserted that mass-production industries could be organized on an industrial-union basis only, that craft unionism could not do it. Workers would not join unions which divided them between skilled and unskilled, nor could collective bargaining be effectively carried on on this basis.

The gist of the craft-union view was that the AFL constitution was in the nature of a contract between the Federation and its constituent unions with jurisdiction as the *quid pro quo* for affiliation. The AFL had therefore no constitutional sanction for granting industrial charters transgressing existing jurisdictional grants. The mass-production workers were, moreover, insubstantial stuff on which to build permanent unions; only crafts-

10 William M. Leiserson, *Right and Wrong in Labor Relations* (Berkeley: University of California Press, 1936), p. 27.

men have what it takes to stay with the union in good times and bad. Industrial unionism had been tried and found wanting, William Green argued.

Immediately after the convention, Lewis organized the Committee for Industrial Organization which was composed of Lewis representing the Mine Workers, Charles P. Howard of the International Typographical Union, Sidney Hillman of the Amalgamated Clothing Workers Union, David Dubinsky of the International Ladies Garment Workers Union, Harvey C. Frenning of the Oil Workers, Max Zaritsky of the Millinery Workers and Thomas H. Brown of the Mine, Mill, and Smelter Workers. The CIO claimed as its purposes the

> encouragement and promotion of organization of the unorganized workers in mass production and other industries on an industrial basis . . . ; to foster recognition and acceptance of collective bargaining in such industries; to counsel and advise unorganized and newly organized groups of workers, to bring them under the banner and affiliation with the American Federation of Labor.[11]

The CIO met with unprecedented success.

In 1936, the AFL Executive Council directed the CIO to dissolve on pain of suspension. The CIO denied the authority of the executive Council to suspend their unions. The unions making up the CIO were thereupon suspended by the Council, a decision later upheld by the AFL convention with the CIO unions excluded from voting. In 1938, the CIO became a permanent federation, the Congress of Industrial Organizations with John L. Lewis as the first president.

Beneath the debaters' arguments of AFL and CIO were conflicting temperaments and ideologies. There was first the traditional AFL distrust of government despite the New Deal, a distrust which increased since it appeared that the CIO was a protégé of government. What government gave, the AFL spokesmen argued, it could also take away. There was also the numbing effect which the organizing failures of the postwar period had on the aggressiveness of the AFL leaders. At this point, the differ-

---

[11] International Ladies Garment Workers Union, *The Position of ILGWU in Relation to CIO and AFL, 1934–1938* (December 1938), p. 13.

ence between AFL and CIO may well have been in the will to organize. The CIO had it and the AFL did not.

There were also important conflicts in personalities. Many of the CIO leaders were ambitious men who had been denied positions of prominence in the AFL councils until the very end. Many of the older AFL craft-union leaders saw the CIO group as an alien movement and were determined to get the CIO unions out of the AFL, even if they had to use doubtful law to do so. At the end, there was a paralysis of AFL leadership when confronting the CIO challenge. William Green, kindly but ineffectual, was incapable of providing the kind of aggressive leadership to hold the craft-union chieftains in line; many have speculated that Gompers might have. The CIO had Lewis who, after the New Deal, may have been one of the decisive elements in the success of industrial unionism at this stage.

INDUSTRIAL UNION ORGANIZING

Immediately on its launching, the CIO mounted a vigorous organizing campaign on industrial-union lines in the steel industry. It created the Steel Workers Organizing Committee (SWOC), followed later by organizing committees for textile, packinghouse, paper, petroleum, public utilities, insurance, and construction. The organizing committee became the CIO's structural adaptation to the problem of combining central direction and financing with indigenous participation by the union leadership of the industries to be organized. In addition, the CIO was composed of (1) recently AFL-chartered internationals (United Auto Workers, United Rubber Workers, United Electrical Workers, for example) who left the AFL to become part of the CIO; (2) secession groups from established AFL internationals like the National Maritime Union headed by Joe Curran and the International Longshoremen's and Warehousemen's Union headed by Harry Bridges; (3) long-established unions like the Miners, International Ladies Garment Workers (which withdrew from CIO in 1938), Amalgamated Clothing Workers, and the Mine, Mill, and Smelter Workers, all of whom were to experience a rebirth of strength and power as CIO affiliates.

The CIO's year of decision was 1937—the year of the UAW

sit-down strike in the General Motors Fisher Body plants in Flint, Michigan, which achieved General Motors' recognition of UAW; the John L. Lewis-Myron Taylor agreement by which SWOC gained U.S. Steel recognition; and the U.S. Supreme Court validation of the Wagner Act by a five to four vote. But the CIO also suffered a tragic defeat in 1937—the loss of a five-week strike against the "Little Steel" companies, in the course of which ten strikers were killed outside of the South Chicago plant of the Republic Steel Corporation.

INDUSTRIAL UNIONS STABILIZED

By the opening years of World War II, it was evident that CIO industrial unionism was a durable accomplishment, and the sizable collective-bargaining and membership gains in the course of World War II underscored this fact. The craft unions grew in this period, too, but many of them abandoned their doctrinaire position and took on industrial-union-like characteristics. Notable instances of the "industrialization" of the traditional craft unions have been the Machinists in the aircraft and metal-working industries generally, the Boilermakers in the shipbuilding industry, and the Electrical Workers in the mass-production electrical products industry. The AFL had done so well, in fact, that far from being eclipsed by the CIO, the AFL became the more numerous of the two federations. AFL unionism was plainly not obsolete if union membership was a valid measure.

CRAFT AND INDUSTRIAL UNIONS MERGE

In the postwar period, the industrial unions were put to the decisive test as to whether they could stand on their own without a favorable administration for at least part of the time and without the restrictions imposed on anti-unionism by a war emergency. The 1946 elections brought in a Republican Congress. The 1945–1946 period was rocked by the greatest strike upheaval since 1919.

Unlike the post-World War I period which was a burial ground for industrial unionism, the post-World War II period ushered in a strike wave on which the industrial unions rode to new heights in collective bargaining and union membership. A one-hundred-thirteen-day United Auto Workers' strike against General Motors was the most significant contest in a period that included industry-wide strikes in steel, oil refining, electrical manufacturing, and meatpacking. Only agriculture, white-collar, service, technical, and professional employment remained (and continues to remain) substantially outside of the orbit of unionism.

By the 1950's, it was apparent that the period of economic expansion was over, and with it, a union slowdown ensued that may have begun as early as the closing 1940's. The enactment of the Taft-Hartley Law in 1947 restricting activities of unions may have been the harbinger (some unionists say the cause) of the plateau. The election of Republican President Dwight D. Eisenhower after twenty years of Democratic rule in the White House was an indisputable sign of a new tide in the American political situation which, if it was not hostile, was at least restrictive. These factors and sudden changes in the leadership of the AFL and of the CIO—the deaths of the respective presidents William Green and Philip Murray—within a few days of each other and their replacement by George Meany and Walter Reuther respectively provided a new opportunity for the reassessment of the rivalry that ultimately led to AFL-CIO unity.

Twenty years after the CIO was established, the AFL and the CIO merged in 1955 to become the AFL-CIO. The unity talks which had gone on sporadically for years began in earnest when newly designated AFL President Meany established a principle of merger based on equality between the merging parties rather than on the CIO's return to "the house of labor," as Green had stated it. To give additional meaning to the principle of equality, the new constitution put its seal of legitimacy on both the craft- and industrial-union forms and sanctioned the establishment of an industrial-union department.

The AFL was, however, asserting the principle of equality from a position of strength. On the eve of merger, the AFL probably had twice as many members as the CIO even after allowing for the margin owing to CIO losses from the secession of the UMW and from expulsion of eleven unions on grounds of communist domination. The AFL-CIO split had been, it would seem, advantageous to both parties up to the end of World War II—rather more so for the AFL than for the CIO. CIO membership, one may speculate, was brought to a halt by the situation that there were no more viable organizing situations of the industrial mass-production kind on which the CIO had thrived earlier. The AFL unions on the other hand were more adaptable to the rapidly growing service industries. In any case, both AFL and CIO unions had proved their survival value.

INDUSTRIAL UNIONISM'S REVOLUTION

The rise of industrial unions has meant something more than the emergence of an inclusive form of unionism. The quality of inclusiveness in the industrial unions has interacted with corporately managed mass-production systems, a welfare state, an "affluent" society, a well-established two-party system resting on a pluralistic power base, to induce profound changes in the industrial, political, and economic spheres. Industrial unionism operating in this dynamic setting has produced an elaborate system of industrial government at the worksite, a program-oriented political movement, a new power center in the total society, an integrating force for masses of ethnic workers, a challenge to the quality of the management performance, and new realignments of forces and interests *within* the labor movement.

The industrial unions put the grievance procedure to new uses in such issues as job classification, seniority, and work pace. To make the most efficient use of the grievance procedure, the industrial unions have been training a corps of stewards to handle the grievances expertly on their own power with intervention by higher officials only in the later stages. This shop-based grievance procedure is a source of great strength for the industrial unions.

If the industrial unions have not had the most members, they have the greatest impact on the content of the agreement. Negotiated wage supplements, including health and pensions and supplementary unemployment benefits and sick leave, have created a vast private social-insurance system for employees and their dependents. Paid leaves for holidays, vacations, and recently, thirteen-week "sabbaticals" have replaced the reduction in the hours of the workweek as the vehicle for increasing the workers' leisure. Currently the main interest of industrial unions is the use of collective bargaining to ameliorate the effect of work displacement caused by technology, relocation of industry, corporate mergers, and retrenchment. The innovative role of the industrial unions in this period stems from the fact that these unions bargain in industries which are undergoing rapid change; the innovation consists of collective-bargaining responses to these changes.

The collective bargaining of industrial unions is more than a simple transaction over hourly wages and piece rates. It is now part of a system of constitutional government in the enterprise which consists of a charter (as it were) in the form of a detailed agreement, a continuing procedure for the enforcement of this charter and its adaptation to change, and a private, impartial judiciary to settle disputes after the parties have failed on their own. None of this is new in concept. What is new is the pervasiveness of this system throughout American industry and the expertise which the union- and management-participants bring to the process.

Industrial unions have had to enter into a mode of political action which is programmatic. Programmatic politics stands somewhere between pressure-group politics which stresses the re-enforcement of job interest, on the one hand, and, on the other, labor-party politics which stresses what are often called "socialist programs." Programmatic politics' middle ground consists of a concern with domestic and international policies within the framework of a welfare-state capitalism. This interest in programmatic politics stems from (a) the greater sensitivity of mass-production unionism to economy-wide forces and (b) the greater sensitivity of the public to the impact which mass-production unionism can exert on the economy.

In any case, these active political interests of the labor movement could no longer be served by simply passing resolutions. In consequence, the industrial unions have had to pioneer in the development of a vast and intricate network of their own political institutions and functions compatible with the American situation.

The rise of industrial unionism has gone hand-in-hand with the widespread economic enfranchisement of diverse ethnic groups who have been the main reservoir for unskilled and semiskilled labor in the hitherto unorganized mass-production industries. Industrial unionism blasted the myth that these ethnic groups of workers were inherently unorganizable. This has been most notably demonstrated by the Negro workers as union members.

UNION GOVERNMENT

The inclusiveness of the industrial unions has induced counter-movements by sectional interests seeking representation within the industrial union. Industrial unions have responded by developing a complex variety of internal governmental forms to speak for craft, occupational, regional, employee, and product pressure groups. When containment of the craft or craft-like interests within the inclusive unit has not been possible, "craft severance" representation action under the NLRB has not been infrequent.

Industrial unionism has not eliminated conflict over job interest with craft unions. The conflicts now center on the issue of contracting-out—maintenance work to outside employers. The industrial unions—that is the unions whose main strength is in heavy industry—are against contracting-out because this would reduce the volume of work for their members. The building trades unions favor subcontracting because it increases the volume of work for their members who are employed by the outside contractor.

In the pre-1933 period, the inclusive structural types were regarded as more compatible with social reform and the revolutionary objectives of unionism, and the narrower types, with pure and simple trade unionism. Within substantially narrower confines, the contrast between building tradesmen and autoworkers still has some merit. But the industrial unionists no longer seek anti-capitalist objectives, and the most conservative craft unionist is a supporter of the welfare state. The difference is more temperamental than ideological, although as the industrial unionists have settled down, even this difference is diminishing.

In the upsurge period of the CIO, the lack of experienced union leadership created a vacuum which the organizationally skilled Communists and their followers exploited to their great advantage. Combined with the wartime alliance between the Soviet Union and the United States, it was possible for Communists to influence the political programs and the international labor-movement affiliations of the CIO. In 1949 and 1950, the CIO expelled eleven affiliates on grounds of Communist party domination.

There is now no radical labor movement of consequence in the United States. There are a few unions whose leaders may profess left-wing objectives, such as Harry Bridges of the International Longshoremen's and Warehousemen's Union of the West Coast (ILWU). But Mr. Bridges' ideological radicalism is limited to words. In action, Mr. Bridges' relationship with the Pacific Maritime Association seems to have become a model of constructive, collaborative labor–management relations in meeting the challenge of automation.

As the worker's defense against industrialism, unionism has been a permanent feature of the terrain for more than a century and a half. But the prevailing winds in union forms, philosophies, and functions have shifted over this period. We have seen how industrial unionism was aborted for a century, even though developments in industry seemed to have been ready for it.

The question may now arise, are we witnessing the emergence of a new period in industrial unionism? Is industrial unionism losing the initiative? Is the membership stagnation of the industrial unions an indication that industrial unions are being displaced by new modes of employee representation? Is the union substitution policy of large-scale corporations providing an alternative to labor movement unionism? Is the association the new industrial unionism of the professional employee?

The signs are not clear. As this is written—late 1964—the industrial union in automobiles has scored great collective-bargaining victories. Yet American management is beginning to assert initiating power in collective bargaining deriving from its strategic power in technology.

12 UNIONIZATION OF WHITE-COLLAR WORKERS

Everett M. Kassalow

Articles about the "crisis" or the "stagnation" of the American trade-union movement have become common, one is tempted to say "fashionable," in recent years. This crisis-ridden or stagnant institution nevertheless still seems to be very much alive, judging by some of the monumental collective-bargaining advances of recent years or by its heavy participation in the recent election campaign. There is, however, some important evidence of slow-down in union growth, and a kind of semi-isolation which seems to have overtaken the unions in the past decade.

The simplest standard which can be applied in this respect is the membership test—has union membership grown in recent years? Latest surveys of the U.S. Department of Labor, covering the year 1962, put union membership at 16.6 million. This is a formidable figure, but it represents a decline of nearly one million from the peak reached in 1956. Of even greater significance is that this decline took place in the face of a growing labor force. As a result, union membership which made up over 33 per cent of all nonagricultural employment in 1956 was down to less than 30 per cent in 1962.

Doubtless many factors have contributed to the reversal of union growth which had been a continuous process from the mid-thirties into the mid-fifties, with time out only for the postwar adjustment period. But no other factor has been more important than the sweeping changes which have occurred in the labor force in the past decade. Most notable of these changes has been the rise to first place, among the major occupational divisions in the labor force, of the white-collar group. The American labor movement, much like labor movements in other industrial nations, has always based itself primarily on manual workers, and it is now confronted with the fact that its base is eroding.

WHITE-COLLAR WORKERS OUTNUMBER BLUE BY 1957

To the extent that any image of the typical American worker was valid, by 1960, the clerk, the typist, the teacher, the engineer, the manager, had become more typical than the automobile assembly worker or the truck driver. It is not coincidence which makes us date the decline in union membership most clearly from the 1956–1957 years. It was just in that very period that the United States became the first major industrial nation in the world in which white-collar workers had come to outnumber manual workers. By the time of the decennial census of 1960, white-collar employees made up over 43 per cent of the employment total, with manual workers accounting for less than 39 per cent. Service and agricultural workers constituted the other 18 per cent of the labor force.

The decline of the extractive industries, such as mining and agriculture, has been underway for many, many decades in the United States. During most of this period, however, both industrially employed manual workers and white-collar employees were both advancing their relative positions in the labor force, although the gains of the white-collar group were more rapid. Between 1900 and 1930, for example, white-collar employees grew to be 30 per cent of the total labor force, contrasted with less than 18 per cent in 1900; in the same period, farm employment declined from 37 per cent to 21 per cent. During these same years, the share of nonfarm manual workers in the total labor force also advanced steadily, though less spectacularly than the white-collar worker.

What stands out most vividly since the end of World War II is not just the continued increase of white-collar employment, but the equally significant, relative decline of the manual worker. In 1950, white-collar employees formed 37 per cent of total employment, and manual workers were over 40 per cent. By 1960, white-collars were 43 per cent, and the nonfarm manuals were less than 39 per cent. Projections of labor force growth made by the U.S. Department of Labor into the mid-seventies indicate a continuation of this trend, with white-collar gains at the expense, relatively, of blue-collar groups. These great employment shifts in the 1950's, and every percentage change represented a shift of seven or eight hundred thousand workers, reflected far-reaching technological changes in the American economy as well as major innovations in the American style of life.

In important industries such as manufacturing, the spread of advanced technology has compelled employers to seek more clerical, technical and professional employees, and fewer manual employees. Computers in all industries, continuous flow processes in steel, oil, rubber, chemicals, and textiles, automatic tool machines, and large transfer machines in metal fabricating—all these were reducing industry's dependence on semiskilled assemblers, laborers, and other manual workers.

BLUE-COLLAR WORKERS ALSO DECLINE IN MANUFACTURING

Between 1947 and 1963, manufacturing output nearly doubled in the United States, but the number of manual employees in manufacturing declined over 400,000. White-collar employment in manufacturing rose by nearly 2 million in the same period. In the manufacturing segment of the economy, normally regarded as the backbone of manual work and of the modern, mass-union movement, white-collar employees now make up over 26 per cent of the employment total.

Not only have technological changes been reducing the job markets for manual workers, but changes in the consumption demands of the American people are having similar effect. The strong tide of prosperity since the end of World War II has gradually influenced American consumers to shift more of their dollars to the purchase of services and to spend relatively fewer dollars on goods. Automobiles, homes, and appliances continue in good demand; but more of the consumers' new dollars are being spent on travel, recreation, education, and other services.

Employment changes have followed these shifts in spending. In 1947, the goods-producing industries supported over 51 per cent of all employment in the U.S., with service-producing industries, including government, accounting for less than 49 per cent. By 1962, service industries were employing over 58 per cent of all workers in the United States. It is not that union members have been leaving the labor movement in any large or unusual numbers in the past eight or nine years; rather, it has been the case that where union membership has been high, industries have experienced substantial declines in employment, thereby cutting total union membership.

GOVERNMENT EMPLOYMENT

Government, as an employer, has been a prominent "gainer" in this period, as consumers have sought more public services. By 1962, government employed over 15 per cent of the work force, a gain of 50 per cent over the 1947 period. It is important to understand, in the face of this rise in government employment, that unionism among government employees in the United States has been rather limited, and much less extensive, for instance, than among great mass-production industries. Of significance on the government side has been the huge increase in teacher employment—from a little over 1,000,000 in the public schools in 1950 to over one and one-half million in 1960, and still rising rapidly.

The striking increase in teacher employment serves to highlight the general growth of professional and technical work. In the decades of the fifties and in recent years, although nearly all major white-collar occupations continue to show growth, it is especially the professional categories—engineers, draftsmen, teachers, scientists, and medical personnel—that have surged forward most rapidly. Total employment in the United States increased 14.5 per cent in the 1950–1960 decade, but professional and technical employment rose 47 per cent.

Until now, most of these growing white-collar segments have barely been touched by unionism. To judge the prospects for unionism among white-collar workers, one is virtually compelled to speculate about the future on what is admittedly only scanty evident today, but there is some evidence to go on.

THE CHALLENGE OF WHITE-COLLAR UNIONISM

The problem of the unionization of this rapidly growing white-collar force is, in reality, at least two problems. In the first place, the problem is posed about what white-collar workers can, should, or are likely to do about the matter themselves.

American society, like most Western democratic societies, has been one in which group action has become more and more essential to preserve democratic decision-making. Indeed, it would be widely agreed that the development in the past thirty years of mass unionism among manual workers has vitally strengthened democratic processes in the U.S. by providing representation and participation channels for millions of industrial workers. Without unions, these millions would otherwise be largely powerless in effecting the day-to-day and year-to-year decisions which govern their lives, their jobs, and the economy generally.

The same problem is increasingly going to be posed for the millions of clerks, teachers, engineers, and other white-collar groups that are swelling the labor force. So long as the white-collar worker was only a small factor in economic life, so long as he enjoyed a very unique relationship with his supervisor, so long as he was the rare professional engineer employed by the firm, the need to find representation channels, as opposed to purely individual contacts, was not pressing.

Today when insurance companies or industrial firms employ thousands of clerks in huge batteries on vast open office floors, the older direct relationship between clerk and supervisor tends to disappear. When aircraft and aerospace companies employ thousands of engineers, an inevitable change in their status has occurred. In contrast to his pre-World War II position in American industry when the engineer was almost automatically regarded as a part of management, he has become an employee.

I am quite convinced that one way or another these "new millions" in American economic life will demand and establish their own channels of representation and influence. In a society which is increasingly characterized by group bargaining and by group consultation on the part of government, no major economic group will long be without its organization form and channel.

PRESENT STATUS OF WHITE-COLLAR UNIONISM

The other side of the problem of unionizing the white-collar worker is the response of the existing labor movement, and most notably the AFL-CIO to the erosion of its blue-collar or manual-worker membership base, brought about by the growing numerical importance of white-collar workers.

The organized union movement is not starting from scratch in meeting this white-collar challenge. Though manual-worker unions have been predominant in U.S. labor history, significant union organization among postal employees, railway clerks, retail clerks and a few other white-collar groups goes back many decades. Musicians, actors, artists, airline pilots, and journalists have also been well unionized for years.

Moreover, a closer examination of union-membership figures reveals that the white-collar and government unions have been the fastest growing in the United States in recent years. The Retail Clerks International Association increased its membership 25 per cent in the past ten years. The American Federation of Government Employees, whose membership is substantially, though not exclusively, white-collar, has just about doubled in the past six years. AFL-CIO unions, notably the American Federation of State, County and Municipal Workers, covering state and local government employees, both manual and nonmanual, and teachers have also registered membership gains at a time when large manual-worker unions have been declining.

Taken as a whole, however, the figures on white-collar and public employee unionism cannot be comforting to the leaders of organized labor. The latest U.S. Department of Labor survey of union membership reports there are some 2.3 million white-collar unionists against more than 14 million manual-worker union members. Over 50 per cent of the organizable potential in the manual field are in unions, as opposed to a 10 to 12 per cent unionization among white-collar employees.

AFL-CIO RESPONSE TO WHITE-COLLAR GROWTH

Needless to say, the AFL-CIO is aware of these labor-force changes that are affecting its membership growth. In the past few biennial conventions and in its periodic reports, the labor federation has commented on this issue. As yet, however, it is fair to say that the main center of organized labor as such has not modified its policies, its structure, its tactics, or the allocation of its resources in any major way to meet this new challenge. It has not taken advantage of this new opportunity to organize. A possible exception can be noted in the case of the teachers' union whose organizing effort during the successful campaign for union recognition in New York City in 1961 was supported by large sections of the AFL-CIO, including the national headquarters, notably by its Industrial Union Department.

The generally slow response to the white-collar organization challenge by the AFL-CIO is hard to explain. Certainly the AFL-CIO has never been a class-conscious labor federation for the purely industrial proletariat or manual workers, which might feel ideologically inhibited about unionizing white-collar employees. On the other hand, however, in the tradition of the AFL which predates the merger with the CIO, it has been reluctant to assume major responsibility for new organizing as such. There have also been conflicts between AFL-CIO affiliated unions as to which union or unions has the right or responsibility to organize particular groups of white-collar workers. Viewing such conflicts, the Federation tends to play a relatively passive role in white-collar organizing.

Again, whereas the AFL-CIO leadership is not revolutionary proletarian in ideology, it does come out of a manual tradition. The largest unions in the Federation as well as most of its influential leaders have a manual background and base. They do not take easily to the white-collar workers' outlook or needs. Moreover, many of these leaders today find their own unions caught up in complex problems of adjustment to automation and other major technological developments. They do not lack the usual number of important problems to occupy their time! Nonetheless, several of the originally CIO-affiliated large industrial unions, like the Auto Workers and the Steel Workers, do give special attention to organizing the salaried workers in their industry and have scored some successes. One must also add that although union membership has declined slightly in the most recent years, the American labor movement still can count great successes over a relatively short span of time. It has grown over five-fold, from 3 million to more than 16 million, in less than thirty years.

Member unions continue to record important successes in wages, hours, and working conditions. The thirty-hour workweek established by the New York City electricians just a few years ago is one outstanding example. The United Steel Workers' negotiation of the so-called sabbatical leave, thirteen weeks of vacation every fifth year, for steel workers with long company service is another case in point. Just this past year, the United Automobile Workers successfully bargained for an early retirement system, entirely paid for by the automobile companies which will permit high seniority employees to retire at sixty with pensions ranging up to 400 dollars a month.

Coupled with the continued successes of AFL-CIO unions and their leaders often is their feeling that any group that wants to organize or needs to organize should help itself. There are also still some lingering feelings of resentment against the white-collar workers' air of social superiority so characteristic in the past. As yet, the AFL-CIO leadership hasn't felt a sufficient threat to its position as spokesman for the American worker to divert large resources for the purpose of organizing white-collar employees on a mass scale.

WHITE-COLLAR UNIONISM, PROBLEMS, AND PROSPECTS

Yet there are signs of change both inside and outside the AFL-CIO which suggest the white-collar union picture may be shifting. We have already alluded to the membership advances made by AFL-CIO affiliates in the public employment field in recent years. A Presidential Executive Order issued by the late President Kennedy in January 1962 places the U.S. government squarely in the position of encouraging collective bargaining and unionism for government employees. It accords to unions operating in the federal government the right to gain full recognition, sign written agreements, and carry on many of the activities until now limited to private employment. Although this directive repeats the traditional prohibition of strikes by U.S. employees, it is not viewed as a serious union deterrent since most public employee unions had already voluntarily renounced the right to strike.

Union recognition and collective bargaining in the public service have made important progress in the two years since this Executive Order was issued and, with concerted effort, even more progress can be anticipated in the future. The legitimation of unionism and bargaining for public employees is likely to enhance its acceptance in other white-collar fields.

A few of the hitherto manually dominated worker unions in private industry have also begun to increase their efforts in the white-collar field. The automobile workers' union, the UAW for one, has been overhauling its organization, structure, and techniques in order to unionize more white-collar employees in the automobile and related companies. A new department has been created within the union to offer service exclusively to professional, technical, and office employees. In recent negotiations with the Chrysler Corporation, the automobile union insisted on a new program that will enable unionized salaried employees at Chrysler to participate in the company's stock purchase plan. It was only a few years ago that the large unions in the mass-production industries, including the Automobile Workers' union, were resisting company efforts to involve unionized employees in such company-sponsored plans, on the ground that this was undesirable company paternalism.

The Automobile union's flexibility in this respect is a sign of change. In the past, one of the weaknesses of most AFL-CIO union efforts to organize white-collar employees was the failure to realize that there are some differences between the socio-psychological outlook of white-collar and manual workers. Often the union organizer with experience limited to campaigns in the blue-collar field would begin by informing white-collar employees they were no better off than blue-collar workers so far as social and economic opportunities were concerned; therefore, they should form unions as the manual workers had done. No worker really wants to feel the best he can do is to be "equalized." The union should be a road up for him, not some kind of leveling device. This is especially important for white-collar workers whose "upward aspirations" are known to be much greater than those of blue-collar workers.

Although the enormous increase in white-collar employment may be reducing these advancement opportunities somewhat—there can only be just so many supervisors and higher level jobs —the union, to appeal successfully, must convince the upward aspiring employee that it can reinforce his prospects and not downgrade or level them.

One other point is worth noting on the role of supervisors in influencing the future of white-collar unionism in the United States. Unlike most other industrialized countries, labor-relations law in the United States makes it very difficult for supervisors or foremen to organize or join unions. Judging by the positive way in which unionized supervisors and foremen helped influence favorably the spread of white-collar unionism in other countries, obstacles to supervisory unionism may also be something of an obstacle to general white-collar unionism in the United States.

OFFICE AUTOMATION MAY ENHANCE UNION OPPORTUNITIES

The impact of automation on many aspects of office work may also enhance the opportunity for white-collar unionism. Studies to date indicate that many traditional white-collar careers are being severely jolted when automation, in the form of large data-processing machines, takes over the modern office. Many older, highly sought-after jobs in filing, recordkeeping, accounting, and the like are wiped out. Although some new, well-paid high-status jobs such as programmer are created by office automation, the numbers of these jobs are relatively few, and often the companies want newly recruited employees to fill them.

In the automated office, many clerical employees now find their old freedom of movement restricted. The high-speed office machines require close and constant attention. Sometimes night-shift work for office employees is introduced for the first time as companies seek to take full advantage of the expensive equipment.

Clearly new frustrations and insecurities attend developments like these; but to be successful in translating these insecurities into successful organizing appeals, the union will have to appear as guardian of the white-collar worker's threatened status. It can, for instance, insist that new jobs created by office automation be open to employees whose status is being undermined, and that senior employees be given the chance to train for the new posts. In a few cases, unions have already succeeded with such demands.

Offsetting some of these new opportunities for unions is the fact that routine office positions continue to be filled primarily by women workers. Many of these women are not committed to permanent work careers. It is, therefore, more difficult to convince them of the need to join unions and pay dues since they regard their jobs as temporary. So the president of a British union of clerical workers remarked: "It is not that they feel superior to trade unions—they just aren't interested." This lack of job commitment on the part of women is also an obstacle to white-collar unions organizing in other fields such as retail trade and department stores.

WHITE-COLLAR UNIONISM OUTSIDE THE AFL-CIO

Within a few white-collar occupations, the most interesting organizational stirrings are going on outside the AFL-CIO. This is true of several professional groups which have been experiencing the development of that group consciousness and sense of employee group-need which is a prerequisite to union formation.

The American Nurses Association, for example, has gradually been transforming its structure to add bargaining functions on behalf of nurses to its regular professional association activities. The first impulses in this direction came during World II when nurses found their wages frozen under government wage regulation. Several state associations of nurses put themselves forward as bargaining agents for their members to represent themselves before government bodies since it was impossible for individuals to plead for wage changes.

A few years later, the national body, the American Nurses Association, accepted the necessity for collective bargaining; it continues, however, to insist on the distinction between bargaining and unionism and rejects the latter. Studies of the actual collective agreements negotiated by nurses, however, reveal that they closely resemble collective agreements in other occupations, and typically cover wages and other working conditions. Some of them provide for a union shop and the "check off" of nurses' union dues. Unlike most unions, nurses do oppose the use of strikes and seek some form of terminal arbitration for unresolved disputes.

The National Education Association, the professional society for public school teachers, has also been drawn, albeit reluctantly, into bargaining activities. While continuing to insist on "professional" participation with boards of educations in many states and localities, NEA seeks to resist the usually accepted government procedures and agencies for handling labor disputes on the grounds that these are designed for unions and not for professional groups. Yet in the past few years, NEA affiliated bodies in different localities had to compete against the American Federation of Teachers in regular collective-bargaining elections, held under the auspices of state labor agencies to determine which group should hold exclusive bargaining rights to represent teachers. Just this last fall, new wage disputes between teachers and public authorities flared up in such scattered areas as Georgia, Oklahoma, Kentucky, and Louisiana. There were highly spontaneous outbreaks which attest to widespread teacher unrest. One way or another, increasing numbers of teachers have been caught up in bargaining processes and forms of unionism.

A study of the grievances of both teachers and nurses indicates that their desire to protect their professional status is generally as important as purely economic factors in impelling them to organize. Teachers, for example, almost unanimously object to the tendency in many school systems to assign them to supervising the cafeteria during lunch periods or to working long, extra hours in after-school activities in no way related to their professional training and expectations. Clearly, unionism among groups like these will build on professional as well as economic grievances and goals.

Similar discontents led to an upsurge of unionism among groups of engineers ten or fifteen years ago. Engineers' concern with excessive subdivision of work, their lack of full professional recognition, as well as insecurity of employment resulted in the formation of engineering unions in major aircraft and engineering development companies on the East and West coasts. Once again, these were mainly unions independent of the AFL-CIO.

The tide of engineering unionism has, however, receded considerably in recent years. Conflicting feelings about the compatibility of professionalism and unionism seem to lie at the base of this downturn in engineering unionism. Employers have played heavily on this point, insisting on the incompatibility of professionalism and unionism. Obviously engineers are professionals; but just as obviously, when they are employed by the hundreds or the thousands in large companies, they are also employees with some of the same needs as other employees. The engineers do not seem to have progressed as far as other professionals, such as nurses or teachers, in reconciling these varying, but by no means necessarily contradictory, needs of unionism and professionalism.

Finally, mention must be made of the large number of semi-professional associations covering nearly 400,000 employees in state and local public employment. These, too, lie outside the AFL-CIO, and only in some cases have such associations begun to assume union-type activities.

In the light of these developments among professionals and government employees, however, there is a very serious possibility that the largest number of white-collar workers may unionize or form bargaining associations independent of the AFL-CIO.

WHITE-COLLAR ORGANIZATION LIKELY TO INCREASE

Objective circumstances, such as loss of individuality in white-collar work, pose a threat to genuine professional status and create the need to be represented in private and public decision-making—these and other forces seem slowly to be moving large masses of white-collar workers toward group organization. Just what forms this organization may take, how it will be related to already existing labor organizations, and how rapid its progress may be in the face of managerial opposition and some continued feelings of white-collar worker superiority only the coming years will reveal.

13 THE PHILOSOPHY OF AMERICAN MANAGEMENT TOWARD LABOR

Neil W. Chamberlain

Let us begin by taking this rather portentious title apart. Dissection is often conducive to analysis. When we speak of the philosophy of "American management," we lump all managers together in what is presumed to be a common mold, as though they thought alike about, and reacted alike to, some other homogeneous entity which we label "labor." But this is, of course, a literary fiction. We are scarcely warranted, even in pleading the theorist's right to abstract and to generalize, to engage in such sweeping characterizations. We have to fall back on a journalist's impressionism, which is admittedly not without its value. Historians do the same when they try to catch the spirit of a time or place.

DIVERSITY OF MANAGEMENT ATTITUDES

But we should pause long enough, before plunging ahead on this impressionistic basis, to appreciate the diversity that we embrace within these two categories. Management attitudes toward labor range over a whole spectrum. At one pole, we have employers who take a generally optimistic and favorable attitude toward labor, who try to understand labor's objectives and to work out a cooperative relationship. One example of such a managerial approach on the contemporary American scene is provided by the Kaiser Steel Company in California. This is the business firm that joined, a few years ago, with the Steelworkers

Union in exploring methods by which they could jointly share the fruits of progress. They enlisted the imaginative assistance of a trio of professional industrial-relations experts, and the result was an agreement that workers would receive a specified proportion of all the savings which accrued from the introduction of improved techniques, along with certain employment guarantees. Thus, progress and rising productivity no longer loom as a threat to the workers in this company, but bring financial benefits of a very substantial magnitude.

I will not try to point the finger at any management located at the opposite end of our spectrum, where attitudes toward labor are pessimistic and even cynical. Such managements do, of course, exist. Instead, let me take a company which I would be inclined to put somewhere in the negative half of the range as another example with respect to attitudes toward labor, even though it does not belong in the nether hell of any personnel inferno. I refer to the General Electric Company. There are people who would disagree with me on this point, but I shall explain why I regard it as I do.

The General Electric Company is by no means anti-labor. It has established terms and conditions of employment that a great many workers would be only too happy to have for themselves. But its attitude tends to be distinctly paternalistic. It has developed an explicit philosophy, to which its former vice president of industrial relations, Lemuel Boulware, has lent his name, so that it has become known as Boulwareism. The heart of this philosophy is that General Electric wants to do what *it* believes is right for its employees. In order to do so, it constantly re-examines its own policies, takes note of what other companies are doing, listens to the requests of its employees and the demands of its unions, and then decides for itself what is the fair thing to do. It avers that it stands ready to change its decision in the light of any new information, but the heart of the matter is that when *it* decides that it has all the relevant data, then *it* will announce what terms and conditions of employment it believes are fair, and it will not budge from that position into which it has put its full measure of wisdom and sense of justice. Some people applaud it for this earnest effort to adhere to its considered convictions, but others, among whom I would include myself, are less enthusiastic.

In adopting this philosophy, General Electric is arrogating to itself a kind of infallibility of judgment, a paternal policy of "papa knows best." The treatment of employees in terms of wages and conditions may be excellent, but its attitude toward its employees is that of a superior father-figure.

In between Kaiser Steel and General Electric, there are many shades of management philosophy, and, as I have already noted, there are managements whose philosophical position is a good deal more austere or severe than General Electric's. With all this diversity then, whenever I speak of the attitudes of American management as a whole, I am engaging in a rather sweeping characterization.

LITTLE WORKERS AND BIG LABOR

The same thing is true when I talk of labor. Management's attitude often differs depending on what kind of labor we are talking about. Some managements have one kind of stance relative to salaried professional and technical employees, for example, and a different stance toward hourly-paid production employees. Even with respect to production workers, there is sometimes a different point of view relative to the skilled groups in contrast to the unskilled.

But the really basic distinction is that between organized labor and the individual. The distinction is neatly pointed up by the statement of one industrial-relations director, in the course of a private conversation, that we love our workers but we hate the unions. Workers as individuals are one thing. Workers organized into unions are another thing. Most managers today adopt a rather equalitarian point of view toward workers as individuals. Social distinctions are minimized rather than stressed. Worker–manager relationships are often on a first-name basis.

One of the most popular subjects in executive programs is human-relations training, in which managers explore, among other things, the importance of understanding another person's springs of action, and of interacting with him in a positive manner. Such programs are not restricted to relations among executives but often stress manager–worker relations and means of improving them. Ambition and initiative are approved and re-

173

warded. The notion of "career training" is becoming current, and there is a spreading acceptance of the view that the only condition necessary for advancement into managerial ranks, other, of course, than native ability, is formal education. The rising proportion of college-trained people in the population-at-large means that every year more children of workers' families are able to satisfy this condition. Moreover, even for those who have not completed higher educational programs, a good many companies make it financially possible for any interested worker to continue his formal education. Thus management is now less a closed social class than it ever was. The manager's attitude toward the individual employee is what we might appropriately call a "wholesome" one.

But unionized workers are Labor with a capital "L," and as such are regarded quite differently by managers. Labor with a capital "L" is sometimes regarded as a faceless and often misled mass, an organized pressure group, an adversary, sometimes a guerrilla army, even legalized extortionists. Even the more temperate managers usually view the introduction of a union into their firm with sorrow and misgiving, and sometimes with guilt. The latter reaction occurs when they see the union as a mark of their own failure. It is the price that they have to pay for not being as good managers as they should have been.

In some way their personnel policy was deficient, so that their workers—whom they thought they had known and understood and treated fairly—were driven to form a union. It is scarcely surprising that managers would not respond affirmatively to an organization whose very presence and especially whose opposition tactics often give them an uneasy feeling of personal inadequacy, whether or not they are willing to admit this. Where unions and union actions are subconsciously regarded as the wages of managerial sins of omission or commission, it is easy to understand why they are not likely to be looked on with favor. They stand as perpetual reminders of management's own failings. I do not intend to suggest that this is a reasonable attitude, but I am quite sure it is a prevalent one.

Since World War I, there has been another attitude toward unions which has grown in importance. This constitutes a recognition that in modern large-scale corporate organization, personnel policy cannot be administered on an individual basis. Terms and conditions cannot be tailored to meet each separate case. General policies have to be hammered out. A case can be made for involving workers, in some representative fashion, in the drafting of such general policies. Some form of unionism is thus almost necessary in modern economic society. But this idea does not mean that management need feel any particular sympathy, rapport, or even respect for such worker institutions—any more than workers need feel sympathy, rapport, or respect for a corporation. They can be treated impersonally, as one would not treat an individual worker. They can be sharply opposed, as one might take issue with someone of a different political persuasion or with a business rival. They can be charged with incompetent and even corrupt leadership, as one might charge any faulty organization. And none of these attitudes toward labor, in its institutional sense, has any necessary relationship to management's attitude toward labor as individual workers.

This last position, which we might label management's "institutional" philosophy of labor, is, I think, the dominant attitude today among businessmen. But the other two points of view coexist, often in the same mind.

Many managers still pride themselves as at least partially responsible for the absence of a union in their plants or offices. "Good management" keeps the union away, and the absence of a union conveys a nice sense of righteousness. In times of labor strife, particularly during prolonged strikes in which exacerbated feelings give rise to some violence, the belief that unionism is easily converted into a legalized form of extortion often asserts itself. The hearings in the U.S. Senate a few years back, presided over by Senator John L. McClellan, which laid bare before the public some of the less savory practices of a relatively few but quite large unions, encouraged this view.

In general, then, the tendency in American management's thinking is to the effect that the impersonal corporation gives rise to the impersonal labor union, both of which can perform well or badly. Accompanying this is a belief that the better management performs its functions, the less the union is necessary. On the whole, managers think they have performed pretty well, and therefore they see only a limited role for the unions. The fact that unions refuse to be limited, but remain assertive and demanding, is ascribed to the self-interest of the union chiefs who endeavor to build up their own importance by belittling management's performance. The union bureaucracy entrenches itself by stirring up unrest and dissatisfaction among workers who would otherwise be relatively content. This is a disjointed philosophy which requires considerable subtlety to be integrated into an internally consistent doctrine. Probably most managers tend to emphasize one or another of its facets—the institutional impersonality of organized labor, the influence of management performance on its functional specifications, and the influence of self-serving union officials on its actual behavior. The greater the emphasis on any of these three facets, the more distorted becomes the image of the union.

CONCEPTS OF THE MANAGEMENT FUNCTION

The philosophy of American management toward labor has been very much conditioned by its philosophy of the management function. The notion that the role of manager carries with it certain inalienable prerogatives is deep-seated. Let us pause briefly for a little historical perspective. Even within the last half-century there were prominent employers who attributed divine sanction to managerial authority. One of these, President George Baer of the Philadelphia & Reading Coal and Iron Company, did in fact achieve a degree of immortality by a public assertion in 1902 that God in His infinite wisdom had lodged an authority with management that was not to be challenged by those who were managed.

Not many businessmen were so blunt in their beliefs, but far more common throughout the last century—and equally effective —was the view that the market system was a gift of Providence, and the terms and conditions which were the result of free competition in the labor market, however onerous they might appear to those working under them, actually were conducive to the common good. This miracle was achieved through the "invisible hand" about which Adam Smith had written so compellingly.

The free market made no provision for labor unions, so that their attempted intervention could be regarded as a challenge to the invisible hand of Providence. Does this sound a little far-fetched? Let me quote, then, the words of a Protestant minister resident in Scranton, Pennsylvania, published in 1887, which— we can say with another of our sweeping generalizations—represented a point of view more or less characteristic of the clergy of the time. "Competition, and not selfish combination, is the essential foundation upon which the whole structure of industrial society must stand, in a free country, and under true Christian civilization."[1] With this kind of theological fortification, American management erected a credo of the managerial prerogative. The management prerogative—that is, the right of management to set its own terms, leaving it to workers to accept or reject them as they chose—was indivisible from the free market system. Thus, by happy coincidence (or should we say the rigors of logic?), managerial self-interest was readily identified with social welfare. Union interference with managerial discretion could be branded as anti-social and even un-Christian. Thus, when the Typographical Union made demands on the *New York Journal of Commerce* in 1851, it elicited a response the vehemence of which arose from what was conceived as an affront to its constituted authority. In rejecting the union's request for rules which would limit the number of apprentices and female compositors who could be hired, whom the male journeymen regarded as a threat to their employment security, the publishers thundered in their editorial columns, with more than a touch of self-righteousness:

... Sooner than be restricted on these points, or any other, by a self-constituted tribunal outside of the office, we would go back to the employment of our boyhood, and dig potatoes, pull flax, and do anything else that a plain, honest farmer may properly do on his own territory. It is marvelous to us how any employer, having the soul of a man within him, can submit to such degradation.[2]

1 Samuel Logan, D.D., *A City's Danger and Defense* (Philadelphia: The Jas. B. Rodgers Printing Co., 1887), p. 327.

2 George A. Stevens, *New York Typographical Union No. 6* (N.Y. State Dept. of Labor, Annual Report of the Bureau of Labor Statistics, 1911), Part I, 241.

BUSINESS RELIANCE ON PRIVATE PROPERTY

This vigorous assertion of management right is obviously linked to the notion of business as private property. Property rights are an essential ingredient of a competitive society, and a union effort to infringe on such rights is an attack on the system itself. For workers to combine to bring pressure or power to bear on management, to force it to concede certain of its rights of property, could readily be construed not only as unlawful but immoral. Thus property rights, managerial authority, and the competitive system could all be linked together as a kind of holy trinity, and the unions could be cast in the role of Beelzebubs who would attack the kingdom of economic righteousness for personal power and enrichment. This is not a fanciful figure of speech, but comes very close, I think, to capturing the spirit of the management view prevailing in the nineteenth century.

Now we are in the midst of the twentieth century, and, in the intervening years, several things have happened to modify the commercial scriptures. For one thing, some corporations grew so enormous in size and had such obvious power over employees, customers, and the public at large that the notion that they still remained private property and could be used as the owners and managers saw fit began to fall out of fashion. The large corporation became a frequent subject of journalistic attack.

Second, recurring financial crises and economic depressions, culminating in the Great Depression of the 1930's, robbed the competitive system of a large measure of its claim to being a beneficent gift of Providence. It obviously needed a little human assistance as well. That meant that private managers, the special custodians of the competitive system, were obliged to share discretion with others, notably with government. But government in turn allowed organized labor to participate in making economic decisions through the device of collective bargaining, which has been legally protected since the NIRA in 1933 and, particularly, the NLRA of 1935.

Third, despite effective management opposition, over the years the unions have gained ground. Episodically and spasmodically, they won concessions on hours of work, protest over discipline, work loads, the speed of assembly lines, pensions, promotions, and a variety of other matters. And in doing so, they inevitably weakened the basic credo of the management prerogative. It became increasingly difficult to argue that a union's demand for a guaranteed annual wage, for example, or for job-security provisions somehow endangered the managerial prerogative, when management had already surrendered that prerogative on a score or more of other fronts.

As a consequence of these several developments, the management-prerogative issue which played such an important part in management-thinking and in union–management relations in previous years has by now become much less significant. The tendency is for management to guard the discretion which it believes it needs to do a good job of management, even while recognizing that this discretion may be chipped away, from time to time, by unions exercising their bargaining power in what they conceive to be the interests of their members.

From time to time, "management rights" in these more modest terms flare up into a sharply drawn issue, notably during the 1959 national steel strike when the companies sought to recapture the authority to institute changes in work rules even in the absence of major changes in job content. The General Motors strike in 1964 provided an example of what might have been an equally sticky wicket, as our British friends would say, but which was glossed over in the final settlement by a union and management both anxious to find a peace formula. The UAW asked for a new contract clause which would have read:

The Corporation and the Union both subscribe to the moral principle that the dignity and worth of the individual human person transcend all other values. Accordingly, it is agreed that the Corporation will exercise its managerial authority in the light of that principle, and any failure on its part to do so may be taken up by the Union under the Grievance Procedure.

That last clause would have meant that any union protest not met by the company could have been appealed to an outside umpire, who would have been authorized—indeed, directed—to determine whether an action of the management hierarchy failed to recognize the "human dignity" of the workers affected, or whether disciplines meted out by the company had been exces-

179

sively harsh in the sense that another person might reasonably be expected to behave the same way under similar circumstances.

The difference between the apoplectic response which could be expected of management to any such union proposal, both now and a hundred years ago, is that formerly this would have been regarded as interference with an "inherent" if not a divine right of management; whereas, now, it would be treated primarily as a threat to the efficient performance of the managerial function.

Property rights and the authority which goes with them no longer constitute the chief philosophical bastion of defense of management against labor. It is not that belief in property rights has lost status; it is simply that, like so many other orthodoxies in our times, it has lost its power to arouse strong passions, except among small proprietors when they are beset by large unions. At least some of the managers who run the giant corporations and who provide the flavor of the contemporary business creed, while they still regard private property as the cradle of freedom, experience uneasiness in legitimatizing their own actions in terms of someone else's property—that is to say, in terms of the dispersed property claims of a shifting base of stockholders, most of whom have little knowledge of or affinity with the corporations they presumptively "own."

COMPETITION AS A WAY OF LIFE

Managers' attitudes toward organized labor are now rooted in two separable but related propositions. The first is that the role which society expects them to play demands that their principal concern be with efficient business management, tested by the making of a profit. It is true that most corporate public-relations departments profess multiple concerns—the "balanced best interests" of employees, shareholders, suppliers, customers, and community. But in the last analysis, it is the profit performance which is essential not only to survival, but also to the kind of progressive, innovative spirit which American society believes *should* characterize its business operations. American managers are not expected to relax, they are expected to fight. They are not supposed to be satisfied with present accomplishments, but to engage restlessly in a search for new achievements.

However the characteristics of economic competition may differ from those pictured by the Anglo-American economists of the nineteenth century, the business world within which managers operate remains one of continuing struggle. Despite occasional violations, the federal anti-cartel laws are very much on the minds of businessmen, and in recent years that body of legislation has been enforced even more rigorously than in the past. Three years or so ago, a number of high officials of major electrical companies were given jail sentences, and their firms were subjected to legal suits and penalties, for attempting to circumvent the law by collusive agreement. The U.S. Supreme Court has been increasingly reluctant to approve the merging of rival firms, or the acquisition by one company of another operating in the same general product area, on the ground that this would lessen competition.

Thus a businessman can never settle back in the comfortable assurance that his market position is a relatively secure one. Markets have a way of being lost unless they are continually defended and expanded. The rise and decline, or decline and rise, within a decade or so of major firms like Ford, Chrysler, Studebaker, Singer, Underwood, Remington-Rand, and many others, attest to the reality of the struggle. The competition comes in part from firms making the same products in the same way but more efficiently, from firms making the same products by improved technologies, and from firms making entirely new products which render old ones obsolete.

Thus the competitive environment impresses on the American manager the importance of efficient and profitable performance, not as a matter of selfishness, or of a myopic disregard for social values, or even of choice. The American culture demands that kind of performance of its businessmen, it has created a role for them which requires attention to the rate of return obtained on investment.

CONFLICT WITH UNION GOALS

When a businessman strives for cost reduction, quality control, an improved rate of output, he is simply conforming to the institutional role which has been written for him by the society of which he is a part. But inescapably, that role brings him into conflict with organized labor, whose own institutional role is bound up with preserving the income continuity of its members, protecting the value of their learned skills, relaxing disciplinary and production pressures. It is not a matter of one of these groups being right and the other wrong, or of one being narrowly preoccupied with money values and the other more broadly concerned with human values. It is simply that American society has written different scripts for these two sets of economic performers, and the roles in which they are respectively cast *call* for a clash of objectives on the economic stage.

But both managers and organized labor understandably enough tend to forget this cultural determination of each other's attitudes when they are immersed in the daily struggle. The charges and recriminations sometimes fly back and forth as though each were undermining the fabric of society instead of preserving it. It is difficult to be objective when one is directly involved. The consequence of this continuing encounter is readily predictable. In terms of management's philosophical disposition toward organized labor, it leads to a state of mind where unions are identified with efforts to interfere with that efficient performance which society expects of business—to interfere by such tactics as fighting for the retention of outworn work rules and customs, opposing new technologies, insisting on rewards for long service rather than ability. One can hardly expect managers to look benignly on those who are impeding it in doing its job, however sincere or well motivated they may be.

Thus management's institutional role helps to mold its conception of organized labor as a barrier to efficient performance and, in consequence, to economic progress. But there is a second and related consideration which confirms management in this point of view. Regardless of any professions or denials by union officials, managers suspect that unions are carriers of the seeds of government control if not socialism. It is not so much that the unions want it that way, but that their actions are driving the United States in that direction. By demanding employment guarantees and cradle-to-grave welfare programs, they enlarge the state's scope of economic intervention. Who but the state can give such open-ended assurances? By demanding the profit motive and impeding industrial efficiency, they pave the way for throwing more of the burden of society's economic operations into subsidized bureaucracies or government initiative. Who but the state will provide or insure the capital for risky and large-scale ventures when the probability of reward is so reduced by the persistent, importunate demands of one's cohesively organized employees? By creating collective-bargaining stalemates and threatening the disruption of industry, once again the unions are responsible for forcing governmental intervention and even the dictation of the terms of settlement. Who but the state can bring together two such powerful protagonists as a big union and a big corporation?

SHORT RUN AND LONG RUN

Thus the actions and institutions of organized labor can be viewed not simply as making management's role difficult, but even as threatening the system of free private enterprise from which management derives its very authority. The consequence is that managers often find themselves adopting an ambivalent attitude toward organized labor. As we noted earlier, many if not most of them are ready to admit that large-scale economic organization creates a need for some form of worker representation. They will often concede, and even catalogue, the useful contributions that unions have made. At the same time, accompanying this short-run, limited acceptance of a union function goes the longer-run, deep-seated concern that unions are likely to be responsible for remaking economic society in a shape not to management's liking, a concern which recommends a policy of containment.

It is this time perspective, then, which creates a philosophical ambivalence. Short-run accommodation has its place, but, if not kept within close bounds, it may lead to long-run disaster. The danger of appeasement is a lesson that the modern world has learned well. But to some extent, and from another perspective, this attitude reflects the same kind of opposition to change that management imputes to the unions, though in a larger social setting.

A few thoughtful high-level managers are paying serious attention to the new planning programs that have arisen in Western

Europe as devices for achieving national goals of rising income and full employment, programs which attempt to work out a cooperative relationship between the public and private sectors. By and large, however, business opinion in the United States is still opposed to all forms of national economic planning. If it persists in that opposition, it is likely to be the instrument for making its own worst fears come true. Worker unrest at the economic insecurity introduced by the accelerating pace of technological change may well force the government into more sweeping programs than would be necessary if business recognized the validity of labor's fears and worked cooperatively with government to meet the problems posed.

Without making any forecasts as to the likely developments on this front, I will conclude by saying that I have considerable confidence that the capacity to adapt to the pressures of social change which American managers have shown in the past, even though sometimes tardily, will stand them in good stead again. In the meantime, their attitude toward organized labor is one which calls for neither wholesale condemnation nor approval, but for understanding.

14 WORK AND LEISURE IN THE ROUND OF LIFE

Arthur M. Ross

VALUATION OF WORK AS A CENTRAL ACTIVITY

These days it is fashionable to believe that the valuation of work as a central human activity has declined as leisure opportunities have increased along with economic development and real incomes. If one looks back through the long sweep of history, however, the opposite conclusion emerges. Work has never been so highly valued as in the current era.

The ancient Greeks and Romans thought of work as painful drudgery suitable only for slaves. The Hebrews regarded it as punishment for sin, and the early Christians deprecated acquisition and wealth. "Behold the fowls of the air," Jesus said, "for they sow not, neither do they reap nor gather into barns; yet your Heavenly Father feedeth them." During the Middle Ages, material pursuits continued to be viewed as the opposite of spiritual salvation. Nobility, clergy, and gentry abstained from labor, while there were scores of festivals and holy days for the commonality.

Only as economic activity began to quicken toward the end of the medieval period did the Catholic Church develop a more tolerant attitude toward worldly activity. But the basic reassessment came with the Protestant Reformation, which for the first time assigned a positive spiritual value to one's "calling." As capitalism came into full flower, socialistic critics and conservative defenders of the existing order found themselves in full agreement on the central importance of work.

Secular philosophies have become dominant in the twentieth

century, but the concept of work continues to enjoy augmented status. In the older industrial societies of Europe, occupational achievement is fast becoming the sole source of personal prestige. The time has passed when inherited wealth, ownership of land, and a distinguished family name were sufficient to guarantee a place in the top ranks of social structure. The vestigial leisure class, like the European nobility, serves as an object of attention for tabloid readers and conducts experiments in far-out styles of life, but no longer stands at the center of the power structure. Professional or business achievement is the *sine qua non*. The communist nations continue to glorify and sentimentalize manual labor and ascribe putative ownership of their economic systems to the workers and peasants. And the developing countries are sparing no effort to instill motivation, commitment, and work discipline into large populations formerly occupied with casual, unrationalized agricultural activity in the villages.

Since the time of De Toqueville, the United States has been known as the country where work is at the top of the agenda. Recent developments indicate that work-oriented values are not receding but are being generalized throughout the whole population. Never shrinking from arduous assignments, the United States has now resolved that even the slum-dwellers of Harlem and the isolated mountaineers of Appalachia should be pulled into the mainstream of economic life, inoculated with achievement motivation, and endowed with the requisite education and self-discipline. Poverty is no longer the predominant human condition, but has become a form of moral turpitude. The percentage of women who participate in the labor force has risen from 20 per cent in 1900 to almost 37 per cent in 1964; and whereas the majority of working women were under thirty years of age in 1900, today almost half of all women between thirty-five and fifty-five are in the labor force. One of the most widely discussed books in recent years—*The Feminine Mystique* by Betty Friedan—contends that homemaking and motherhood can no longer be considered a satisfactory career for an intelligent, well-educated woman.[1] At the same time, approximately 4,000,000 Americans are holding two or more jobs, and overtime work opportunities are eagerly prized.

[1] Betty Friedan, *The Feminine Mystique* (New York: Norton, 1963).

THE SHORTER-HOURS MOVEMENT

The movement for shorter working hours, which has been one of the principal issues of industrial relations during the past century, must be viewed in this broader historical and philosophical context, if we are to avoid fallacious suppositions and predictions.

The shorter-hours movement was invested with more emotional energy and pressed with greater vigor than any other demand of working people in the nineteenth century. Since the philosophy of work and achievement had attained unquestioned acceptance, how can the strength of the protest be explained?

First, we should note that the character of work had been transformed, particularly in the factories. Formerly, work had been leisurely and spasmodic, carried out in the midst of the family and interwoven with other aspects of life. Then it was segregated, militarized, highly disciplined and abstracted from the natural rhythm and spontaneity of human activity. Physical conditions of work were often degrading in the extreme; supervision was harsh. In the 1840's, the twelve-hour day was most common in manufacturing industries, although in some cases Saturday work was shortened to ten hours, for a total of seventy hours per week. There were substantial variations, however. For example, President Van Buren established a ten-hour day in federal shipyards as early as 1835. On the other hand, wool spinners and weavers in New England worked an eighty-four-hour week as late as 1859.

Van Buren's proclamation may be regarded as the first success of the shorter-hours movement. By 1850, the building tradesmen in the larger cities had obtained the ten-hour day, although other workers lagged behind. During the 1850's, Ira Steward developed a theory which concluded that shorter hours of labor automatically led to increases in wages. This theory became very popular, and lay behind the early resolution of the American Federation of Labor that "eight hours shall constitute a day's labor from and after May 1, 1886."

Actually the process of shortening the workweek was spasmodic and irregular. For many years large differentials persisted, in contrast to the predominance of the forty-hour week at the present time. In 1890, for example, locomotive firemen were working seventy hours per week on the average; cotton spinners and bakers, sixty-five hours; blacksmiths, sixty hours; and building craftsmen, fifty-five hours. Scheduled hours for all industries averaged sixty-six hours in 1860, sixty hours in 1890, and fifty hours in 1926. (Because of chronic absenteeism, average hours worked were considerably less.)

In 1938, Congress enacted the Fair Labor Standards Act, under which the basic forty-hour week became effective in 1940. The forty-hour week is, of course, merely the standard; it does not prevent overtime assignments when work is plentiful, nor curtailed schedules when work is scarce. Nevertheless, average weekly hours have fluctuated narrowly in the neighborhood of forty since the end of World War II, the fluctuations being closely correlated with business and employment conditions, for manufacturing industries as a whole. The average was 40.3 hours in 1946, 39.6 hours in 1954, and 40.4 hours in 1963.

As the prevailing workweek has thus been stabilized in the United States, Western European countries have been slowly moving in the direction of forty hours. In Austria, for example, average weekly hours declined from 44.5 in 1954, to 42.6 in 1962. In France, the corresponding change was from 44.2 to 42.9; in West Germany, from 48.7 to 44.7; in Norway, from 44.2 to 42.4. One major exception is found in the United Kingdom, where weekly hours have remained in the neighborhood of forty-six, reflecting the unusual reliance on overtime assignments in some British industries. The International Labor Organization has lent its support to the principle of the forty-hour week, and it is likely that there will be further reductions in the European countries. Information about working hours in other regions of the world is so spotty that very little can be said.

In appraising the future of the shorter-hours movement, it is logical to begin by examining the present strength and validity of the various arguments which have traditionally been invoked in favor of this policy. Some of the considerations which made the issue so poignant during the nineteenth century are no longer very significant. For example, it cannot be claimed that the forty-hour week is injurious to health, except in a few extraordinary occupations. Neither can it be contended that the forty-hour week deprives a worker of family life or the opportunity to participate in civil or social activities, or that it keeps him at the level of a farm animal, or that it saps his productivity. It does remain true that if weekly hours are reduced while weekly earnings are maintained, an hourly wage-increase has been achieved. But hourly wage-increases have now become so regular, particularly in the unionized sector of the economy, that shorter hours can no longer be viewed as a necessary device for accomplishing that purpose.

Two major arguments remain, however: first, that hours must be cut in order to eliminate unemployment and retain the available work opportunity in an age of automation; and second, that more leisure can and should be provided for its own sake, as one of the fruits of higher productivity.

WORKING HOURS AND UNEMPLOYMENT

The current debate on working hours in the United States is focussed almost entirely on the work-sharing principle. According to the AFL-CIO,

> The aim of organized labor's campaign for a reduction of working hours is clear, simple and direct—to spread job opportunities and reduce unemployment. . . . Reduction of working hours and an increase in the overtime premium to discourage employers from scheduling overtime work are elements of the needed series of measures to increase unemployment and ease the growing job displacement that results from automation.

Business organizations such as the Chamber of Commerce and the National Association of Manufacturers reply that these proposals would make it more costly to hire workers and therefore diminish the amount of employment. President Johnson and Secretary Wirtz oppose the AFL-CIO demand for a standard thirty-five-hour week, but favor the idea of higher overtime rates in certain industries. The President has stated:

I believe the enactment of a 35-hour week would sharply increase costs, invite inflation, impair our ability to compete, and merely share instead of creating employment. But I am equally opposed to the 45- or 50-hour week in those industries where consistently excessive use of overtime careers increased unemployment. I recommend, therefore, legislation authorizing the creation of tri-partite industry committees to determine, in an industry-by-industry basis, as to where a higher penalty rate for overtime would increase job openings without unduly increasing costs.

It is certainly true that the technological revolution has speeded up, that the end is nowhere in sight, and that the social equilibrium is being shattered in massive and unprecedented ways. Still there is really no evidence to support the popular view that automation is eliminating work as such—as distinguished from the many specific jobs and occupations which are obviously being eliminated. Unemployment has been too high in the United States throughout the past seven years; nevertheless, the average unemployment rate since 1957 has been lower than in previous periods, such as 1908–1915 and 1921–1924—to say nothing of deep depressions such as those of the 1870's, the 1890's and the 1930's. Furthermore, those countries experiencing the most rapid technological change at the present time (as indicated by trends in output per man-hour) are the same countries enjoying the "economic miracle" characterized by full employment and labor shortages. Agreed, it is difficult to envisage exactly how the labor force will be deployed fifty years from today; but it would have been equally difficult in 1910 to predict the industries and occupations of 1960.

Even on the assumption that most clerical work will eventually be computerized, along with many managerial tasks, no one has any difficulty in thinking of things which need to be done—clearing the slums, providing more transportation, improving education, restoring the purity of air and water, multiplying recreational facilities, and so on. The real problem is that many of these neglected activities have traditionally lain in the public sector. This circumstance creates institutional and political difficulties, but it does not prove that work opportunity is drying up in any general sense. In the long run, man's wants for goods and services still appear to be unlimited.

Thus, the fashionable cliché that automation and cybernation will drastically reduce the opportunity (or need) for work is not supported by the evidence. On the other hand, there are sound reasons to reduce working hours as a means of spreading the remaining opportunity in certain industries and occupations. These are activities with a declining employment trend, a middle-aged labor force, and specialized occupational skills with limited transferability. Even if economic growth succeeds in restoring and preserving a satisfactory general employment level, an unemployed fifty-five-year-old coal miner may well find it impossible to make the transition into one of the growth sectors.

Workweeks of less than forty hours have already been established in some industries through collective bargaining. These industries include longshoring, garment manufacturing, brewing, baking, rubber manufacturing, and printing. Perhaps 10 per cent of production workers already have shorter workweeks. In addition, about half of the office workers have schedules of less than forty hours. In the case of office workers, however, the problem has not been fear of displacement, but rather the long commuting distances traveled by women who live in the suburbs together with their household responsibilities.

With respect to the employment argument for shorter hours, the following conclusions seem justified. (1) Reducing hours without cutting take-home pay would have the same economic effects as a general wage-increase. Purchasing power would rise, but costs of production would rise to an equal extent. Under these circumstances it cannot be predicted that total employment opportunity would expand. (2) A given quantum of job opportunity can be rationed among a greater number of people by reducing or eliminating overtime. (3) Despite the dramatic progress of technology, however, there is no convincing evidence that society is running out of work. (4) Nevertheless, employment problems in declining industries and occupations can be mitigated by rationing the remaining job opportunity. (5) For handling localized problems of this type, collective bargaining is a more effective device than legislation.

LEISURE FOR ITS OWN SAKE

The case for a general reduction in working hours therefore comes down to the question of whether additional leisure is desirable as a general proposition. When the issue is put in these terms, it is important to keep in mind that fewer hours per day and fewer days per week are not the only methods of reducing work time. Vacations, holidays and retirement are probably the more significant forms of leisure. The first and second have the effect of reducing the amount of work time in a year, and the third reduces the number of work years in a life span.

Three weeks of vacation and eight paid holidays are equivalent to a 9 per cent reduction in annual working hours. Of course, some employees worked during vacation periods and allowed holidays before these fringe benefits became general during the past quarter-century. Nevertheless it is safe to assume that there has been a considerable reduction in annual working hours, even though average weekly hours were almost the same in 1964 as they were in 1941. So far as retirement is concerned, only 28 per cent of men over sixty-five are now in the labor force as compared with 48 per cent in 1947.

Many solemn questions have been raised concerning the quality of this additional leisure—the incredible amount of time devoted to television programs, the popularity of spectator sports, the high consumption of liquor, and so on. In fact, one widely discussed book—*Of Time, Work, and Leisure* by Sebastian de Grazia—denies that leisure has increased at all.[2] De Grazia defines leisure as time which is truly unfettered or uncommitted, and contends that the reduction in working hours has been balanced, or even overbalanced, by the increase in commuting time, compulsory do-it-yourself chores, and babysitting by husbands while their wives go to work.

We cannot make the assumption, however, that more leisure is necessarily and universally desirable. Before this proposition can be accepted, three questions have to be answered. Do people prefer more leisure, on the one hand, or more goods and services

[2] Sebastian de Grazia, *Of Time, Work, and Leisure* (New York: Twentieth Century Fund, 1962).

on the other? Does leisure yield diminishing returns to the point where it eventually becomes a burden rather than a benefit? Will important positive values and satisfactions be sacrificed if work is reduced to the status of an incidental or peripheral activity?

The choice between more leisure and more goods and services confronts us continuously as output per man-hour increases. It might have been thought that the pressure for leisure would increase as basic material needs were satisfied, but the evidence is to the contrary. The statistics on this point go back to 1910. They show that in the 1910–1920 decade, 70 per cent of the potential benefit of higher productivity was "taken out" in greater leisure. (During that decade the standard workweek declined by about four hours.) In contrast, since the end of World War II, approximately 89 per cent of the potential has been devoted to more goods and services. (The average workweek has changed very little in the postwar period, although paid vacations and holidays have become more common.)

Some of the phenomena we have already noted—"moonlighting," more working women, and the popularity of overtime— attest to the fact that the concept of the "good life" seems almost infinitely expansible. The hunger for affluence in the nations of Western Europe seems equally evident. David Riesman claims that in sophisticated social strata "there is a tendency for people, more accustomed to upper-middle-class norms, to less eagerness for bounteous spending on consumer goods," and that "the younger generation of reasonably well-off and well-educated Americans do not seem . . . drivingly or basically materialistic." I must say that this alleged decline in materialism is not very evident in the middle-class suburbs, and even Riesman concedes that it "may be a long time appearing in the working-class and white-collar groups."

Does leisure yield diminishing returns and eventually become a burden? Riesman has come to this conclusion. When he and his collaborators wrote *The Lonely Crowd*, they took it for granted that as the trend toward automation accelerated the effort to increase work satisfaction might as well be given up, "with the meaning of life to be sought henceforth in the creative use of leisure." Clark Kerr and his associates reached a similar conclusion in *Industrial Man*. "For most people, any scope for the independent spirit on the job will be missing," they said; but "the great new freedom may come in the leisure of individuals." Since then, however, Riesman has changed his mind. He says that he and his associates had failed to recognize "that there would come a point where additional increments of leisure would prove more stultifying than satisfying and that the mass of men would be incapable of absorbing any more."

A case in point is found in the thirteen-week "sabbatical leaves" recently negotiated for employees in the basic steel industry as a device for spreading work opportunity and perhaps providing a realistic foretaste of retirement. Actually the analogy with the academic sabbatical leave is not very good. The professor on sabbatical has control over his own time, but employs it purposefully in furtherance of professional objectives. The steelworker, on the other hand, merely has a thirteen-week vacation. Some of the early beneficiaries of the program during the winter of 1963–1964 were described as staring moodily out the window and remarking that thirteen weeks is a long, long time. It was not difficult to predict that the employers and the union would soon engage a corps of social workers and vacation planners to assist the steelworkers in making better use of the time. And if thirteen-week vacations are to be offered, organized programs of recreation, travel and adult education do seem indispensable.

Thus, it is not clear whether man can successfully be re-educated for a life in which work is the exception and leisure the rule. The positive values and satisfactions from work must also be weighed in the balance. It has commonly been assumed, especially in economic analysis, that work is an unpleasant dis-utility which has to be accepted in order to obtain the wherewithal for goods and services. From this it would follow that if the goods and services could be obtained without the work, utopia would have arrived. Today many proposals for breaking the connection between work and income are being voiced; and in some circles the concept of full employment is condemned as a reactionary program which would sentence people unnecessarily to continuing their life of toil.

But work has always been one of the great balance wheels of life along with other sources of profound satisfaction such as love, play, and faith. A large and growing proportion of the labor force—which Galbraith calls "the new class"—finds creative fulfillment or "self-realization" in its work. Many jobs are too dull for this, but all competent research studies have led to the conclusion that even a dull job is better than no job—and not merely because it brings in money. As Morse and Weiss have said,

> For most men, having a job serves other functions than the one of earning a living. . . . The typical employed man does not at present have alternative ways of directing his energy and internal resources, and does not at present have alternative ways of gaining a sense of relationship to his society, which are sufficiently important to take the place of working.

And as Wilensky states, "Modern philosophies of work both reflect and reinforce a highly developed propensity for the activity itself."

In the long run, the question of work and leisure involves the malleability of human personality. Throughout history, most men have found the meaning of leisure in its rhythm with work. Even the tiny leisure class of former days has now virtually disappeared. Is resistance to unlimited leisure only a temporary cultural lag? Can man be re-educated so that work is no longer a central need or can nonwork activities be redefined so that they will contribute to man's self-definition and self-esteem in the same way that work has traditionally contributed? Perhaps so. Science has performed many wonders. God labored six days and rested on the seventh. Already man is resting more than two days for every six he works. But revolutionaries are chronically disappointed with the obduracy of the human animal; and the apostles of unlimited leisure must consider the limited malleability of the material they are working with. There is no doubt that much more leisure can be *imposed* on the workers by consensus of employers, union leaders, government officials, scientists, and other authorities. But this does not mean that it will necessarily be a blessing.

For the first time in history, the place of work in man's life is becoming a matter of choice rather than brute necessity; and the choice cannot be avoided. As Gerald Piel, the editor of *Scientific American,* has said,

The enormous power made available to modern societies by industrial technology must be brought under the control of democratic institutions, still to be perfected, that will submit this power to rational management in the interest of human welfare.

As time goes on, the content of jobs will change greatly and the concept of work itself may be altered; but if human welfare is really to be the standard, the importance of work must be kept well in the foreground.

15 WAGE POLICIES OF AMERICAN UNIONS

Harold M. Levinson

Because of the considerable size and complexity of American unions, any attempt to discuss their wage policies briefly must involve much simplification. Nevertheless, at least their dominant characteristics can be described, so long as we keep in mind that important exceptions can be found to almost any generalization that might be made.

To begin with, a fuller understanding of the wage policies of American unions must rest on a knowledge of the basic economic and political philosophy of the movement itself which I will only mention briefly. Of primary importance is the fact that American labor has fully accepted the institutions of private capitalism and has not supported programs calling for government ownership or operation of industry. And second, American unions have rejected all attempts to establish an independent political labor party along the lines adopted in Britain and elsewhere on the continent. In these respects, our labor movement has been highly conservative in its economic and political ideology.

The term "conservative" in this context, however, should in no sense be interpreted to reflect any lack of militancy or aggressiveness. In fact, American unions have been extremely aggressive in pressing for higher wages through *direct* collective bargaining with employers. In addition to wage increases, unions have also placed great emphasis on obtaining, through direct collective bargaining, several types of so-called "fringe benefits," including employer-financed pension and medical-care programs, paid vacations, paid holidays, supplementary unemployment benefits, severance pay, and many others. Similarly, the labor movement has been active politically, operating within the framework of the existing pro-capitalist political parties, in pressing for broad social-security, minimum wage, and protective hour legislation, and in promoting more aggressive government policies designed to achieve a high level of employment in the economy. Thus, American labor's conservative ideology does not stem from weakness. On the contrary, it stems precisely from the belief that a high degree of centralized economic and political power in the hands of the government—indeed, even of a labor government—represents a threat to the ability of the individual unions to utilize their economic power fully in their collective bargaining with employers. In essence, the American unionist wants to be free to establish his *own* wage policies and to bring economic pressure to bear directly on his *own* employer, with a minimum of government intervention or control.

This philosophy also extends to the power structure within the labor movement itself. There are, at the present time, about 80,000 local unions in the United States, most of which are affiliated with one of approximately 200 national unions. About two-thirds of these national unions, representing about 80 per cent of the total union membership in the United States, are in turn members of the central labor federation, the American Federation of Labor-Congress of Industrial Organizations, known as the AFL-CIO. Unlike the situation in most European countries, however, the AFL-CIO has *no power* in the formulation of union wage policies. This power is reserved instead to the individual national or local unions, which are as opposed to the centralization of power in the hands of the AFL-CIO as in the hands of the government.

A final stage in this process of decentralization of power—and the one which diverges most sharply from the European practice —arises from the fact that, with few exceptions, American collective bargaining is not conducted on an industry-wide basis. Instead, the most common practice is for negotiations to be carried on by the national and local union representatives with the officials of an individual company. It is true that in some industries having many small employers, such as building construction or apparel, multi-employer bargaining is common; even in these cases, however, the scope of negotiations is usually confined to one city or a small region. It is also true that in a few other industries, most notably in trucking, there has been a trend toward more centralized bargaining on an industry-wide basis. Nevertheless, decentralization still predominates, with the result that approximately 150,000 separate collective-bargaining contracts are estimated to be currently in effect in American industry.

THE DETERMINANTS OF UNION WAGE POLICY

In view of this highly decentralized decision-making process, it is pertinent to question which major factors may affect the wage policies adopted by any particular union. In analyzing this issue, two broad types of pressures may be distinguished. On the one hand, the decentralized bargaining process generates considerable political pressures on the leadership of each union to obtain wage or fringe-benefit increases at least equal to those being negotiated by other unions. For if the leaders fail to achieve this, they face the danger of being voted out of office by a dissatisfied membership. In addition, rivalry among the leaders of the strongest unions accentuates these political pressures for continual wage and fringe improvements.

An alternative view, commonly referred to as the "economic" theory of union wage policy, places greater emphasis on the economic environment. This viewpoint holds that the union leadership, in formulating its wage policy, is strongly influenced by the amount of actual or potential unemployment of its members, by the level of profits being earned by the employer, and by the general conditions of economic activity as a whole.

Undoubtedly both points of view contain important elements of truth for particular unions at particular times. Particularly during the years 1946–1951, collective bargaining in the United States was characterized by a series of "wage rounds," under which a major agreement was first negotiated in an important basic industry—usually automobiles or steel—which was then widely followed in other sectors of the economy. Although this experience tended to support the political hypothesis, these were also years during which economic conditions throughout the economy were very favorable, so that all unions were operating without serious economic constraints.

Since 1951, however, I believe there has been ample evidence to support the view that the wage policies of most American unions are most importantly affected by the varying economic environments within which each union is operating. Several studies of wage movements in manufacturing industries have shown a strong inverse relationship with the rate of unemployment and a strong positive relationship with the level of profits. In addition, other investigators have found that even such strong national unions as the United Automobile Workers and the United Steel Workers of America have been flexible in adjusting their demands to fit the varying economic conditions of the large number of firms within their jurisdictions.

A final important influence which should be stressed in any evaluation of union wage policy is the role of the employer. Particularly during periods of adverse economic conditions, the decisions of unions to modify their demands may be more strongly affected by the increased resistance offered by employers than by the union's own concern about unemployment or profits. Thus, in some industries where employer strength has been weak, as in bituminous coal and in maritime, the unions have sometimes continued to press for and to obtain large wage increases even in the face of rising unemployment and declining profits.

The allocation of responsibility for the determination of the wage policies to be adopted in bargaining also varies among unions, though there has been a long-run trend toward a greater share of power to be centered in the national union. This has developed because the national union can provide more skilled personnel, can coordinate the bargaining policies of the several local unions more effectively, and can utilize all the financial resources of the union to achieve the best over-all gains. In general, the national union is most influential in policy formulation in industries with national product markets where the maintenance of an over-all bargaining strategy is necessary in order to prevent some local unions from undercutting the wage standards of other locals which are producing goods for the same final product market. Where the geographic extent of the product market is limited, however, as in the construction industry or the local service trades, the goods or services produced in one locality do not compete with those produced in another. Hence there is less necessity for over-all coordination, and the local unions still commonly retain much power to establish their own policies.

THE STRUCTURE OF BARGAINING

We have already noted that American collective bargaining is usually conducted on a company-by-company (or a limited regional) basis, but with the national union often playing an important role in establishing and coordinating the union's strategy for the industry as a whole. In very broad terms, three major approaches to this process of "decentralization with coordination" may be distinguished. The first of these is used by many of the strongest unions which have organized a major proportion of the workers in their industries and which are operating in manufacturing sectors characterized by large companies, limited entry of new firms, price leadership, and national product markets. The basic steel, automobile, aluminum, farm equipment, and rubber industries are examples of this type. Here, the usual bargaining strategy has been for the national union to negotiate an original and usually a relatively liberal "key" bargain with one or with a group of the dominant companies in the industry. Once the key bargain has been established, the union then moves on to the smaller firms, using the key bargain as the basis for its demands. Although the union will usually insist on terms equivalent to those of the key bargain if it believes that the economic condition of the smaller firm is strong, the union will also commonly agree to more moderate terms if the company's "ability to pay" is weak. By using this over-all strategy, the strong unions are able to concentrate all their efforts on first negotiating a favorable "key" bargain with the larger and usually more profitable firms in the industry. Yet it also gives the unions a high degree of flexibility to "bargain down" from this higher level in subsequent negotiations with less profitable concerns, so long as these concessions do not have a serious adverse effect on the union's over-all bargaining strategy.

It is interesting to contrast this approach to wage-bargaining with the industry-wide negotiations preferred by most European unions. Since, under an industry-wide contract, the terms of employment must accommodate the bulk of firms in the industry, those terms must usually be set at a relatively low level if marginal firms are not to be forced out of business. It then becomes necessary, if advantage is to be gained from the superior position of the more profitable firms, for the local unions, works councils, or shop steward committees to "bargain up" from that minimum level. Although this process may yield equivalent benefits in the end, it appears to "downgrade" the role of the national union in obtaining higher benefits as compared with its American counterpart.

A second group of unions are those operating in industries having a national product market, but characterized by many small firms, ease of entry, considerable price competition, and relatively low profit levels. Leading examples of this type are the textile, lumber, leather, furniture, and apparel industries. Because of the ease with which new nonunionized firms can enter these industries—particularly in the southern region of the country where union influence is weakest—union strength is relatively low. Consequently, although the national unions do play an important role in establishing wage policy in these industries, they are forced to follow a much more moderate approach in order to prevent the employment opportunities of their members from being reduced or eliminated by the rise of nonunion competition. In addition, local union influence is stronger because of the need to adjust quickly to the more severe competitive pressures on the unionized employers.

A final important and more heterogeneous group of strong unions is found primarily outside manufacturing. These include many powerful craft unions in the railroad, construction, and some local service trades, as well as among the teamsters, longshore- and offshore-maritime workers, mineworkers, and a few others. The structure of bargaining in this group of industries has also depended largely on the nature of the product market. Where that market has been local, as in the construction or service industries, the responsibility for policy-formulation and wage bargaining has generally remained with the individual locals. On the other hand, where the scope of the product market has been nationwide, as in coal mining, the national union has taken over control. Since most of the unions in this broad group of industries are firmly established and well protected from the possible entry of nonunionized producers, they have also been quite successful in obtaining favorable wage and fringe benefits.

In recent years, there has been some evidence in a few industries to suggest a trend toward more centralized bargaining. The most dramatic example has been in trucking, where the rapid rise in the importance of long-distance freight shipments has been accompanied by a marked shift in power away from the local toward the national unions and by a strong trend toward the establishment of nationwide wage and fringe-benefit standards. In the steel industry, several of the largest firms have preferred to bargain as a unit with the national union, though final contracts are still signed separately. Similarly, some greater degree of coordination or centralization of bargaining, either among employers or within the union, has recently developed in the automobile, construction, telephone, and a few other industries. Whether or not these trends will be maintained or expanded into the future is, however, difficult to judge at this time.

POLICIES TOWARD GENERAL WAGE ADJUSTMENTS

The American labor movement's lack of any broad ideology is most clearly reflected in its approach toward general wage adjustments. In this area, little can be said beyond the observation that each union's policies are highly pragmatic, aimed primarily at obtaining as large an increase as appears feasible at a particular time, within the constraints imposed by the economic environment and the relative bargaining power of the union and the employer. Though exceptions to this general description can, of course, be cited, such as periods of national emergency, any attempt to attribute a more rational or a more long-run philosophy to American unions would be misleading. Thus the commonplace observation that American unions simply want "more, now" contains a considerable element of truth.

In a general way, it may perhaps be said that American unions do hold to a broad philosophy that wages should be increased at least as much as increases in productivity. This view is supported both on grounds of equity—that is, that workers *should* share in the "fruits of progress" as a matter of right—and on the economic ground that failure to do so will result in a deficiency of purchasing power and, thus, in a decline in employment and output. This "purchasing-power theory" is also often advanced by union spokesmen to support wage increases in excess of productivity gains on the ground that higher wage incomes will stimulate, demand, and encourage growth. In very large part, however, these views represent rationalizations designed to provide justification for pragmatic wage policies which would be adopted in any case.

The significance of this approach to general wage adjustments can perhaps be understood more fully in the light of a policy adopted in 1962 by the Council of Economic Advisors to the President. The Council set forth certain broad rules or guideposts for noninflationary wage and price behavior which it suggested should be followed voluntarily by strong unions and large companies. With respect to wages, the Council proposed that union bargaining demands be sufficiently moderate so that total hourly labor costs would not rise more rapidly than productivity per man-hour. Furthermore, in order to prevent increasingly serious distortions of the wage structure, the Council proposed that *each* union adjust its demands roughly in accord with the *over-all* increases in productivity in the economy as a whole.

Given the nature of American collective bargaining, however, it will be extremely difficult, if not impossible, to obtain the acceptance of any such broad wage policy. For even if some unions were disposed to adopt a more moderate approach, the decentralized structure or decision-making in collective bargaining plus the strong rivalries among union leaders would probably generate such strong political pressures on the unions' leadership that the policy of moderation would be abandoned. This problem may pose a serious dilemma in the future as stronger efforts are made by the government to lower the rate of unemployment in the American economy from its current level of about 4½ to 5 per cent to a "full employment" level of 4 per cent or less. On the basis of past experience, it is estimated that a 4 per cent rate of unemployment would generate a rate of price inflation of about 2½ to 3 per cent per year. Since this is a higher rate of inflation than the American people have been prepared to accept in the past, some self-restraint on private wage-price decision-making or some change in government monetary-fiscal policies may be required. It is always possible, of course, that over time and under government and public pressure, the guideposts approach will gradually acquire some relevance in a few key industries. Thus far, however, its effects have been minor.

Another important development of wage bargaining in recent years has been the widespread adoption of long-term contracts which extend over a period of two and often three years. During the year 1964, for example, only 119 out of a total of 307 major collective-bargaining contracts studied by the U.S. Department of Labor were subject to negotiation. Of the remaining contracts, 116 did not expire until 1965, and 72 were in effect until 1966 or later. In order to protect the interests of workers under contracts of such long duration, deferred wage increases are provided to become effective at specified future dates. In addition, automatic cost-of-living adjustments are sometimes included, tied in to possible changes in the cost of living while the contract is in force. The major advantage of this approach has been, of course, to avoid the continual uncertainty and expenditure of effort involved in annual bargaining and to permit the representatives of labor and management to concentrate their efforts on other longer-run problems of industrial relations.

POLICIES TOWARD THE WAGE STRUCTURE

I would like to turn finally to a discussion of the policies of American unions toward various aspects of the wage structure, or of wage relationships. In this area, it must always be kept in mind that the wage structure has been significantly affected by underlying economic conditions of supply and demand for various types of labor, so that the effects of union policies, if any, are impossible to isolate. Nevertheless, at least the broad objectives of American unions toward wage relationships may be identified.

With respect to occupational wage differentials, the attitude of various unions has depended primarily, of course, on the character of their membership. With few exceptions, the strong craft unions, which have represented highly skilled tradesmen, have long attempted to maintain or to increase their margin of superiority over the wages of semiskilled or unskilled workers. Where several crafts have been represented by the same union, or where a union representing many occupational levels has had a craft-union origin, wage increases have usually been negotiated on a percentage basis in order to maintain existing percentage differentials. Conversely, most of the industrial unions established during the 1930's have stressed a more egalitarian approach by negotiating equal cents-per-hour wage increases for all occupational groups, thus reducing the percentage differentials between various skill levels.

Superimposed upon these varying union objectives, however, have been many basic economic forces contributing to a long-run narrowing of occupational differentials in the United States. Thus, such factors as the rising availability of education and the sharp reduction in immigration after World War I resulted in a narrowing of occupational differentials, desipite the efforts of the craft unions to maintain them. During the 1930s, skill differentials were narrowed much more sharply by the adoption of minimum wage legislation and by the rapid growth of unionism among the semiskilled and unskilled workers. And finally, occupational differentials continued to narrow during the 1940's and early 1950's because of wartime labor shortages and wage controls, plus the continuing rise in the influence of industrial unionism.

During the past decade, however, there is evidence to suggest that this long-run trend has been slowed considerably and that many industrial as well as craft unions have become more concerned with protecting the relative position of the skilled workers within their jurisdiction. One reason for this change has been that the demand for skilled workers has improved relative to the unskilled, so that employers have become more insistent on maintaining differentials in order to attract an adequate supply of skilled personnel. In addition, the skilled workers within industrial unions have threatened to withdraw their support and to join or form rival organizations, unless their interests were more fully represented in wage negotiations. Thus, both economic and political developments of recent years have forced a considerable modification of the preferences of some unions for a narrowing of skill differentials. It is highly unlikely, however, that past trends will be reversed; rather, what is suggested here is that union policies will be more oriented toward the *mainte-nance* of existing percentage differentials than has been the case in recent decades.

Another aspect of union policies toward occupational wage differentials involves the problem of establishing appropriate differentials among the hundreds and sometimes thousands of job classifications within a plant. All American unions place a great deal of emphasis on this aspect of wage determination, and insist that the wage rates for different jobs be appropriately related to the requirements of skill, effort, responsibility, or to other factors which may be involved. In a few instances, notably in the steel industry, unions have cooperated with the company management in setting up a complete system of job evaluation and in establishing a wage structure for all jobs within a plant or company. This type of approach to the problem is, however, still the exception. Most unions prefer that the management take the initial responsibility for establishing an internal wage struc-ture, with the union reserving the right to negotiate if the com-pany's decisions are considered to be arbitrary or improper. As a result, it is very common in collective bargaining for the union to press for the correction of "wage inequities," involving par-ticular job rates that it considers to be too low.

Another aspect of union policy toward the wage structure in-volves the negotiation of geographic or regional differentials. Here again, American unions have varied considerably in their approaches. In general, as we have already noted, the most important factor affecting a particular union's policy on this question is the geographic extent of the industry's product mar-ket. If that market is national in scope, so that the goods pro-duced in one area must compete with those produced elsewhere, the union is strongly motivated to equalize the rates paid by all employers in order to "take labor out of competition." In the steel and automobile industries, for example, it has been a major objective of the unions during the postwar years to eliminate the substantial North–South wage differential which had existed in these industries for many decades. Over several negotiations, these differentials were gradually reduced and finally were completely eliminated. In other industries, however, such as electrical equip-ment, the unions have also wished to get rid of regional wage differences, but have not had sufficient bargaining power to be able to achieve this objective.

By contrast, where the product market is local in scope, as in construction or newspaper printing, interarea wage differences are of much less importance, so that wage equalization has not been stressed, and the local unions have a great deal of power to negotiate as they wish. It may well be the case, in fact, that in these industries the effect of union bargaining-policy has been to *increase* interarea differentials, since the strongest locals, which are already receiving the highest wages, are also in the most favorable position to negotiate even more favorable terms.

The area in which virtually all American unions have been most consistent in their wage policies has been in pressing for "equal pay for equal work" in the payments made to individuals doing the same job in the same plant. On the ground that interpersonal differentials based on managerial discretion often lead to favoritism or discrimination, the great majority of unions have attempted to establish a uniform rate or other standardized method of payment for a given job, irrespective of sex, age, color, or other personal characteristics. It should be noted, however, that local union discriminatory policies against Negroes are still found, particularly in the craft unions and in the South, though such policies have been condemned by both the national unions and the AFL-CIO.

In some cases, this preference for interpersonal uniformity has also been reflected in resistance to the use of piece rates or other methods of incentive pay. The Automobile Workers and the building trades unions, for example, have long been bitter opponents of the use of piece rates because of the belief that they lead to excessive "speedup," and that the number of workers required in production may be reduced. On the other hand, unions such as the Steelworkers, the Mineworkers, and the clothing workers have supported—or at least accepted—the use of incentive pay on the grounds that it permits individual workers to increase their earnings and that it helps unionized employers to compete more effectively with nonunionized producers. Thus no broad generalization can safely be made regarding union policies toward incentive methods of payment, though it is very likely that opposition to such systems is more common in the United States than in the continental countries.

SUMMARY

What, then, can we identify as the dominant characteristics of the wage policies of American unions? Briefly, they can be summarized as follows.

First, American unions have rejected broad programs of social reform in favor of a system of direct collective bargaining with individual employers, supplemented by political pressures on the existing political parties to provide a legal framework which is conducive to union organizing and bargaining activities.

Second, the primary emphasis in collective bargaining is on direct improvements in wages and in a large variety of fringe benefits for unionized workers, again supplemented by political pressures for the maintenance of a broad basic social-security program, minimum-wage legislation, and an aggressive government monetary-fiscal policy to maintain a high level of employment.

Third, the procedures by which union wage policies are established are highly decentralized among thousands of national and local unions, and these policies are implemented by bargaining separately with tens of thousands of individual companies or small groups of companies. However, a considerable degree of centralization is provided in many industries by the participation of the national union in all important company negotiations and by the policy of negotiating a key bargain to be used as the pattern for others to follow. The central federation has no role whatever in the formulation of wage policy.

Fourth, American union policies toward general wage adjustments are highly pragmatic, based primarily on the short-run objective of obtaining as much as is feasible at any particular time within the constraint imposed by the economic environment and by the bargaining power of the employer. This approach has had the advantage of permitting the parties a maximum degree of flexibility in adjusting to the great variety of conditions among different companies, industries, and regions in the American economy. On the other hand, it has the disadvantage of making it extremely difficult, if not impossible, to develop any broadly based wages policy or incomes policy, which would facilitate the achievement of a high level of employment, without generating excessive inflationary pressures.

And fifth, American union policies toward wage relationships among occupations, areas, and individuals are highly varied, depending primarily on the composition of the union's membership and on the type of product market within which the union is operating.

Perhaps the most appropriate final observation which can be made concerning the wage policies of American unions is that they embody a system which is best adapted to the needs and values of the American economy and of American society. The lack of any long-run ideology or of a strong class consciousness, the emphasis on narrow group interests, the distrust of centralized power and the preference for decentralized decision-making are all indigenous to the American frame of reference. Thus, whatever the advantages or shortcomings of these wage policies may be, they have served to fit the American labor movement into the larger society of which it is a part.

16 DISPUTES SETTLEMENT: THE GRIEVANCE PROCEDURE AND THE ROLE OF VOLUNTARY ARBITRATION

Benjamin Aaron

INTRODUCTION

Grievances involve disputes over the interpretation and application of private collective-bargaining agreements between employers and unions. They are thus to be distinguished from disputes over the terms to be incorporated into such agreements at the time they are negotiated. This same dichotomy is known in many other countries as that between disputes over rights (corresponding to our grievances) and disputes over interests (corresponding to our contract-terms disputes). The procedures for settling the latter type of dispute in the United States differ substantially from the established methods of grievance handling and settlement; and they are outside the scope of the present discussion.

THE COLLECTIVE-BARGAINING SYSTEM

Because the grievance and voluntary arbitration procedure is an integral part of this country's collective-bargaining system, which in turn is a reflection of the philosophical, political, and economic values on which our democratic society is based, I want to discuss, at the outset, those values.

Philosophical Values

Public opinion in the United States has traditionally demonstrated an adherence to pluralism, a broad tolerance of ambiguity, and a general agreement on certain ethical postulates. Americans do not usually believe in a single-minded loyalty to any person or institution; our democracy is based on a multiplicity of allegiances: ' to self, family, church, union, employer, and government. The concept of democracy is incompatible with total commitments of any kind, although in our country, as in others, war or the imminent threat of war tends to intensify individual and group allegiance to the national government.

Americans also have a habit of dealing with major issues by compromise. This type of accommodation is frequently ambiguous—sometimes deliberately so. If it does not often prove wholly satisfactory to any given interest group, it is, nevertheless, usually acceptable to the great majority of the people. Great social changes seldom occur suddenly; rather the process is, in Tennyson's phrase, one of "freedom slowly broadening down from precedent to precedent." It took almost one hundred years, for example, for the guarantee in the Fifteenth Amendment to our federal Constitution—that the rights of citizens to vote shall not be denied or abridged by any state on account of race, color, or previous condition of servitude—to be fully implemented by the adoption of the Civil Rights Act of 1964.

Ethical Values

Finally, most Americans agree on certain ethical principles, however lax they may sometimes be in observing them in daily life. Among these principles are the dignity of the individual, the superiority of persuasion over force, and the importance of what we call "due process." The concept of the dignity of the individual needs no elaboration; it is intrinsic in the ideal of ordered liberty, wherever that ideal is pursued. Americans prefer persuasion over force, not only because the use of force usually entails a limitation or denial of someone's freedom, but also because we believe, with John Milton, that truth will not be "put to the worse, in a free and open encounter" with falsehood. The concept of due process, which may be loosely paraphrased as a belief that all citizens, regardless of their station in life, are entitled to fair treatment by those in authority, lies at the heart of our democratic faith.

Political Values

The structure of the United States government is that of a republic. Decisions are made by elected representatives of the people, but those decisions are influenced, if not actually dictated, by the pressures of a wide variety of pressure groups in our pluralistic society. The framers of our federal Constitution concluded, on the basis of their personal experience and knowledge of history, that even good men are corrupted by power; hence, the familiar system of checks and balances among and between the three major branches of our government: the executive, the legislative, and the judicial. Our federal system also entails a division of functions between the national government and the state; and experience with the problems of federalism has taught us that this division cannot be predetermined by fixed and formal rules, but must be conceived of as a flexible and constantly evolving process.

Economic Values

The economy of the United States has developed in a tradition of individualism and of competition. The doctrines of the classical economists found a favorable environment here; for many years, laissez faire was the dominant economic philosophy, and interference by either government or private associations, such as labor unions, with the supposedly "automatic" adjustments of the price mechanism in respect to both commodities and labor was strongly disapproved. Although the Great Depression of the 1930's marked a permanent shift in attitudes toward the role of government in economic and social affairs, the tradition of self-determination and resistance to governmental regulation remains strong.

Collective Bargaining as a Reflection of Societal Values

All of the foregoing history, values, and attitudes are reflected in the American collective-bargaining system, which may be broadly described as one of balanced conflict and cooperation.

Fundamental differences continue to exist between employers and unions, not so much over ultimate objectives as over the best way to achieve them. At the same time, the adversaries typically compromise these differences and negotiate collective-bargaining agreements under which they are able peacefully to pursue their common goal of greater prosperity for all concerned. Moreover, whatever their disagreements, they are generally united in their resistance to governmental interference in respect to the substantive terms of the bargain. Thus, for example, the traditional exhortations by presidents of the United States urging labor and management to practice restraint in raising wages and prices have never proved especially effective.

The pluralism that characterizes our society is reflected in the diversity of forms within the collective-bargaining system. The scope of the bargaining may be on an industry-wide, company-wide, or area-wide basis, or it may be limited to an individual plant. In some instances, bargaining policies at the plant level may be completely controlled by the top officials of a company and by officers of the parent union, in others, they may be largely determined by the local representatives of the parties. The relations between employer and union may be extremely formal or completely informal, hostile or friendly. The completed agreement may consist of a detailed, printed document purporting to cover every aspect of the relationships, or it may consist of several typewritten pages setting forth only a few broad governing principles.

The bargaining process, which can be analogized to the legislative process in the broader society, is conducted by elected or appointed representatives of the employees and the employers. These representatives are subject to the same types of pressures from interest groups within their own constituencies as are legislators in the state and federal government, and sometimes they are removed because of the dissatisfaction of their constituents with the results of the bargaining.

Finally, the element of due process is embodied in the grievance and arbitration procedure which is almost invariably included in the collective agreement. It is to this aspect of the bargaining process that I shall direct the remainder of my remarks.

THE GRIEVANCE PROCEDURE

Collective bargaining, as practiced in the United States, consists of more than periodic negotiations of wage increases and other terms of collective agreements. Indeed, the major part of collective bargaining is made up of the daily adjustments of the multitudes of problems which arise during the relatively lengthy periods—typically ranging from one to three years—between contract negotiations. The process is designed not simply to enhance the bargaining power of the employees or to provide them with increased financial rewards for their labor; its further purpose is to endow them with a sense of worth, recognition, and participation, without which they would react against the system and seek another. These needs are continuous and must be continuously met. Therefore, the execution of a collective agreement, far from obviating the necessity for joint consultation between employer and employee representatives, signals the commencement of that process insofar as it applies to the daily problems of the enterprise. The grievance procedure is the mechanism which regulates these discussions and adjustments. Hence, it is frequently said to constitute the heart of the collective-bargaining relationship.

Types of Grievance Procedure

Some form of grievance procedure is included in virtually all of the more than 125,000 collective agreements in the United States. Although these procedures vary widely in their specific characteristics, almost all of them have certain common features. Thus, most of them provide for successive stages in the procedure. A typical arrangement provides three such stages: at the first step, with or without his union steward or shop representative, the employee presents his grievance to his immediate supervisor or foreman; at the second step, the grievance or shop committee, usually consisting of from three to five employee-members of the union, discusses the grievance with the employer's industrial-relations supervisor or director; and at the third step, the shop committee or the union's business representatives, or both, discusses the grievance with the employer's plant manager or super-intendent.

Purpose and Advantages of a Multi-step Grievance Procedure

Of course, there are many varieties of this multi-step procedure, but the underlying purposes remain the same. Most grievances are settled at the first step which is also the most informal. At this stage, the employee may simply make an oral complaint to his foreman, and the latter may either agree to remove the offending cause or persuade the grievant that his complaint has no merit. If the grievance goes beyond that stage, however, it is usually reduced to writing, and the alleged facts are studied by representatives of both parties before the matter is again discussed jointly at the second step. The chief value of this procedure is that it serves to verify the alleged facts and to clarify the issue between the disputants. Frequently, it is discovered at this stage that either the facts alleged by the grievant or the answer given by his foreman is incorrect, or perhaps that the grievant has a sound basis for his complaint but has not stated it, or that he has misstated the relief to which he is entitled under the agreement.

The principal value of the third step is that it serves to involve higher officials on both sides and, thus, to broaden the area of authority for the ultimate decision. The union's business representative is usually a full-time employee or officer of the union who does not work for the employer. Coming from the "outside" and representing the full authority of the union, he carries a prestige greater than the grievant or any other employee in the local plant. Similarly, the plant manager is the top spokesman for management at the local level and is to some degree removed from the daily administrations of labor–management relations. These men have the authority to dispose of the grievance on terms which their subordinates may, for one reason or another, be unwilling to accept. Moreover, at such third-step meetings, both men frequently learn about conditions within the plant of which they were previously unaware. Indeed, one of the principal values of a well-functioning grievance procedure is that it provides a reliable two-way communications system between the employer and the union.

Differing Attitudes toward Administration of Grievance Procedure

The diversity of forms of grievance procedure is matched by the wide variety of attitudes that employers and unions bring to its administration. The word "grievance" is itself frequently a matter of contention. Should it be interpreted broadly, so as to include workers' complaints about any matters affecting their employment, or should it be narrowly construed to apply only to alleged violations of specific terms of the collective agreement? The solutions of this problem are worked out in the individual bargaining units, usually on a trial-and-error basis. In some instances, the parties find that a broad definition of "grievance" is preferable, because it brings all dissatisfactions quickly to the surface, where they can be dealt with more effectively. In other cases, the parties decide that their procedure will function more quickly and efficiently if grievances are confined to issues arising out of the interpretation and application of the collective agreement. In still others, the parties may compromise the issue by allowing any complaint to be the subject of a grievance, but limiting the types of grievance that may ultimately be submitted to arbitration—the terminal step in the grievance procedure, which I shall discuss presently.

Perceptive students of labor–management affairs can usually tell from the way that the grievance procedure is administered in a given enterprise whether the relationship between the employer and its employees is a healthy one. The grievance record can, indeed, be thought of as an industrial fever chart, although we must be careful, of course, not to apply that metaphor too literally. It is clear, however, that a heavy backlog of unresolved grievances, perpetuated by a constant influx of new ones, signifies an unhealthy situation which is likely, sooner or later, to erupt into a strike, slowdown, or some similar breach in the labor–management relationship. On the other hand, the lack of any grievances is also a danger sign. Some complaining by employees about working conditions is normal, and, when no such complaints are made known through the grievance procedure, it may be that genuine collective bargaining is no longer possible. Under such circumstances we may expect either an attempt by the employer or others to get rid of the union entirely, or an effort by the employees to redress their grievances by resorting to self-help on the job.

VOLUNTARY ARBITRATION

The vast majority of the collective-bargaining agreements provide for arbitration as the terminal step in the grievance procedure. Although the device of voluntary arbitration has long been known in this country and has been part of the collective-bargaining structure in a few industries for many years, its broad acceptance is of relatively recent origin, dating from the early 1940's.

Variation of Arbitration Procedures

As is the case with bargaining structures and grievance procedures, the types of arbitration arrangements adopted by individual employers and unions are richly diverse. Some are extremely informal: the arbitration step is simply an extension of the grievance procedure, and the arbitrator serves primarily as a mediator whose function is to assist the parties to reach an agreement. Others are very formal: the arbitration step is consciously distinguished from the preceding stages of the grievance procedure, and the arbitrator serves primarily as a judge whose function is to hand down a binding decision on the basis of the record made at the hearing. Between these extremes exist a myriad of other arrangements, representing every intermediate shade and nuance in the relationship between the arbitrator and the parties.

The diversity is manifested in a variety of other ways. In some enterprises, virtually all unsettled grievances are appealed by the union to arbitration without regard to their relative importance or merit. This practice may result from a strong feeling of equalitarianism within the union, or from the political weakness of the union officers; on the other hand, it may simply be a response to the employer's refusal to settle grievances at the earlier stages of the procedure. In other enterprises, however, great emphasis is placed by the parties on settlement of all grievances at the earliest possible stage; unsettled grievances are carefully screened, and only the most important ones are submitted to arbitration. In this latter type of situation, the relationship between the employer and the union is usually well established and reasonably friendly, and the union officers are in firm control of the organization's affairs.

Permanent Arbitrators

Because there is such a great variety in the conception of the role which arbitration should play in the administration of the collective agreement, it follows that the arbitrators themselves are called on to serve in many different ways. At the one extreme is the permanent impartial umpire or chairman, so called because he serves in a continuing capacity under the agreement and hears, either individually or as chairman of a tripartite board, all the grievances submitted by the parties. Do not be misled by the word "permanent"; it reflects the initial intentions of the parties who engage the umpire, but not necessarily their subsequent behavior. Permanent umpires are frequently dismissed when their decisions are no longer acceptable to one side or the other, or when continuing tensions within the union- or management-structure require that some dramatic change in the arbitration be made. It is an accepted fact, and one considered to contribute substantially to the vitality of the system of voluntary arbitration in this country, that arbitrators are always expendable and that the parties must have full freedom to change arbitrators or to modify the arbitration procedure itself to fit their own particular needs.

Ad Hoc *Arbitrators*

Although the practice of employing permanent impartial umpires or chairmen is well established, especially in giant enterprises such as the leading automobile, steel, and rubber companies, exactly the opposite approach is followed by most employers and unions in this country. The typical collective agreement provides for the selection of an arbitrator by the parties whenever a grievance is appealed to arbitration. The arbitrator so chosen serves for that particular occasion only; hence he is commonly referred to as an *"ad hoc* arbitrator." Of course, an *ad hoc* arbitrator may be repeatedly invited to serve the same parties in that capacity, but he has no formally recognized continuing relationship with them. Moreover, under most *ad hoc* arbitration arrangements the parties customarily use a number of different arbitrators.

Advantages and Disadvantages of Permanent and Ad Hoc *Procedures*

It is generally recognized that both the permanent and the *ad hoc* procedures have special advantages and disadvantages. The former is practical only for those enterprises in which a large number of grievances are arbitrated each year or in which the matters submitted to arbitration, although not numerically great, serve as precedents for the disposition of large numbers of grievances at an earlier stage, or even determine the policies to be followed by the employer and the union in regard to issues of vital importance to them both. In such a situation, the parties prefer to submit all unresolved disputes to one impartial umpire or chairman. In so doing, they can educate him in the special problems of the business, give him a deeper insight into the relations between the parties, and obtain the benefit of advice which he, as a skilled and objective observer of the labor–management relationship over a continuous period, sometimes lasting for many years, is able to give them. To achieve these purposes, they are willing to pay the permanent arbitrator for his availability when needed, as well as for the time he spends in deciding the cases submitted. In some instances the parties contract for the full-time services of the umpire and insist, as part of the arrangement, that he not engage in similar work for anyone else. Almost invariably in such cases, the umpire develops, over time, close personal relationships with representatives of both sides and learns much about underlying problems in the enterprise which he could not possibly discover during an arbitration hearing, however informal its character.

The arrangement that I have just described is neither necessary nor practicable, however, for the typical small firm in which only a few cases are arbitrated each year. Resort to *ad hoc* arbitration is preferable in such circumstances because it is less expensive; it also allows the parties to try a number of different arbitrators and to choose the one who has, in their judgment, the best qualifications for dealing with a particular type of problem. Whether permanent or *ad hoc,* few arbitrators can handle all types of problems with equal skill. Parties who employ a permanent umpire may find his decisions in grievances involving complicated piecework rates, for example, less satisfactory than his decisions in respect to disciplinary problems. Parties who use only *ad hoc* arbitrators are, on the other hand, free to employ an expert on piecework rates for that type of grievance and to engage someone else to dispose of a disciplinary grievance.

It would be a mistake to assume, however, that all the advantages are on the side of *ad hoc* arbitration. *Ad hoc* arbitrators usually have some other profession, such as teaching or the practice of law, to which they devote most of their time, and they are not always readily available when called on to serve. Moreover, even the best arbitrator cannot function at top efficiency when, as frequently happens, he is completely unacquainted both with the parties and with the situation out of which the dispute arose.

Acceptance of Arbitration Awards

Far more significant than the varying types of arbitration procedures to be found in the United States is the tradition of acceptance of the arbitration award. Refusal by either party to abide by the award is so rare as to be statistically and practically insignificant. To a slightly lesser extent, the same may be said about refusals by the parties to abide by the commitment included in the collective agreement to arbitrate grievances instead of resorting to self-help or to the courts. Such refusals are now virtually unavailing in any event. A provision in the federal Labor Management Relations Act permits employers and unions to bring suit against each other in federal or state courts for breach of their collective agreements. In 1957, the United States

Supreme Court ruled that under this provision a court could order specific performance of an agreement to arbitrate grievances arising during the life of a collective-bargaining contract.

The Issue of Arbitrability

Most of these contracts provide, however—either implicitly or explicitly—that some issues shall not be subject to arbitration. In recent years, there has been a noticeable increase in the tendency on the part of some employers to refuse to arbitrate grievances on the ground that such grievances are not arbitrable under the terms of the collective agreement, and their position has frequently been upheld by the courts. This trend was abruptly halted and reversed, however, by a series of decisions handed down by the Supreme Court in 1960. These decisions held that on questions of arbitrability the courts have authority to determine only whether there is a collective agreement in existence, whether there is an arbitration clause, and whether there is an allegation that a provision of the agreement has been violated. If a court concludes that the arbitration clause is broad enough to encompass the alleged dispute, it must order arbitration. By these and related decisions, therefore, interpreting and effectuating the will of Congress, the Court has assigned to voluntary labor arbitration a position of central importance in the national labor policy.

The word "voluntary" is crucial here. Bear in mind that the court decisions that I have just mentioned apply only in cases in which the parties have previously agreed to arbitrate. No law compels such an agreement, and, in fact, a small number of collective-bargaining contracts do not provide for the arbitration of disputes. By the same token, the parties may, if they wish, expressly agree that questions of arbitrability shall be decided by a court rather than by an arbitrator.

SUMMARY AND CONCLUSION

In conclusion, I should like to re-emphasize that the collective-bargaining system in the United States and especially the grievance and arbitration procedures are reflections of the basic values which underlie our society. The diversity among procedures is but another manifestation of its pervasive pluralistic spirit. The repeated rejection of proposals to establish labor courts in place of private arbitration tribunals is to be expected in a society which, despite its increasing dependence on government for economic protection and assistance, continues to oppose governmental regulation of the substantive terms of collective agreements and the details of their administration. At the same time, the wide acceptance of the proposition that disputes arising under existing agreements between employers and unions should be voluntarily submitted to adjudication by neutral third parties is further evidence of our national dedication to the principles of due process and fair play.

To be sure, the system is far from perfect, and it is constantly subjected to criticism, not only by those who speak from ignorance, but also by those who are most intimately involved in its administration. Such criticism is, on the whole, helpful; it lends vitality to the system and provides the impetus for change. And change itself is relatively easy because it does not depend on the general will expressed in legislation, but only on the joint decision of the partners to a given collective agreement. By any pragmatic test—which is the kind Americans prefer—our collective-bargaining system is a success; and that success is in large measure a result of the efficient functioning of the thousands of private grievance and arbitration procedures which, despite their wide diversity of form, have a common purpose and a common result—the peaceful, democratic, and fair adjudication of labor–management disputes.

17 GOVERNMENT REGULATION OR CONTROL OF UNION ACTIVITIES

Charles Gregory

EARLY JUDICIAL CONTROL OF LABOR UNIONS

Before 1910, the regulation and control of American labor unions was chiefly by judge-made law. Workers who used economic pressure to spread union organization in the early 1800's were held guilty of common-law criminal conspiracy. But this device for controlling unions was abandoned around 1850. Courts soon began to allow peaceful strikes for immediate benefits. But most judges thought that campaigns to extend union organization were unlawful. Actions for damages had become the only recourse in these cases. Then around 1880, state courts developed a far more effective device—the labor injunction. This remedy protected only against the tortious invasion of property rights. But our state courts soon invented theories making most peaceful union self-help pressures unlawful.

The courts had always allowed business combinations to eliminate trade rivals and control markets. No legal wrong was done if they were pursuing self-interest and gain. But if *unions* sought to protect *their* standards by eliminating nonunion employers and workers, the courts held this to be wrongful for the spread of unionization led to monopoly. And though monopoly was not tortious according to common law, the courts declared it to be an illegal purpose for union self-help. This was enough to support the labor injunction. Moreover, peaceful secondary boycotts and organizational picketing were made torts in themselves. Thus the courts applied a double standard by denying to unions what they let business groups do.

THE LABOR INJUNCTION

The labor injunction was the most ruthless anti-union weapon ever devised. It was used to protect business only when unions threatened employers with organizing pressures. This remedy was far more effective than other legal sanctions. Criminal prosecutions and damage suits required extensive pleadings, months of waiting, and jury trials. But a judge could issue an injunction without a jury trial. And he could issue a temporary injunction without any trial at all. Thus strikes, picket lines, and boycotts could be smothered before they really got started. Anyone disobeying an injunction was summarily thrown into jail for contempt of court, again without jury trial.

SHERMAN ANTI-TRUST ACT—1890

As industry grew larger, employers began to produce for markets in other states and buy materials from outside. Then the Sherman Anti-Trust Act was passed in 1890. It was believed to be designed to apply only to business organizations as an anti-trust measure. This act was enforced by indictments, triple damage suits, and injunctions. Under its terms, federal courts soon began to apply it to labor unions and to regard most union interferences with the movement of goods in interstate commerce as unlawful restraints of trade. Unions exerted organizational pressures on nonunion employers by peaceful secondary boycotts. Because they disrupted the interstate movements of goods, the Supreme Court ruled that these boycotts violated the Sherman Act. But clearly they were not restraints of trade at all. The unions were simply trying to improve their conditions of work— not to monopolize the market for goods. They obstructed the transit of goods; but so did train robbers. And nobody would think of suing *them* under the Sherman Act.

But the Supreme Court refused to declare simple strikes unlawful under the Sherman Act merely because they disrupted the flow of goods in commerce. To show a violation in this area required proof that the strike was intended to unionize the employer—and for the purpose of eliminating competition between union-made and nonunion-made goods in interstate markets. Thus bargaining strikes which also obstructed the flow of goods in commerce would never be violations. Clearly the Supreme Court was using the Sherman Act merely as a device to stop the spread of union organization. And its concern over the movement of goods in commerce was only *incidental*.

ANTI-INJUNCTION MEASURES: THE CLAYTON ACT OF 1914 AND THE NORRIS-LA GUARDIA ACT OF 1932

At the same time, the labor injunction flourished in common law in federal and state courts. In 1914, Congress passed the Clayton Act to limit use of the injunction against union self-help pressures in labor disputes. Section 6 of the Act declared that the labor of a human being was not a commodity. Section 20 seemed to offer some relief from the court's injunctive process. But this measure was so narrowly construed that injunctions against union organizational drives continued. All that the Clayton Act *actually* did was to allow further injunctive relief against unions under the Sherman Act. In the 1920's, Professor Felix Frankfurter headed an attempt to promulgate a *really* effective anti-injunction law. The result was the Norris-La Guardia Act of 1932. This act defined permissible labor disputes broadly enough to include organizational drives against nonunion employers. It required only that the union have an economic interest in employment conditions at the nonunion plant. Then it described the permissible union self-help techniques—the strike, the secondary boycott, and picketing. Such devices when used in a labor dispute as defined were nonenjoinable in federal courts.

CHANGING FEDERAL POLICY—NATIONAL LABOR RELATIONS ACT OF 1935

While this act did not legalize organizational pressures, it removed the injunction, employers' only effective defense against unions. Certainly it meant congressional approval of union expansion throughout entire industries by economic self-help. But it left employers free to fight back with economic weapons by discriminating against employees who supported unionism. The National Industrial Recovery Act of 1933 and the amended Railway Labor Act of 1934 had introduced the principle that employees could join unions without employer interference. But in 1935, Congress passed the National Labor Relations Act, or Wagner Act, to replace the NIRA which was ruled unconstitutional. That statute prohibited anti-union conduct by most employers. If an employer interfered with his employees' attempts to organize unions or tried to dominate such unions, if he discriminated against employees for their union interest or refused to bargain with newly formed unions, he was committing unfair labor practices. The National Labor Relations Board, set up under the terms of the Wagner Act, ordered these unfair practices stopped and granted remedies such as reinstatement of employees with back pay. And the federal courts enforced these orders. Thus, Congress proclaimed the national policy of strong affiliated labor unions organized throughout entire industries. In upholding this statute, the Supreme Court greatly expanded the commerce power of Congress to cover virtually all important units of industry and production. Thereafter unions began to form and grow rapidly.

REPRESENTATIONAL FUNCTIONS OF THE NATIONAL LABOR RELATIONS BOARD

The Labor Relations Board administers an elaborate procedure enabling workers to select or reject unions. Many employers voluntarily recognize unions formed or chosen by their employees. The Board conducts elections when necessary, especially where two or more unions are competing for representational rights. The Board has strict rules governing attempts by outside unions to displace already recognized unions. It will protect an established employer–union contract relationship for three years. Then an outside union may call for an election. To avoid needless conflict, the AFL-CIO has developed no-raiding pacts, administered by an impartial arbitrator. The Board's enormously complicated task of handling these representational matters is a most important aspect of regulating and controlling unions today.

UNION IMMUNITY FROM ANTI-TRUST LAWS

The anti-injunction and Wagner acts clearly made the expansion of union strength the prevailing national policy. At the same time, the interpretations of the Sherman Act remained unchanged. Under them, union self-help pressures to extend unionism and eliminate nonunionism were still illegal. The Supreme Court should have recognized this contradiction and have overruled its earlier decisions, making organizational strikes and boycotts illegal under the Sherman Act. But what it did in the 1941 Hutcheson Case was to indulge in some judicial sleight of hand. It said that since peaceful union self-help conduct in a broad labor dispute context is no longer enjoinable, it is lawful for all purposes—even under the Sherman Act. It based this incredible inference on Section 20 of the Clayton Act which was rejuvenated by the later Norris-La Guardia Act. In effect, the Hutcheson doctrine removed labor unions from the jurisdiction of the Sherman Anti-Trust Act. However, it could still be applied if the unions' conduct was violent or if they connived with employers to restrain trade.

PEACEFUL PICKETING AND FREE SPEECH—1937–1949

By 1930, a few state courts allowed peaceful organizational picketing and secondary boycotts. But most of them curtailed such conduct by injunctions or criminal statutes. In 1940, however, the Supreme Court declared peaceful picketing to be constitutionally protected free speech. This placed it beyond the power of states to control. Most lawyers accepted the identity of picketing and free speech; but many thought it palpably untenable for even *peaceful* picketing cannot be dissociated from a pattern of coercion. And if it *were* merely free speech, Congress could not regulate it. Fortunately, the Supreme Court withdrew protection from peaceful picketing wherever its compliance would force the picketed employer to commit a crime. Thus, his refusal to sell ice to nonunion peddlers in compliance with picketing demands would be a violation of the state anti-monopoly law. Soon states were freely allowed to circumvent this constitutional doctrine simply by making the union's demands on the picketed employer contrary to public policy.

The Supreme Court then extended the doctrine of federal preemption to prevent states from regulating unions. In the Wagner Act, Congress had guaranteed employees and unions the right to promote their interests by concerted activities, and the states were powerless to impose conflicting controls over union conduct guaranteed protection in federal statutes, except when violence occurred.

RAILWAY LABOR ACTS—1926 AND 1934

After decades of bitter strikes, the railroad brotherhoods were firmly established. In the 1926 Railway Labor Act, Congress provided mediation and voluntary arbitration of bargaining disputes, with emergency powers vested in the President. This was unsatisfactory since the carriers still interfered with the union organization of their employees. The amended Railway Labor Act of 1934 created boards of adjustment to dispose of grievances and the National Mediation Board to handle all unsettled bargaining and representational disputes. It clarified and enforced the rights of employees and unions to organize and bargain collectively, introducing the principle of majority rule. Moreover, in 1951, Congress permitted the carriers and brotherhoods to contract for the union shop.

Changes in labor relations laws and policies were constant from 1935 to around 1950. But World War II dominated this period. Thus, although there were many strong unions by 1941—unions maintaining a tremendous pressure for higher wages and other concessions—in industries that had never been organized before, and this continued during the war, a war economy could not afford to have strikes. The War Labor Board was created to handle the constantly recurring disputes between unions and employers. Although strikes never were prohibited, the unions made voluntary no-strike pledges that were honored almost 100 per cent.

War Labor Board tripartite panels held hearings on bargaining demands. Sometimes they persuaded the parties to settle. Usually they made recommendations on issues that remained unsettled. The War Labor Board affirmed or modified these, in the end promulgating final contracts. The War Labor Board kept wages at a reasonably stable level, made a sensible compromise on the issue of union security, and refused to include novel items in collective agreements. But most important for the future of labor relations, it added grievance arbitration to thousands of contracts.

POST-WORLD WAR II CHANGES

After the war, the big unions sought wage increases, union security, stronger seniority provisions, vacations, and paid holidays, as well as pensions and insurances of all kinds. With wartime restrictions off, they conducted industry-shaking strikes. Simultaneously, the National Labor Relations Board expanded the employer's duty to bargain, including many new items. These great strikes provoked widespread demands for compulsory arbitration. Australia and New Zealand have long arbitrated their bargaining disputes; but early experiments in the United States were declared unconstitutional by the Supreme Court. At present, industry and organized labor would both rather continue free collective bargaining with strikes than share the dismal experience of countries having compulsory arbitration.

COMPULSORY ARBITRATION OF BARGAINING DISPUTES

Many states later passed laws forbidding strikes in public utilities. A few states required all unions to give advance notice of intention to strike. The Supreme Court declared these statutes unconstitutional because they interfered with the federally guaranteed right to strike. Unfortunately, experimental compulsory arbitration was thus thwarted in an area where it might have done some good. Of course, Congress can still pass such laws and permit states to do so. A few states allow public-utility strikes with plant seizures, operating with regular personnel who are temporarily appointed public employees.

TAFT-HARTLEY ACT—1947

The intensive strikes for money items and the closed union shop immediately after World War II contributed to Congress' passage of the Taft-Hartley Act in 1947. Title I of this statute is the amended National Labor Relations Act. The original National Labor Relations Act designated only unfair labor practices of employers. Unions were free to exercise any organizational and bargaining pressures. Unions were guaranteed the right to strike, and employees the right to engage in concerted activities. The National Labor Relations Board protected most of this conduct from employers' reprisals. When labor organizations had become very strong, extreme union self-help tactics were regarded as intolerable. This conduct included pressures against employers to force their employees to organize, pressures directly against employees themselves, secondary picketing and boycotting which implicated neutral employers and their employees, and even pressures against employers to ignore National Labor Relations Board certifications of other unions. Most unions sought the closed or union shop.

UNIONS' UNFAIR LABOR PRACTICES

Congress amended the National Labor Relations Act by defining six unfair labor practices of unions. The first made it unfair for unions to restrain or coerce employees. The second prohibited unions from trying to make employers discriminate against non-union employees. The third was a union's refusal to bargain in good faith with the appropriate employer. But the fourth was the most elaborate: Subsection A outlawed union secondary labor boycotts; whereas, Subsection B allowed secondary tactics if the union was certified to the employer against whom the pressure was aimed. Subsection C outlawed union attempts to make an employer deal with a union when another union had been certified to him by the National Labor Relations Board. Subsection D made it an unfair practice for unions to engage in work-jurisdiction disputes, where two unions claim the right to do certain work, and each strikes if the employer gives the work to members of the other union.

The fifth unfair labor practice was to prevent excessively large initiation fees under a valid union-shop agreement. In a union shop, an employer is free to hire anyone he pleases, but he must agree to discharge an employee who refuses to join the union or who does not pay his dues. Under the Wagner Act, federal policy accepted the closed union shop if the employer agreed to hire only union members. This is forbidden by the 1947 statute. But employers, now free to hire anybody they please, may make and enforce agreements requiring both new and old employees to join the union. However, Congress deferred to the states in 1947 by specifying that any state was free to forbid agreements making employment conditional on union membership. Now there are about twenty of these so-called right-to-work statutes. A corporation with plants in forty states may have a master contract with one union covering all these plants; but half of these plants might be union shops and half of them not because of local right-to-work laws.

Whether to have union security or right-to-work statutes is a contentious issue. Supporters of right-to-work laws say that they allow employment without paying tribute to unions. Opponents of these acts say they are meant to keep unions weak by denying them financial support from workers who profit by union bargaining gains. They call such nonunion workers free riders. A compromise is the so-called agency shop where an employee pays the equivalent of union dues without actually joining the union. The National Labor Relations Board finds this compromise acceptable; but right-to-work states are in disagreement about the agency shop. Unions want Congress to permit union shops throughout industry as it did on the railroads in 1951.

Featherbedding

Another union unfair labor practice which was declared unlawful was featherbedding, the device of gaining employment and pay for unnecessary and unwanted services. In 1946, Congress had declared it illegal for the musicians' union to compel broadcasting stations to hire more performers than they needed. This law accomplished nothing because the standard of guilt was so elusive and vague. Under the Taft-Hartley sanction, it was unfair for a union to make an employer pay money for services not performed or not to be performed. Two unions, the Typographers and the Musicians, brought pressures compelling employers to pay for unnecessary and unwanted work. But the union members always stood ready to perform this unwanted work—and in some cases did perform it although it was not used. Hence, the National Labor Relations Board and a majority of the Supreme Court held that the unions were not in violation of the Act. This sort of thing makes people very angry, and the public wants it stopped. However, workers claim that they have long been the victims of a speedup and want to compensate for the effects of technology and automation. The resulting compromise, according to the late Senator Robert Taft, is unintelligible legislative and judicial line-drawing. Union regulation and control in this area has proved almost impossible to articulate in enforceable terms because there is no workable standard.

ORGANIZATION OF GOVERNMENT EMPLOYEES

The 1947 statute contained additional restraints on unions. Strikes by government employees were declared unlawful, and individual offenders are summarily discharged. Government employees have long been allowed to organize, but their use of collective strength in bargaining has always been discouraged. Recently an effective representational procedure was established to enable organization of government employees. And plans are afoot to develop some type of negotiation—possibly with arbitration—to set terms and conditions of work for public employees. Collective bargaining by government workers has become a critical issue in states and municipalities. School teachers, policemen, and firemen, hospital workers, and other public employees also understand and seek to use the advantages of organization. Their strikes would generally be thought to be illegal. Everyone but the public employees themselves seems to think that their services cannot be suspended. Since we all hate to pay higher taxes in order to improve public working conditions, how else can group bargaining be made effective than by the strike? Negotiation with expert mediators might suffice, but eventually arbitrators may have to break the log jams. This is an extreme recourse, but if strikes of public workers are to be forbidden, a substitute must be found. The only answer seems to be some sort of arbitration.

NATIONAL EMERGENCY STRIKES

In the Taft-Hartley Act, Congress provided a method of controlling national emergency strikes, except those handled under the Railway Labor Act. Whenever the President thinks an industry-wide strike imperils the national health or safety, he sets up an emergency board to investigate and report to him. The President may then direct the Attorney General to have the strike or lockout enjoined. Federal mediators undertake to secure agreement between the parties. If the dispute is not settled in sixty days, the National Labor Relations Board files a supplemental report containing the employer's last offer to the union. The National Labor Relations Board then conducts a secret ballot among the employees to see if they wish to accept the offer. The injunction is then dissolved. If settlement has not been reached, the strike may be resumed. By that time, the President has made a complete report to Congress.

This device has been invoked twenty-four times, and the Supreme Court upheld this procedure in the steel strike of 1959. It declared that by "national health" Congress meant that of the economy as a whole and the general well-being of the country. Another technique used during the war was seizure and public operation of strike-bound plants. The Supreme Court declared that the President has no such power of seizure, however, in the absence of specific legislation granting him such authority. The President has appointed groups to handle disputes between unions and employers under contract with the Atomic Energy Commission or engaged in missile construction. When mediation fails, the appropriate panel takes jurisdiction, requesting the parties to appear and submit their claims. After hearings, the panel makes recommendations disposing of the various demands presented. The parties' submission to this procedure is entirely voluntary, but it has been effective in avoiding disruptive strikes.

ENFORCEMENT OF COLLECTIVE BARGAINING

Since 1935, a kind of self-government, far more effective than any imposed control or regulation, has evolved in collective bargaining. This is chiefly a result of increased union responsibility. A generation ago, labor unions generally could not sue or be sued. The Wagner Act greatly increased the number of unions and resulting collective agreements, but provided no means for their enforcement. Finally in 1947, Congress provided that the parties might sue each other in the federal courts if the employer operated in interstate commerce. Under this vague provision, the Supreme Court would not let unions directly sue to enforce promises dealing with the terms and conditions of individual employment. Federal courts could enforce promises to unions, however, including commitments to arbitrate unsettled grievances arising under contracts.

GRIEVANCE ARBITRATION

Since World War II, thousands of collective agreements provided for such arbitration. Now that unions could compel employers to comply with promises to arbitrate, it became possible to enforce provisions dealing with individual terms and conditions of employment. This whole development of grievance arbitration has become one of the most stabilizing controls in modern labor relations. Strikes seldom occur now, except when new agreements are bargained. With longer and longer contract terms, arbitration of unsettled matters arising under them will greatly minimize wasteful disputes.

The largest single issue in grievance arbitration is the discipline and discharge of employees for just cause. To justify a discharge, an employer must show that the penalized employee was guilty of something like theft, insubordination, or fighting, or was in violation of a plant rule meriting this extreme penalty. This power of the employer to impose discipline in proper cases is an effective method of controlling employees and even unions themselves. The privilege of employers to hire permanent replacements in bargaining strikes affords another control over unions.

Moreover, unions may not terminate collective agreements and call bargaining strikes without a sixty-day notice to mediation officials. The Taft-Hartley Act also lets employers recover damages from unions for harm caused by specified unfair labor practices. In such cases, Congress requires the National Labor Relations Board to seek injunctions. Unions violating no-strike pledges still remain free from injunctions; but they are subject to damage suits, and employers may discharge employees who participate in such strikes.

POLITICAL CONTRIBUTION BY UNIONS

The Taft-Hartley Act makes it unlawful for unions to contribute money to support political candidates in federal elections. It forbids unions and their officials to demand or accept money from employers and to condone payments to employees where no services are performed. These are largely to prevent bribery and shakedowns.

REGULATION OF INTERNAL UNION AFFAIRS

Traditionally, courts refused to interfere with the internal affairs of labor unions, treating them like clubs and lodges. They would protect vested property rights of members, but only when remedies within the organization were exhausted. Many unions would not admit Negroes or would only let them join auxiliaries, with no voting rights. But some courts now regard this as a denial of equal protection under the Constitution. The National Labor Relations Board recently revoked the certification of a union that refused to admit or represent Negroes. Unions are under fire where they prevent Negroes from obtaining employment by denying them membership. Since 1959, in the Landrum-Griffin Act, Congress has required unions to file elaborate reports with the government concerning their internal affairs. This statute also grants redress to employees against union officials who deny them the right to participate in union meetings and elections. But its chief concern is to prevent union officials from misappropriating funds. As unions have become more powerful, a greater measure of control has been necessary to insure their fiduciary responsibilities. Furthermore, unions are now sufficiently public in nature so that disclosure of their internal affairs is essential.

FUTURE POLICY CONSIDERATIONS IN CONTROLLING LABOR UNIONS

There is now much concern over the size and power of our nationally affiliated unions. Many believe that unions should now be brought within the reach of the anti-trust laws to prevent them from abusive practices. This is anathema to labor unionists who recall how the Sherman Act was used to render them powerless a generation ago. A better proposal may be to exempt unions from the anti-trust laws and to outlaw their abusive practices under the National Labor Relations Act.

At present, labor unions continue to enjoy almost complete immunity from the anti-trust laws. Their great power must always present a temptation to abuse it. And our free labor unions may some day become so strong and large that Congress may be forced to curtail their power by measures similar to anti-trust controls. There is even talk that widespread and crippling strikes should be outlawed. Whether this does happen depends largely on how our labor unions shoulder their increasing responsibilities. With the growing maturity of bargaining relationships between employers and unions, it need never occur.

18 THE POSITION OF MINORITIES IN THE AMERICAN LABOR MOVEMENT

F. Ray Marshall

Before discussing the position of minority groups in the American labor movement, it is necessary to clarify the meaning of minorities because many nationalities, economic, religious, or ethnic groups have at some time been in the minority. As successive waves of immigrants have been assimilated by the American society, more recent arrivals have taken their places at the bottom of the occupational ladder. Indeed, the nationality compositions of various occupations and trade unions have reflected both the time of arrival of these groups to the United States and the tendency of some groups to concentrate in particular occupations. As time went on, the older immigrants from northern and western Europe tended to move into better jobs, making room at lower levels for later arrivals from southern and eastern Europe. These latter groups have, in turn, more recently moved up the occupational ladder, making room at the bottom for Negroes and various Spanish-speaking groups. Indeed, Negroes started being drawn out of the rural South and into the non-agricultural work force at an accelerated rate when the flow of immigrants from Europe was cut off by World War I.

I do not wish to imply, however, that the Negro problem is identical with the nationality or religious problems of an earlier time, because the Negro has encountered much greater obstacles to his economic advancement. And although Orientals have had more difficulties than Europeans, they too have found greater acceptability than Negroes. American Indians, Mexicans, and

Puerto Ricans also have suffered from discrimination, and their economic conditions are often worse than those of Negroes; but discrimination against these groups is limited geographically and has become much less significant since World War II. Thus, although these other groups still have serious economic and social problems, the main minority group problem for both the unions and American society is the assimilation of the Negro. I shall therefore direct this chapter to the Negro problem. After outlining the historical relationship between unions and Negroes, I shall discuss the main changes in union racial practices since 1930.

HISTORICAL RELATIONS BETWEEN UNIONS AND NEGROES

In addition to his easy racial identification, the Negro finds it more difficult to assimilate because he was a slave. Slavery created an image of inferiority for Negroes which survived emancipation. The slave system also made it difficult for Negroes to maintain stable family relations and acquire other characteristics which were useful to European and Oriental immigrants in their advancement in America. Although most slaves were kept at a very low level of education and training, some of them acquired such skills as were needed in the plantation economy. Direct and indirect competition between slaves and white workers generated animosities which survived emancipation.

Race relations also were exacerbated by the tendency of Negroes and whites to blame each other for the economic difficulties in which they found themselves, following the Civil War. Most Negroes remained in agriculture after emancipation and became sharecroppers and tenant farmers in the cotton belts. Under this agricultural system, Negroes as well as whites suffered as a result of shortages of capital, heavy debts, high interest rates, depletion of the soil, large families, ignorance, and lack of incentive. But the Negro suffered handicaps that the whites did not face: racial discrimination limited the nonagricultural jobs available to him, inferior education made it difficult for him to compete on equal terms for the few available jobs with whites, and disenfranchisement made it difficult for him to improve his lot through political action.

239

The policies developed by unions in the South depended mainly on the number of Negroes in the unions' jurisdictions and their strategic location. Wherever they had the power, unions usually excluded Negroes from membership and the better jobs. Not only did these early Southern labor organizations bar Negroes because of a desire to limit the supply of labor, but since Negroes were regarded as inferior people, unions would have encountered stiff community opposition if they had accepted Negroes into the same locals with whites.

But many unions found it impossible to ignore Negro workers. In trades with many Negroes, discriminating unions found their positions weakened by the employers' ability to play Negro and white workers against each other. Under these circumstances, it was necessary for unions either to admit Negroes or to cooperate with Negro labor organizations. Some Bricklayers' locals, for example, attempted at first to exclude Negroes, but later either took them into white locals or chartered separate locals for them. Where the Bricklayers maintained integrated locals, their leaders found it desirable to avoid publicizing their racial practices for fear of community opposition.

Besides the Bricklayers and other trowel trades unions, the major integrated locals were in the coal mines whose geographic isolation protected them from community pressures. Unions also used their political and economic power to perpetuate the pattern of job discrimination which had been established before labor organizations entered most industries and occupations.

Although these patterns of discrimination were more rigid in the South, they were by no means restricted to that region. In the North, Negroes actually had fewer opportunities to work in the skilled trades because there were not enough of them to force the craft unions to admit them to membership or to permit them to work.[1] And in the North as in the South, skilled building trades unions barred Negroes from membership in their organizations and restricted their work mainly to Negro neighborhoods. Almost all of the craft unions on the railroads had national constitutional provisions which barred Negroes.

[1] Charles H. Wesley, *Negro Labor in the United States* (New York: Vanguard Press, 1927), p. 112; E. R. Turner, *The Negro in Pennsylvania* (Washington, D.C.: American Historical Association, 1911), pp. 25–29.

THE AMERICAN FEDERATION OF LABOR

The American Federation of Labor (AFL), organized in 1886, at first refused to admit national unions which limited membership to whites. As time went on, however, it became increasingly difficult for the AFL to enforce its equalitarian racial policy. For one thing, powerful organizations, like the Machinists which originated in the South, refused to drop their racial bars as a condition of membership in the AFL. In its early days when the Federation was weak and its survival uncertain, its leaders wanted very much to gain the affiliation of all strong national organizations. The AFL's leaders therefore became willing to accept these discriminating unions, and, in 1895, the Machinists were permitted to affiliate with the Federation by transferring the race bar from their constitution to their practice. Thereafter the AFL accepted a number of organizations with racial bars and even permitted affiliates to change their constitutions to debar non-whites.

The need to accommodate its racial policies to the attitudes of the South also undoubtedly influenced the AFL's practices. The acceleration of industrialization in the South during the 1880's and 1890's brought Southern workers increasingly into competition with unionized workers in other areas. In order to protect their unionized bases, therefore, the AFL and its affiliates intensified their organizing efforts in the South during the 1890's, and AFL President Gompers toured the South in 1895.

The AFL's racial policies were also influenced by the use of Negro strikebreakers and the anti-union attitudes of many Negro leaders. These leaders opposed unions, partly because the latter discriminated against colored workers, but also because they considered it wise to ally themselves with employers who controlled jobs, even though Negroes usually were paid less than whites for the same work. Negro–employer alliances were political as well as economic, however, because most Southern whites were Democrats, and employers and Negroes were Republicans.

After the AFL compromised its earlier racial position, it adopted a policy of chartering directly affiliated locals and central labor unions where its affiliates having jurisdiction over colored

241

workers would not accept them. But these discriminatory practices by the AFL and its affiliates were slowly challenged because of their fundamental incompatibility with sound collective bargaining and union growth—an incompatibility which became increasingly clear to union leaders during and after World War I, when they found many Negroes in their jurisdictions who were difficult to organize because of the restrictive racial policies. Some unions, like those in the garment and coal mining industries, responded by organizing these colored workers on an equal basis, but the reaction of others was to continue to exclude Negroes or to restrict them to inferior membership status.

Although equalitarian racial policies might not have averted the destruction of many unions during the so-called open-shop period of the 1920's, there can be little question that such a policy, if widely adopted throughout the labor movement, would have made it more difficult for employers to use Negroes as a part of their program to destroy unions.

THE CONGRESS OF INDUSTRIAL ORGANIZATIONS

The social ferment in the United States during the 1930's produced a profound change in the status of Negroes in the labor movement. The Roosevelt Administration's encouragement of union growth and the formation of the Congress of Industrial Organizations (CIO) gave colored workers and their leaders alternatives to the AFL and the Republican party. The CIO was made up mainly of industrial unions which had little incentive to bar Negroes from membership. Unlike craft organizations which organize workers in particular crafts or occupations and often supply workers to employers, industrial unions organize all workers in an industry, have no control over employment, and therefore must attempt to organize all workers hired by employers. Since Negroes had entered strategic positions in many of the basic industries during and after World War I, the CIO's success depended to a significant degree on its ability to gain the support of the Negro community.

The nature of the CIO's leadership also influenced its racial policies. The principal leader of the CIO was John L. Lewis of the United Mine Workers, whose organization had consistently followed equalitarian policies. In addition, CIO leaders were younger and more idealistic than those of the AFL and had broader social objectives which required support from Negro communities in political as well as union matters. It therefore became imperative for the CIO to change the traditional anti-union and Republican attitudes of Negro leaders.

In order to accomplish its objectives, the CIO adopted many programs to gain a favorable image in the Negro community. These measures, which were implemented by a Civil Rights committee, caused a profound change in the Negro community. With the formation of the CIO, Negro leaders who had been suspicious of the labor movement realized that Negroes had an opportunity to ally themselves with a new, different, and perhaps powerful labor movement and consequently actively supported the new organization.

Although there can be little question that the alliance between Negroes and the CIO was an important factor causing the AFL and its affiliates to abandon their discriminatory policies, it would be misleading to give the impression that all CIO affiliates consistently followed equalitarian policies and got Negro support, while AFL locals discriminated and were shunned by Negroes. A few CIO locals excluded Negroes from membership; others were segregated. At first Negroes either segregated themselves or were segregated by whites in most of the "integrated" CIO locals in the South. And in the South, with a few exceptions like the Packinghouse Workers, CIO unions did very little to eliminate the historical pattern of job segregation which restricted Negroes to inferior jobs. Despite these qualifications, however, the CIO had relatively equalitarian racial policies, and many of its international affiliates actively supported Negro causes, especially when the changes were initiated by Negroes or employers.

THE AFL-CIO MERGER

Although the AFL-CIO adopted a much more equalitarian racial position than either the CIO or the AFL, a number of features of the 1955 merger tended to exacerbate Negro-union relations. In the first place, two-thirds of the official positions in the merged federation went to the AFL which was never able to overcome its unfavorable image in the Negro community. Secondly, the AFL-CIO Executive Council admitted the Railroad Trainmen and the Locomotive Firemen to the merged organization, even though these two unions restricted membership to whites. There was, at the same time, a number of widely publicized cases of discrimination against Negroes by unions, especially on the railroads and in the building trades, in Northern cities with large Negro populations. And in the South some local union leaders were openly allying themselves with segregationist elements to resist integration in the schools and in the labor movement.

The merger also came at a time of important changes in the mood of the Negro community. Most important, the migration of Negroes out of the South had greatly increased their political power. Therefore, it lessened their dependence on unions. In addition, the persistence of segregation and discrimination in the North as well as in the South had generated a much more militant mood among Negroes. This mood helped in turn to produce a growing body of anti-discrimination laws and orders by the federal government and states outside the South. Although the labor movement as a whole was an important force supporting these anti-discrimination measures, unions—especially on the railroads and in the building trades—were among the most intransigent of the discriminating organizations prosecuted under these laws and orders.

The growing militancy of the Negro community also produced a proliferation of Negro organizations competing for leadership. It was perhaps natural, therefore, that it would become increasingly difficult for any organization like the National Association for the Advancement of Colored People (NAACP) to work closely with unions whose discriminatory practices brought them under increasing attack from the Negro community. Beginning in 1958, the NAACP responded to these pressures with a series of public attacks on the AFL-CIO and its affiliates. The attacks on unions by Negro community organizations were accompanied by mounting criticism of unions from Negroes within the labor movement who formed the Negro American Labor Council in

1960 to fight discrimination by unions and to promote other interests of Negro workers.

Relations between the AFL-CIO and the Negro community seem to have improved following the 1961 AFL-CIO Convention, in spite of a number of violent demonstrations against AFL-CIO building trades unions in several Northern cities during the summers of 1963 and 1964. This improvement has come about primarily because the AFL-CIO has exhibited an increasing awareness of a need to combat discrimination, and because such Negro leaders as Martin Luther King have emphasized that Negroes and unions have many common objectives. Negroes also were reminded that, with all of the faults of unions, the latter had probably done more to promote the Negro's economic opportunities and civil rights than any other nongovernmental organization outside the Negro community.

Another factor which helped heal the Negro-labor breach was the revitalization of the AFL-CIO Civil Rights Committee in 1961. This committee had been a disappointment to its founders and supporters because of internal difficulties and attacks on it from Negro union leaders and civil rights organizations during its first five years. The Civil Rights Committee's first two chairmen had resigned because of these difficulties, and AFL-CIO President George Meany had some trouble finding a new chairman until AFL-CIO Secretary-Treasurer William Schnitzler agreed to accept that position in 1961. At the same time, the Committee's compliance procedures were strengthened and Donald Slaiman, who had a good reputation among civil rights leaders, was appointed director of the Civil Rights Department and its staff was enlarged. The AFL-CIO also played an active role in the passage of the Civil Rights Act of 1964, which the federation said was needed to help the labor movement eliminate discrimination from its ranks.

The unity between union and civil rights groups also was symbolized by organized labor's support of such important civil rights demonstrations as the 1963 March on Washington and the 1965 march from Selma to Montgomery, Alabama, to protest voter-registration discrimination in that state. Although the AFL-CIO Executive Council refused to endorse the March on Washington, many of its affiliates participated in that march and two of its vice presidents, Walter Reuther and A. Philip Randolph, were on the planning committee.

I do not mean to imply, however, that Negro–union differences have been settled. Much discrimination remains in the labor movement, and civil rights organizations have launched a legal campaign to loosen the craft unions' control of jobs. The NAACP also promised widespread demonstrations against building trades unions and employers during the spring and summer of 1965, unless Negroes got more jobs in that industry. There are also likely to be differences between Negroes and labor leaders over the priority to be assigned civil rights matters. Thus, the future relationship between unions and Negroes is likely to be one of both conflict and cooperation.

UNION RACIAL PATTERNS

Perhaps the best way to indicate both the nature of the progress that has been made and the things that remain to be done is to look at particular union racial practices, especially exclusion of Negroes from union membership, segregated unions and jobs, and the status of Negroes within the union hierarchy.

Exclusion from Membership

The number of international unions with formal race bars in their constitutions or rituals has declined from at least twenty-two in 1930 to only two today, neither of which is affiliated with the AFL-CIO. The AFL-CIO's only affiliates with formal race bars removed their discriminatory clauses in 1960 and 1963 respectively. The last remaining internationals with race bars, the independent Railway Conductors and the Locomotive Engineers, had to remove their racial restrictions by July 1965, when the employment section of the Civil Rights Act of 1964 became effective.

The decline in exclusion by formal methods does not mean, however, that discrimination declined by the same degree because there were many local variations from national policy. Exclusion by informal means or tacit consent continues to be a particularly important form of discrimination by craft unions in the buildings trades and on the railroads.

Although there have been few changes in the patterns of union racial exclusion in the South since World War II, Negroes have gained admission to a number of Northern locals from which they were formerly excluded. The forces causing these unions to relax their racial restrictions include the increasing militance of the civil rights movement, anti-discrimination laws and orders, decisions by the National Labor Relations Board that discriminating unions would be decertified if they discriminated against Negroes, and federal court orders making unions liable for damages when they violated their duty to represent all workers fairly. Even before World War II, however, a number of forces had started eroding the race bars of unions, including expansion of Negro employment into jurisdictions covered by these unions, competition between labor organizations for Negro votes in representation elections, and public criticism of discriminating unions.

Segregation

The main forms of segregation in the labor movement have been auxiliary and segregated locals and segregated jobs. Locals with auxiliary charters are not autonomous and are represented by white officers. These locals have almost completely disappeared because of attacks from the Fair Employment Practices Committee created by President Roosevelt during World War II, court decisions which prohibited the closed shop where auxiliaries existed, NLRB decisions that the auxiliary could not be coupled with the checkoff of union dues, state anti-discrimination laws, the Taft-Hartley and Railway Labor Act amendments making the union shop unenforcible if all workers were not admitted on equal terms, and the Landrum-Griffin Act of 1959 which makes it possible for Negro workers to take legal action to abolish auxiliary locals. Some of the auxiliaries were turned into segregated locals, which are supposed to be autonomous. This distinction is sometimes more theoretical than real, however, because the white local might, in fact, represent the Negro local in dealings with employers. Although segregated locals were most common in the South, they existed in some international unions like the Longshoremen, Carpenters, Musicians, and Railway Clerks, outside the South.

There has been a great decline in the number of segregated locals since World War II, and it has been very rare for new segregated locals to be chartered since 1950.

The anti-discrimination laws mentioned above are the main reasons for the integration of unions. Of course, the increasingly militant mood of the Negro community, which considers racial segregation to be at the root of most of its problems, was mainly responsible for the anti-discrimination laws and executive orders. The desegregation of locals throughout the South after 1960 can be attributed mainly to the activities of the Committee on Equal Employment Opportunity, created by President Kennedy and continued under President Johnson who was chairman of the Committee when he was Vice President. Since labor organizations are not parties to government contracts, the Committee on Equal Employment Opportunity has no power to deal directly with union discrimination. But President Kennedy got around this limitation by ruling that neither the federal government nor its contractors would deal with segregated bargaining units. Faced with a possible loss of government contracts, many employers in the South have used their influence to force the integration of local unions.

Although the Negro community and those Negro workers who had inadequate job opportunities on a segregated basis have favored integration, other Negroes, especially union leaders, are afraid that desegregation will cost them jobs and union positions. Negroes also have been afraid of becoming minorities in white locals. Resistance to desegregation often has been overcome by special arrangements to permit Negroes to retain some control in the merged locals.

The pattern of job segregation is much more important than segregated local unions. There has been a long tradition, for example, that Negroes would be hired in menial or otherwise undesirable jobs from which they could not be promoted into the better jobs held by whites. Sometimes, as in the tobacco, longshoring, railroad, pulp and paper, and some manufacturing industries, occupational segregation was reinforced by segregated locals.

Many seniority rosters were integrated in the North during World War II and many Southern companies have integrated jobs since 1950. Job segregation violates all of the anti-discrimination measures mentioned above. But, since there were no state anti-discrimination laws in the South, the main forces for change in that region were court decisions and the federal contract committees, particularly President Eisenhower's Committee on Government Contracts and the Kennedy–Johnson Committee on Equal Employment Opportunity.

Of course, whether or not desegregation causes Negroes to get many new jobs depends on the particular merger procedures adopted, economic conditions in the industry, and management's sincerity in promoting more equal job opportunities for Negroes.

Although our attention has been mainly on the discriminatory practices of unions, we should also note that unions have done some positive things to improve the Negro's economic opportunities. The labor movement has, for example, been one of the most important forces supporting the passage of civil rights legislation. Indeed, the AFL-CIO promoted the Civil Rights Act of 1964 partly because its leaders felt that such a law would help them eradicate discrimination in the labor movement. Other measures taken by unions to improve the Negro's lot include providing contract protection and grievance procedures, including nondiscrimination clauses in collective agreements; equalizing occupational wage differentials, which helped Negroes more than whites because they were concentrated in lower occupations; and reducing the racial prejudices of white members through union education programs. The labor movement also has provided career opportunities for many able Negroes who were barred from other avenues of advancement because of discrimination.

INTERNAL UNION AFFAIRS

We might also note the changed position of the Negro within the union hierarchy since 1930. Although we have no accurate union membership statistics by race, the number of Negro union members increased from perhaps 50,000 in 1930 to over 1.5 million today. There has been a great increase in the Negroes' power within the labor movement at the same time. Although Negroes held few leadership positions in 1930, today they are found in official positions at every level, including the AFL-CIO Executive

Council. At least twenty international unions have or have had Negroes on their highest ruling boards, and there are hundreds of Negroes on international union staffs and in positions of leadership at the local level. There has also been a change in the quality of Negro participation in the labor movement, particularly in the South.

In the 1930's, relations between Negroes and whites were very formal, even in unions like the UMW. Although the racial ferment in the South following the 1954 Supreme Court school desegregation decision increased tension in the unions, relations have been re-established on a much more equalitarian basis. Sometimes integration causes local unions to discontinue formal social affairs, but even some union social affairs which were almost invariably segregated in 1930 are today conducted on an integrated basis in every Southern state. Of course, one of the main reasons for these changes has been the changing race relations in the larger community, particularly the desegregation of public accommodations, which makes it possible for Negro and white unionists to meet together. But labor organizations, particularly the state federations, contributed to the desegregation of public accommodations by refusing to hold meetings in places that would not accept Negroes.

CONCLUSIONS

Although there have been some significant changes in the Negro's position within the labor movement, many problems remain. Indeed, the complete elimination of all discrimination, which is far from being accomplished, would not equalize the Negro's position because of the handicaps he suffers as a result of past discrimination. It seems safe to conclude, therefore, that although the problem of discrimination has been reduced, at least at the policy level, the labor movement's main concern in the future must be with positive measures to improve the Negro's actual employment *levels* as well as his *opportunities*. This will, in turn, require measures to maintain a high level of employment and to work with the Negro community in preparing Negroes for the opportunities which are now available. If full employment could be sustained over a long period of time, white resistance to job integration would be lessened and Negroes would have greater motivation to improve their conditions.

The material for this chapter is based on my *The Negro and Organized Labor* (New York: John Wiley and Sons, 1965).

19 LABOR IN AMERICAN POLITICS

Charles M. Rehmus

Foreign trade-union delegations and individual union officials who visit the United States almost always show a lively interest in the political role of American labor. This interest ordinarily takes the form of questions such as: Why doesn't the American trade-union movement have its own political party? Why don't your unions have political goals? Is it true that American workers are apolitical? Such questions are not naïve, particularly when asked by trade unionists from countries where the labor movement is closely aligned with one particular political party. Moreover, the view they reflect—that the American labor movement is almost exclusively concerned with collective bargaining as the means to protect worker rights and improve wages and working conditions—is a view shared by many Americans.

There is a widespread assumption that organized labor in the U.S. is economically rather than politically oriented. Such an assumption is entirely erroneous. American labor has been involved in politics at least since the 1820's. In one sense, the history of the American labor movement can be viewed as a record of conflict between leaders who stressed the importance of political activity versus those who argued the primacy of obtaining economic gains for wage-earners.

The final ascendancy was gained by those who believed in business unionism. Even those who most strongly supported this point of view, however, were aware that economic gains must be supported by at least some level of political power. The character and degree of labor's political activity has changed many times. Alliances have formed, separated, and regrouped. Influence has waxed and waned. But there has almost never been a time when

American union leaders were not concerned with politics and some kinds of political action.

LABOR AS A PRESSURE GROUP

In short, it is true that American unions today devote their major attention to control of the job, improved working conditions, and higher standards of living for workers. They seek to achieve these objectives primarily through collective bargaining, rather than through class propaganda warfare or through seeking political office directly. Nonetheless, American labor organizations have engaged in substantial political activities throughout their history—never more strongly than at present. These activities, however, have assumed the pattern of pressure politics—attempts to influence public policy—rather than party politics per se.

This choice to be a pressure group rather than a party makes very good sense in terms of the nature of the American political system. It would have been almost impossible for American labor to develop a major political party with its base solely or primarily in the labor movement. There are a number of reasons for this:

1. The size of the United States and the diversity of interests in this nation make it impossible for a party to come to power by appealing to a single interest or by relying on a single set of issues.

2. The composition of the major parties in the U.S. is extremely diverse, and the parties have always shared the labor vote. The American tradition of family influence on political-party choice militates against a clear-cut ideological division of the electorate based on class differences.

3. The powerful position of the president of the United States in the American political system has meant that any truly national party must be a serious competitor for this office. A national organization must be developed if a party is to have an opportunity to elect a president. Labor's strength has always been concentrated geographically. Today, for example, organized labor has a substantial number of adherents in only ten or a dozen of the fifty states. This makes it practically impossible for labor to develop a national political party.

4. State laws favor existing political parties and encourage tra-

ditional voting habits. In many states, new parties must meet extraordinary requirements in order to get on the ballot. Moreover, American candidates must be residents of the district in which they run for office. There are very few electoral districts that are composed primarily of labor voters. This complicates the problem of electing a substantial number of labor representatives to either state or federal legislatures.

5. American political parties have traditionally had low discipline and little centralized control over officials elected under their banner. American unions have likewise rejected specific direction from national bodies. Both of these traditions of autonomy would make a national labor party difficult to control.

6. Finally, and most important, the existing American political parties have shown a marked ability to come to terms with organized labor. The realism with which the large urban party machines in the U.S. have established political alliances with union leaders has ordinarily drawn off any substantial pressure for organized labor to set up a competing political organization.

In summary, for reasons of ideology and tradition, and because of the basic structure of the American political system, most leaders of organized labor have been uninterested in working toward an independent labor political party. This has been true particularly since the rise of the American Federation of Labor, and is still true today. Labor is very much involved in politics, but as an adjunct to, rather than a competitor with, the existing parties. It is committed to raise funds for political activities and campaigns and is extremely active in lobbying, in public relations, and in attempting to educate union members to favor certain programs and candidates.

Before looking more closely at these contemporary activities, however, let us turn briefly to the history of American labor to see how these strategies developed.

LABOR IN POLITICS IN THE NINETEENTH AND EARLY TWENTIETH CENTURIES

Pragmatism has been the characteristic philosophy of most of American labor throughout its history, and this approach carried over into its attitude toward political action. During the formative years of the modern trade-union movement, the late 1820's and 1830's, American workers were already enfranchised. Organized agitation to obtain the vote was unnecessary. This also meant that many workers developed early a traditional affiliation with an existing party which made it difficult to interest them in independent labor or workingmen's parties. Then, as now, labor represented a minority of the American electorate which, along with the lack of class consciousness of most workers, almost foredoomed any national labor party.

Moreover, throughout most of the nineteenth century, the units of government whose enactments most concerned labor were state and local. Many city and state labor groups quickly established satisfactory relationships with the dominant political machine in their area, regardless of the national party affiliation of the machine. These created a network of local allegiances that militated against the creation of competing labor parties or adherence to either of the major parties of the national level.

Pragmatically then, independent political action made little sense to the early American labor unions. Although they developed local political alliances, it should be noted that only in times when economic recession or intense employer opposition prevented labor from maintaining its position by means of collective bargaining did it turn to concerted political efforts. First, labor ordinarily attempted pressure-group action directed at one or both of the two existing political parties. Only when the major parties proved unresponsive to labor's demands did the union movement turn to independent action. For the same general reasons, labor's independent political efforts ordinarily subsided quickly—either owing to an improvement in the economic climate or, as commonly, because one of the major parties embraced its cause.

Thus, for example, the workingmen's parties that sprang up in a number of American towns and cities in the late 1820's have been attributed to the depression of 1828–1829. An equally important factor in their creation, however, was the indifference shown by both the Federalist and Whig parties to workers' problems. These early workingmen's parties had died out by the 1840's, even though this too was a period of economic instability, primarily because the Jacksonian-Democratic movement had taken many of the objectives of the early labor parties over as its own. During this period, the labor movement was able to exert some pressure within the existing political structure, its greatest efforts directed toward enactment of ten-hour-day legislation.

In the depression that followed the Civil War, labor attempted to gain the eight-hour day through similar pressure tactics. The vehicle for these efforts was the National Labor Union, a federation composed of delegates of local unions, trades assemblies, and national unions. Only when legislation that had been enacted proved inadequate and candidate promises hollow, did the NLU determine to chart its own political course. For that purpose, it created a political arm, the National Labor Reform Party. But that party's first convention was also its last. Experienced politicians, both Democrats and anti-Grant Republicans, simply took it over.

No one party or political movement benefited from the unrest caused by the Panic of 1873 and the depression that followed. General discontent was so great that a number of political alternatives arose, each receiving a share of labor adherents. Some workers joined the Greenback-Labor party; others flirted with socialism. However, by the late 1870's, clearly by the early 1880's, most workers found that the Noble and Holy Order of the Knights of Labor, with its call to all who engaged in "honorable toil," had the greatest appeal.

Although the Knights had both an economic and a political program, it is the latter which concerns us here. For most of its organizational life, the Order refused to endorse any party at the national level. Instead, it concentrated on lobbying efforts in Washington. At the local and state levels, however, its constituent assemblies were heavily engaged in political activity, often in combination with local reformers and state and local trade-union federations. In the East, these coalitions usually worked with the traditional political parties. In the West, they tended to develop their own political organizations, often called United Front or United Labor parties. The effectiveness of these tactics at lower governmental levels is indicated by the substantial number of state laws relating to labor and working conditions enacted during the 1880's.

The year 1886 marked the turning of the tide against the Knights. As prosperity returned, the skilled craftsman, willing enough to join with his less-skilled brethren during the lean years, now preferred to go it alone. By 1890, what was left of the Knights had allied itself with the Populist party. By then, however, the skilled worker was no longer a member of the Noble and Holy Order. His interest in craft unionism had revived. In turn, his union had joined a new national organization—the American Federation of Labor.

THE AMERICAN FEDERATION OF LABOR

Much of the new Federation's policy toward political action was shaped by its long-time president, Samuel Gompers. To Gompers, any national labor organization that engaged in partisan politics was signing its own death warrant. Aside from lobbying, labor's only political activity should be to use its votes to tip the election balance—to reward labor's friends and defeat its enemies. This doctrine of minimal political involvement, which came to be known as voluntarism, had several important functions. It gave labor considerable leverage in close elections in areas where workers were numerous. It avoided the diversion of organized labor's resources and energy away from what Gompers thought was its primary function—collective bargaining to achieve economic gains. It prevented undue community hostility toward the AFL which might have resulted from "radical" independent political adventures. Finally, as noted previously, voluntarism allowed AFL affiliates to maintain beneficial relationships with state and local political machines, regardless of the party with which such relationships had been formed.

After the turn of the century, Gompers and the AFL did relax somewhat their dedication to voluntarism. In 1908, the Federation endorsed the Democratic candidate, William Jennings Bryan for president. Increasingly friendly relationships between the AFL and the Democratic party were maintained throughout the period of World War I. In 1924, the Federation endorsed the candidacy of Robert M. La Follette for president under the banner of the Progressive party, but the failure of this venture reinforced Gompers' general faith in the virtues of nonpartisanship. Even following Gompers' death, the AFL remained clear of partisan politics for another twenty years.

It should be remembered, however, that the AFL during this period represented primarily skilled workers—the "aristocracy of labor." After the demise of the Knights of Labor, there were few traditional avenues of organization open to the less skilled wage-earner. This probably accounts for the rise of organizations such as the Western Federation of Miners and the IWW (International Workers of the World), and, in part, for the increased voting strength of various socialist parties during the early twentieth century.

This gap between the economic power of the organized skilled workers and the largely unorganized mass of unskilled workers remained unchanged until the crash of 1929. Then, skilled or unskilled, in a union or not, the wage-earner was unemployed and helpless.

THE CIO AND THE CHANGE IN LABOR'S POLITICAL ATTITUDES

The worldwide depression of the 1930's profoundly altered many aspects of American society. Its impact on the American trade-union movement was severe, leading to fundamental changes in the structure of unionization. Initially, a split over new organizing campaigns and techniques developed within labor's ranks. A number of union leaders, chief among whom was John L. Lewis of the Coal Miners, thought that the AFL's traditional reliance on union organization of only skilled workers was inadequate to meet the needs of the times. The trade-union movement, they argued, must also organize semiskilled and unskilled workers, particularly in the growing mass-production industries. New Deal legislation, such as the National Industrial Recovery Act, encouraged expansion of union organization across whole industries. By 1935, the split between the traditional craft unions and the newly formed industrial unions had widened to such a point that the industrial unions and their leaders were expelled from the AFL. In 1938 these leaders formed their own federation, the Congress of Industrial Organizations.

In its organizational drives, the CIO relied heavily on alleged government support. Lewis, for example, sent organizers into the minefields claiming "President Roosevelt wants you to join the union." The CIO leaders believed that if their new organization was to be maintained and was to continue to grow, the re-election of Roosevelt in 1936 was a necessity. As an initial step in this direction, Lewis made a gift to the Democratic party of 500,000 dollars from the United Mine Workers' treasury. Other CIO unions also contributed liberally. The CIO's contribution to the Democratic campaign in 1936 came to over 700,000 dollars—an immense sum when compared to the 95,000 dollars contributed by the AFL Executive Board to national political campaigns in all of the preceding thirty years.

Additionally in 1936, CIO leaders created a national body called Labor's Non-Partisan League as a medium for union campaign activities. Initially, both AFL and CIO leaders were represented on the League's governing board, although by 1938, the AFL representatives had withdrawn.

Lewis anticipated that his financial support of the Democratic party in both the 1936 and 1938 elections would result in his being the primary labor advisor to the Roosevelt administration during its second term. When these expectations did not develop and when Roosevelt failed to support the CIO on several occasions, Lewis became disenchanted. In 1940, he actively opposed Roosevelt's campaign for a third term and appealed publicly to CIO union members to support the Republican presidential nominee, Wendell Willkie. Lewis' appeal was rejected by the American voters, including most trade-union members, and Roosevelt was easily re-elected to a third term. As a consequence of this repudiation, Lewis resigned as president of the CIO. Leadership of the CIO and its burgeoning political activities then fell to other men.

In 1943, the CIO Executive Board created a permanent Political Action Committee (PAC). During 1944, the political expenditures of the PAC, nearly a million dollars, were the greatest effort ever made by an American labor organization in politics.

At the same time, the AFL followed its traditional political policies; it published and distributed the voting records of Congress and periodically selected a nonpartisan campaign committee to influence congressional and presidential elections. Unlike the CIO, it maintained no permanent political department. As a result of the passage of the Taft-Hartley Act in 1947, however, and in response to what it deemed the anti-union sentiment of that Act, the AFL established Labor's League for Political Education (LLPE). The LLPE was a counterpart political organization to the CIO's PAC, raising and spending nearly a quarter of a million dollars for campaign activities in each of the 1950 and 1952 elections.

With the merger of the AFL and CIO in 1955, a permanent committee was created to supersede PAC and LLPE. The new organization was known as the Committee on Political Education (COPE). It was given a threefold responsibility: meet the need for political education for workers, encourage workers to register and vote, and urge union members to become active in political life. It is largely through the national COPE organization and through the semi-independent COPE affiliates created by a number of international unions that organized labor in America participates today in the political process.

LABOR'S CONTEMPORARY POLITICAL ACTIVITIES

Currently, American labor engages, both in its traditional role as a pressure group and also as an active participant, in election politics. The first of these functions—pressure-group activities to obtain policy and administrative benefits through lobbying—does not require extended discussion.

Like most interest groups in American society, the AFL-CIO and major individual unions maintain public-relations staffs in Washington. These staff people combine two functions: that of making labor's point of view known to the general public and that of lobbying with legislative and executive officials. The labor lobbyist, like lobbyists in general, performs a genuine informational function vis-à-vis government officials. The complexity of issues in today's world is so great that only the unusual official can be aware of all aspects and points of view on all public policies. Lobbyists marshal the arguments for and against any particular policy decisions, demonstrating to officials the constituent points of view that exist in our society. This function is generally educational, particularly when all relevant points of view are represented in regard to a given issue.

The issues that are of concern to organized labor today are far broader than those affecting wages and working conditions directly. Labor is concerned with the whole range of domestic and international policies that affect Americans generally. Labor's legislative program goes far beyond that of Samuel Gompers' time and considerably beyond the particular causes of labor as a special interest group. Thus, the labor lobbyist speaks for many millions of people on an extremely wide range of issues.

The relation between lobbying and election participation can be stated as a general, if fairly obvious, rule. Recurrent failure to achieve desired policy and administrative goals through lobbying will direct any numerically large pressure group to use electoral means to make policy officials more responsive to it. As we have seen, throughout its history, labor has turned from lobbying to electoral activities whenever existing parties and officials seemed unresponsive to labor's needs and objectives.

This brings us, then, to the contemporary election activities of organized labor. Labor today brings three fundamental things to the election process: money, organization, and votes. Each of these requires separate discussion.

Money

Organized labor is able to extend its political influence outside of those areas in which it has a concentration of votes by offering pro-labor candidates a scarce but essential commodity—money. In the 1960 presidential election, for example, the AFL-CIO's COPE organization and individual unions contributed about 2 million dollars to the campaigns of favored candidates. In addition to this amount, which was contributed directly to candidates, perhaps an equal dollar volume of goods in kind—services, time and educational activities—was put into politics by labor. Although figures for the 1964 election year are not yet available, it is a reasonable assumption that organized labor's political contribution of cash and services will have approximated 5 million dollars.

Recurrent attempts have been made by Congress to limit labor's political spending. In essence, the present state of our law is that organized labor may not contribute the dues money of its members directly as campaign contributions to candidates for office. Thus, unions have had to turn to collecting voluntary individual contributions in order to obtain the funds that they contribute directly to candidates.

The collection machinery for voluntary funds is cumbersome. Most unions are in charge of their own collections, but receipt books for each small contribution are sent from the national COPE to the various national and international unions. These receipt books then have to be distributed to the local unions where shop stewards take charge of collections in the plant. It has been found that the number of union members who refuse to contribute to COPE when asked is negligible. The number of members who are never asked, however, is enormous. The fact that labor is able to raise only about 2 million dollars from 17 million members demonstrates clearly the small fraction of labor's goal of one dollar per union member that has actually been achieved.

In addition to these so-called free funds which can be contributed directly to election campaigns, American law does permit spending of union-dues money for citizenship and educational purposes. Many of these expenditures go into newspaper advertising, and radio and television programs which support certain public policies and, thus, inferentially back candidates favored by labor. Moreover, labor can legally direct the time of full-time union officials to political activities during election years. This contribution of service is, of course, an indirect form of political spending.

In summary then, it can be seen that labor does make a substantial dollar contribution to politics. COPE contributes up to 25,000 dollars to individual senatorial campaigns and 10,000 dollars in races for the House of Representatives. Individual unions give additional large sums of free funds to candidates whom they favor. These amounts may be distributed in as many as thirty senatorial campaigns and a hundred or more House campaigns.

It should be noted, however, that the 2 million dollars that 17 million union members contribute directly to politics just about equals the reported political contributions of about 900 officials of the nation's 225 largest business concerns. Moreover, the total value of the labor contribution of dollars and services to politics constitutes less than 5 per cent of the whole amount that is spent by all political parties in American election years.

Organization

One of the most fundamental contributions made by labor to politics is the sheer manpower that union workers can provide in an election campaign. It probably takes direct personal participation in politics to appreciate what this involves. It means attendance at frequent meetings; it means posting placards and handing out automobile bumper-strips; it means individual workers standing on street corners, collecting contributions and passing out campaign buttons and literature. "Getting out the vote" involves climbing endless flights of stairs, driving through heavy traffic, and pounding the pavements from one block to the next, performing the multitude of unglamorous tasks which are the lifeblood of American politics.

Perhaps as significant as any of these activities are the drives undertaken by labor to increase the number of registered voters in the American electorate. In both 1960 and 1964, COPE embarked on extensive registration drives in metropolitan areas in most of the fifty states. These efforts, financed by donations from each AFL-CIO union at the rate of five cents per member, yielded impressive results. In 1960 in St. Louis, for example, 407 unionists registered 85,000 new voters in one day. In the same year, labor registered 100,000 new voters in Spanish-speaking sections of California.

These registration drives are based on labor's conclusion that, at present, more Americans favor the Democratic than the Republican party. Therefore, registration drives conducted in middle- and lower-income areas will result in six or seven Democratic registrations out of every ten new registrants. One example of the results of these registration drives will suffice. Labor's efforts in 1960 in New Jersey increased registration by 227,000, primarily in industrial cities. John F. Kennedy carried New Jersey by only 22,000 votes. Such examples could be multiplied in fifteen or twenty other states to demonstrate that labor's registration drives were a substantial factor in the election of the Democratic nominee in 1960.

The Labor Vote

It is no secret that the leaders of organized labor in America largely favor the Democratic party and its candidates for public office. Most, though not all, of labor's money and aid goes to the campaigns of Democrats. It is also known that while a majority of union members are inclined toward the Democratic party, there remains a substantial number of union members who are adherents of the Republican party. This has led to much discussion, both by students of voting behavior and by organized labor's opponents.

One question that has frequently been raised is whether individual union members support the political activities of their union and its leaders. Such studies as are available indicate that about one-half the members support their union's political activities. Another 25 per cent are apathetic or uncommitted, and 25 per cent are opposed. Even in the case of the UAW, probably the most active politically of all American unions, 15 to 20 per cent of the members oppose its political activities and refuse to accept their union's recommendations when it comes to voting. Nevertheless, a majority of union members believe that their union is properly engaged in political activity. They generally support expenditures of dues money to inform the membership and the public about union views on policy issues.

A more interesting question that has frequently been debated is whether there is such a thing as a "labor vote." Ever since John L. Lewis failed in his effort to get CIO members to vote for Wendell Willkie in 1940, it has often been stated that the labor vote is a myth. This view was reinforced by labor's failure to defeat Senator Taft for re-election in 1950, despite massive efforts conducted throughout Ohio.

If by "labor vote" one means that unions control a large bloc of votes that can be swung to one party or another, it is quite true that such a vote is nonexistent. American labor unions have never had this kind of influence over the voting behavior of their members. There is a kind of labor vote, however, demonstrated inferentially by the fact that many candidates for the presidency and for Congress desire union support. They do so because the labor vote, if properly understood, fundamentally affects the size of urban majorities for Democratic party candidates. Studies of American voting behavior show that in 1956, for example, labor-union members voted for Democratic party candidates 21 per cent more strongly than the rest of the country. What's more, union members voted 20 per cent more Democratic than other people of the same social characteristics—the same occupational status, race, religion, and so forth—who were not union members. These voter studies also show, however, that this Democratic margin was drawn primarily from among workers who had strong positive feelings toward their union, and that, in addition, their union took a strong pro-Democratic stand.

To put it in other terms, more than four-fifths of the workers who feel close identification with a militantly pro-Democratic union vote for Democratic party candidates. But if workers do not feel closely identified with their union, or if their union does not take a strong stand in favor of the Democratic party, the union member is at least as likely to vote Republican as Democrat.

Thus, the labor vote and labor's political power is a limited tool and can be used only in a restricted way. Through political action, labor can encourage more workers to vote—and to vote Democratic—than they might otherwise do. It cannot, as things now stand, effectively swing this same bloc of votes to the Republican party or to a third party. Labor's political influence is, therefore, almost wholly within the Democratic party in that it can increase or decrease the likelihood that Democrats will be elected. Since this is the source of its political bargaining power, the AFL-CIO's alliance with the Democratic party is firm. Organized labor's political efforts will be, in the main, directed toward support of Democrats in the foreseeable future. The influence of the labor movement within the Democratic party will fluctuate, however, depending upon the important of workers' votes to a Democratic victory in any given campaign.

WHAT OF THE FUTURE?

It is clear that at no time in the foreseeable future will the American labor movement attempt to form a labor party similar to those existing in many other industrialized democracies of the world. No prominent or responsible trade-union leader espouses such a course. Without exception, they realize that the structure of existing American politics—the fact that labor is still a minority group in this country, and the fact that union members are not a class-conscious group—would make any such attempt futile. Moreover, there is no important pressure for a labor third party at any point in American society. This is primarily because both parties, to a reasonable extent, particularly the Democratic party in labor's view, are responsive to the needs and aspirations of workers.

It is equally clear that, in the near future at least, organized labor's political objectives are bound up with the success or failure of the Democratic party. In 1964, the leadership of organized labor was united in support of President Johnson's bid for re-election to a greater extent than ever before in history. No labor leader of prominence supported the Republican candidate, Barry Goldwater. The overwhelming victory that President Johnson gained at the polls does have the effect, however, of reducing labor's political influence. If Johnson had been narrowly re-elected in a close election like that of 1960, labor's contribution to the victory would make its voice more prominent in Democratic party councils. As it is, the labor movement is merely one of the voices that must be considered when decisions on public policy are being made. It is true, of course, that there are more congressmen who are sympathetic to labor's cause in the present Congress than at any time since the mid-1930's. Thus the labor movement now anticipates favorable action on a number of causes that it espouses.

In conclusion, the current political role of American labor is as a pressure group which has taken on some of the vote-mobilizing functions of a political party. It is still a pressure group, but one which has, in part, transcended its traditional role. In areas of the country where organized workers are numerically large, the labor movement has become a quasi-party adjunct to the Democratic party.

Labor also contributes to the increasing democratization of American society. It broadens the base of the electorate, informs those to whom it speaks about the major public policy problems of the times, and encourages workers to participate in politics. Each of these efforts tends to make the average citizen's participation in politics more meaningful and creative. Labor's voice is also one of the more prominent in the attempt to make the differences between the American parties more specific and to bring about a realignment, so that the two parties stand for more distinctive points of view.

The future of labor in American politics appears to be one of continuation of these contemporary tendencies, rather than any radical change in its political activities and orientation.

20 SOCIAL SECURITY IN AMERICA: THE TWO SYSTEMS— PUBLIC AND PRIVATE

Eveline M. Burns

In the United States there are two systems of organized provision for social security. On the one hand, there are the public programs (social insurance, public assistance, and measures for veterans) which are supported by taxes or compulsory contributions; on the other hand, there are the so-called fringe benefits or employee-benefit systems which provide pensions, disability and supplementary unemployment benefits, and some types of medical care as part of the wage contract. But it would be a great mistake to think that the two are equally important. In 1962–1963, the public programs disbursed some 31.58 billion dollars for income maintenance alone; whereas, the fringe-benefit social-security programs, including those which federal, state, and local governments provide as employers for their current or past employees, amounted only to 8.38 billion dollars. Employee-benefit schemes in private industry accounted for only 4.78 billion dollars of this sum. Even in the field of medical-care costs, where governmental activity in America has been much less pronounced than in other countries, public tax-supported expenditures for personal health-care in this same year amounted to a little over 5 billion dollars as against only 4 billion dollars disbursed under employee-benefit schemes.[1]

[1] The figures in this paragraph are computed from Ida C. Merriam, "Social Welfare Expenditures," *Social Security Bulletin*, 26 (November 1963), pp. 3–14 and Joseph Krislov, "Employee Benefit Plans, 1954–1962," *Social Security Bulletin* (April 1964), p. 11.

THE PUBLIC SOCIAL-SECURITY SYSTEMS

The Background

The status of social-security legislation in the United States cannot be understood without recognizing the influence of several important facts. The first of these is the recency of public action in this area. It was not until the 1930's that Americans were forced to recognize that economic insecurity was a widespread threat, and one that was outside the control of the individual to a very large degree. It took the Great Depression to force us to admit that this was an area in which government, and especially the federal government, would have to play a role. The Social Security Act of 1935 was the expression of this changed view; for the first time, it brought the federal government into the social-security field on a permanent basis by introducing old-age insurance and providing financial incentives to the states to enact unemployment-insurance laws and to develop public-assistance programs. These were revolutionary changes for it must be recalled that, prior to 1935, only two states had enacted unemployment-insurance laws, and most of them had no permanent machinery for administering or supervising public assistance. Workmen's compensation laws were practically the only widespread public social-security measures.

Such a major change of policy obviously took some time to digest. Staffs had to be recruited and trained, and administrative experience had to be gained. The effects of the new programs had to be studied. Opposition had to be overcome, and the benefits of the new measures had to be appreciated.

Second, and related to my first point, is the fact that until recently the pressure for public opinion has not been so great as in many other countries. Our high wage levels mean that workers do, in fact, have a greater possibility of tiding themselves over short periods of nonearning, although it must be remembered that ours is also a high current-consumption economy, and that the prevalence and persuasiveness of advertising is not exactly calculated to encourage people to save, but rather to spend on current consumption. The great expansion of private profit and nonprofit insurance, especially in the medical field, has also to some extent reduced the pressure for public action. It is note-worthy that it has been the failure of private insurance to cover a large segment of the aged or to meet any significant part of their medical care costs that accounts for the very strong public interest in some form of health insurance for this age group.

A third factor of the greatest importance is the size and political structure of the United States. Ours is a large country with a population of 193 millions spread over a tremendous area. Their ways of earning a living vary greatly. There is a great difference in per capita income among the states, some having an income that is twice that of those at the bottom of the scale. To some extent, they have different social values, especially in their attitude toward minority groups. This fact puts great obstacles in the way of uniformity, even on a minimum basis. It is doubtful that we could ever envisage a single comprehensive system such as Great Britain has,

The political structure of the country reinforces these social and economic differences. Ours is a federal system, and the states are very jealous of their prerogatives and resistant to what they regard as federal intervention or control. And this is understand-able, for some of them such as New York or California are as large and populous as many independent countries—Texas alone is as large as France. Apart from the program for war veterans, which is obviously a national responsibility, and the relatively small, special program for railroad workers, the only federal social-security program is Old-Age Survivors and Disability Insurance. Such a program has to be federally operated because an old-age insurance program could not be operated any other way with so mobile a population as ours. Only in this way could the worker who might have been paying contributions all his working life in one state after another be certain that, by the time he came to retire, he could count on receiving the promised benefits.

All our social-security programs are jointly the responsibility of the federal government and the states (sometimes of the local authorities as well), or are state programs, or, in a few general relief systems, the sole responsibility of local authorities. The federal role is to provide grants to the states to help them bear the costs. Of course, theoretically, the authority that makes grants can lay down conditions or standards which the recipient states must meet if they are to receive a grant. But here strong state resistance is encountered.

Even those who, like myself, believe that the federal government could be more aggressive both in pressing for the power to set standards and in exercising leadership—especially by way of publicizing the consequences of the absence of standards— have to recognize that we must seek the best possible compromise as in so many other policy areas. In this case it is a compromise between the desire for equality of access to basic security in all parts of the country and equal treatment of people in similar circumstances, on the one hand, and, on the other, the avoidance of an excessively high degree of centralization and federal control in so large and richly varied a country as ours. And one always has to take account of the fact that if the federal conditions for receipt of a grant are too widely at variance with state interests or values, the state may simply refuse to participate in the scheme, in which case its economically insecure people may be even worse off.

Broad Characteristics of the Public Programs

Like all other developed countries except Australia and New Zealand, the United States now uses the institution of social insurance to protect the vast majority of its workers against most of the more common risks to continuity of income. We also have a special and generous social-security program for veterans. And like all other such countries, in principle, America buttresses its social-insurance programs with a public-assistance system which is supposed to assure minimum income for the people who are not or cannot be covered by social insurance, or for whom the normal social-insurance benefit is inadequate because they have special needs. Finally, these public-income maintenance programs are complemented by a series of social services, some of which aim to restore unemployed, needy, or very low-income people to self-support at adequate wages, while others aim to enhance the capacity for self-care or the quality of family life.

But although, in broad outlines, the combination of public measures adopted to provide social security is the same as that adopted in other countries, there are also very significant differences. We make less extensive use of social insurance to provide against the various risks to which people are exposed. What has impressed the foreign observer was the slow development of a program which applied the social-insurance principle to help meet the cost of medical care. Health insurance has been among the first social insurance measures to be enacted in most other developed countries. Until 1965, when Medicare was adopted, we had no public program to utilize social insurance and to make available federal subsidies for insurance against the costs of physician's services. Even though limited to the aged, the passage of this legislation marks an important change of policy.

Finally, the United States is also unique in that we have no child- or family-allowance system. One result of our failure to make more extensive use of social insurance and children's allowances is that a relatively greater burden is thrown on our public-assistance programs in providing income maintenance and in meeting the costs of medical care than is usual elsewhere. And this is unfortunate because these programs are primarily the responsibility of state or local authorities whose financial resources are frequently limited.

The Individual Programs[2]

Far and away the most important of our public programs is the federal Old-Age, Survivors, and Disability Insurance system, popularly known as OASDI. This provides income to aged workers, their aged wives (or dependent husbands), and their children. It grants survivor benefits to aged widows and widowers, to orphans, and the widow who is caring for them, and pays benefits to permanently disabled workers and their dependents. There is also a lump-sum death or funeral benefit.

The system now covers about 90 per cent of the working population and is currently paying monthly benefits to about 20 million people. Eligibility is based on earnings in a specified number of calendar quarters, and because we desired to use the

[2] For a convenient summary of the public programs, see *Social Security Programs in the United States* obtainable from the Division of Research and Statistics, Social Security Administration, U.S. Department of Health, Education, and Welfare, Washington, D.C.

social-insurance technique as our main method for providing security for today's as well as tomorrow's aged, these earnings requirements are very liberal. For aged persons between age sixty-two and seventy-two, there is also a retirement test. We say that a worker has retired if he has not earned more than a stated number of dollars in a calendar year.

Benefits are somewhat loosely related to previous earnings by a formula which replaces a much larger percentage of earnings of the low-paid than of the high-paid worker. The system is financed solely out of wage- and payroll-taxes levied on the first 4800 dollars of a worker's earnings. Unlike many countries, we have no contribution from the general taxpayer. There is also a reserve fund, the income from which is expected to cover the difference between the yield of the maximum contemplated tax rate and anticipated expenditures in future years.

Our second most important social-insurance program is unemployment insurance or unemployment compensation as it is often called. This program is primarily the responsibility of the states, although the federal government pays the costs of administration and levies a somewhat complicated tax, the purpose of which was to equalize the competitive position of employers paying different tax rates in different states. About four out of five wage- and salary-workers are covered by unemployment insurance. The programs are similar to those in other countries in that workers who have had some defined amount of earnings or employment in some specified period are entitled to benefits when involuntarily unemployed, and the benefits are payable for a limited period, usually about twenty-six weeks. But our systems are unlike others in that the entire costs are paid by the employer; workers pay contributions in only two states. And through the operation of experienced rating systems, the amount of tax each employer pays is determined largely by the extent to which his own employees have drawn benefits.

Workmen's compensation laws exist in all states and are wholly state-administered. They also cover about four out of five wage- and salary-workers, and, like unemployment insurance, typically exclude workers in agriculture, small firms, domestic service, and casual labor. They provide for both cash benefits and medical treatment of sick or injured workers, although the amount of the benefits and the extent of medical care vary greatly from one state to another. They are financed almost wholly by employers. Four states have also enacted temporary-disability insurance laws providing cash benefits (and, in one state, some hospital care) for workers suffering disabilities not incurred in the course of their employment.

We also have a relatively small special social-insurance program for railroad workers which provides old-age, survivor, and permanent-disability pensions co-ordinated with the basic OASDI system, as well as short-period disability and unemployment-insurance benefits.

Our public-assistance programs which are usually operated by the states or by our local governments under the supervision of the states currently provide income to some 8 million people. However, the federal government plays an important role because it provides the states with grants-in-aid covering the aggregate 55 per cent of the cost of assistance given to needy aged, totally disabled, or blind persons, and to families with dependent children. General assistance, however, which is supposed to provide for all the needy people who cannot meet the eligibility conditions of any of the "categorical boxes" into which we have divided our assistance programs, does not receive any financial aid from the federal government. It remains a state, or state and local, or even, in some states, a purely local responsibility, and the character of the programs varies widely both within and between states, reflecting differences in financial capacity and local attitudes. In some areas, general assistance is practically nonexistent.

Finally, we have a very generous system of special benefits for veterans, financed and administered by the federal government. This includes cash payments (compensation for service-connected disabilities as well as for nonservice connected disabilities, pensions subject to an income test, and compensation and pensions for survivors), extensive programs of hospitalization, and all types of medical care, rehabilitation, education and training assistance, loans for purchase of houses and businesses, and low-cost government life insurance.

Many of these social-security programs are buttressed by a gamut of service measures looking toward the restoration of people to self-support or self-care. Thus, all states have an extensive network of public employment offices (or exchanges) which endeavor to place unemployed workers in jobs. Under the Manpower Training and Development Act, we now have a nationwide system of training and retraining. Many of the disabled are helped by the federal-state Vocational Rehabilitation system. The Area Redevelopment of the Appalachia Acts aim to revive economic activity and to create jobs in our depressed areas. The very recent Economic Opportunity Act (the so-called Poverty Program) aims to enhance employability, especially on the part of young people. The state public-welfare authorities which are administratively responsible for public assistance are now required to develop a variety of services which have as their object the restoration of people to self-support or to self-care or the strengthening of family life. All states operate a variety of child-welfare programs with some assistance from the federal government.

PRIVATE EMPLOYEE-BENEFIT SOCIAL-SECURITY SYSTEMS

The relatively small role of the private employee-benefit security systems seems, at first sight, surprising in view of the great growth of such plans in the last twenty years. It has been estimated that by the end of 1962, under those plans, about 111 million persons, workers and their dependents, were covered by some form of health insurance, that about 52 million were covered for life insurance, 27 million were included in temporary-disability and sick-leave plans, 23 million were under pension schemes, and 1.8 million were covered by supplementary unemployment-benefit plans. But these figures exaggerate the extent of the protection available. Some of the health-insurance plans covered hospitalization only. Of all workers and dependents covered, only eight out of eleven had any protection against regular medical expenses other than surgery, the costs of which were covered, at least in part, for some 106 million workers. And although pension plans included something like 45 per cent of the employees in private industry, the extent to which workers formally covered by them can count on actually receiving benefits when they retire is limited unfortunately. Not all pension plans are funded. It is common for the employer to reserve the right to terminate, modify, or amend the plan. Vesting, namely the workers' right on leaving a given employer before retirement to receive all or part of the benefits purchased on his behalf by the employer's contribution, is still relatively rare. And the period of service necessary to qualify for reasonably adequate pensions is still quite long. One authority has estimated that not more than half of those currently covered under private pension plans would ever receive a cash benefit because of lack of vesting.[3] There is also very limited protection for survivors in most of these plans.

Little is known about the level of benefits, although it is generally believed to be very modest, except for the higher-salaried and managerial employees. Nor does it seem that these plans will continue their past rapid growth in the future, except perhaps in the field of medical care. Already the rate of growth of pension plans is slowing down. It has been estimated that, by 1980, they may possibly cover as many as 42 million workers, and that the number of beneficiaries may increase from the present 2.25 millions to 6.5 millions. But this will affect no more than a third of the estimated number of aged beneficiaries under the public old-age insurance system by 1980.

Temporary-disability insurance and supplemental unemployment-benefit schemes have shown little growth in the proportion of workers covered in the last seven or eight years. And it must not be forgotten that the vast majority of covered workers have achieved their protection as part of the collective-bargaining process: the unorganized workers and those in the lowest-paid occupations have been, and are likely to be, little affected by this development.

Included among the employee-benefit plans are the very extensive programs for government employees. The 2.3 million employees of the federal government have their own retirement, survivors, disability, life-insurance, health-insurance, and workmen's compensation programs. About three-quarters of the 5

[3] Dan M. McGill, *Pensions: Problems and Trends* (Homewood, Illinois: Richard D. Irwin, 1955), p. 40. A more recent study takes an even dimmer view. See Merton G. Bernstein, *The Future of Private Pensions* (New York: Free Press of Glencoe, 1964), *passim*.

million state and local government employees have similar bene-fit schemes, giving retirement and disability protection; and al-most two-fifths of them are also covered by OASDI. The state employee-benefit systems, however, generally make only limited provision for survivors; and group life- and group health-insurance, where found, are usually on a voluntary basis. I think we can claim that, given our late start, we have done surprisingly well. Year by year, we have improved or extended our social-security programs, and, by now, they are accepted by all political parties as an essential part of our industrial society.

AN OVER-ALL EVALUATION

Yet this brief description of our social-security system will have made it evident that, like many other countries, we in the United States have much unfinished business before us. In fact, there are a number of problems that have been pointed to by almost every report of the many committees of inquiry and by academic studies of our programs that have been made in the last twenty years.

First, what we have is a patchwork of many programs which are far from well integrated. As a result, we have far too many gaps and anomolies and cannot yet claim that every American has equal access to at least minimum security. This results from the fact that our approach is characterized by a high degree of categorization. We use different techniques, such as social insurance and public assistance; we further subdivide people for social-security purposes according to the risk which is responsible for their loss of income. With such an approach, there is always the danger that some people will not be able to meet the eligi-bility conditions of any existing program. This would not matter if we had a residual underpinning public-assistance system avail-able everywhere for which the only eligibility condition was need, regardless of the reason why the person was in need. But our public-assistance programs, which in principle should per-form this function, are the weakest link in our chain of social-security measures.

Our patchwork system not only results in denying some people access to any form of socially provided income; it also leads to very different treatment of people in what would seem to be similar circumstances. In our unemployment-insurance programs, there are considerable differences from one state to another in the amount and duration of benefits that are paid to workers with similar employment histories. In public assistance the differences are even more glaring—the average payments in some states being more than twice as high as those in others. There are also differences of treatment between age groups that are difficult to justify. Children receive much less favorable treatment as a group under our public-assistance programs than do adults.

Second, we have not yet used social insurance, which is admittedly our preferred technique, to cover all insurable risks and all workers exposed to them. As I mentioned ealier, the risks of old age and loss of a breadwinner are indeed very comprehensively covered by social insurance: about 90 per cent of the working population (including the self-employed) are covered by the federal OASDI program. The risk of loss of earning power owing to disability is similarly covered by this program, but only if the disability is total, permanent, and has lasted more than six months. Short-term disability insurance entitles workers to social-insurance benefits in only four states, unless they are railroad employees or the disability was a result of an occupational injury or disease. And here, too, by no means all workers are covered by such programs. Social insurance provides benefits to unemployed workers, but only for relatively short-period unemployment (usually not more than six months), and the federal–state programs cover only about 80 per cent of all wage- and salary-workers. Above all, except for workers with occupational injuries, diseases, and, it now seems likely, for the aged, social insurance is not used to meet the costs of medical care.[4]

Third, in relation to the absolute levels of social-security benefits in most other countries, ours are high. Indeed the benefits of our old-age insurance system form a not insignificant part of the retirement income even of the middle classes. But our record is not so good if we measure these benefits in relation to earnings levels. The OASDI benefit of the single worker with earnings at about the average level amounts to only about 28 per cent of his

[4] In California, the temporary-disability program provides for limited hospitalization, and, in New York, some employers are permitted to offer medical benefits in lieu of cash disability benefits.

previous earnings (42 per cent for a married couple). It is even less for the higher wage-earners, although it is more for the lower-paid worker. Unemployment benefits replace perhaps 36 per cent of the insured worker's normal wages. This is partly because, unlike some other countries such as Germany or Sweden, we have not built any effective *automatic* devices into our social-insurance system for ensuring that our social-security benefits rise with wages and prices. We have, indeed, raised the money amount of OASDI benefits from time to time since 1935, and when we do so, we increase the benefits, not only for those coming on the benefit rolls in the future, but also for those who have already retired. But these changes have necessitated special legislation, and often there has been too long a time lag before the law has been changed.

The monthly payments under our public-assistance programs are even lower in most states. Although, in principle, these payments are supposed to make up the difference between the recipients' resources and the minimum standard of living defined by each state, in many states, especially in the poorer ones in the South, this minimum standard is very low, particularly for families with children. And some states do not even make payments large enough to ensure recipients the minimum standard of living as the state defines it.

Fourth, looking at our policies as a whole, I think it must be admitted that, in the last thirty years, most of the very considerable progress that we have made has been in the realm of the aged, whose security has been immeasurably improved over what it was before 1935. We have not done nearly so well by our children. We have made it clear that social insurance is the preferable type of social-security program. Yet children whose normal breadwinners cannot provide for them receive social-insurance benefits only when their breadwinners die or are totally and permanently disabled, in which case they draw survivor's or dependent's benefits. A quarter of the states provide dependent's benefits under their unemployment-insurance systems. But a very large number of children are in need because of family breakdown—their breadwinner has deserted the family or has separated from the mother without providing for adequate support, or their parents were never married. Such children have to depend on the much less desirable public-assistance system with its means test, its uncertainties in many states, and its relatively low payments. And we make no provision at all for the millions of children who are in poverty, even though they are living with both parents one of whom is employed, but who are members of relatively large families, except in the very few public-assistance programs that are prepared to subsidize wages. We do indeed recognize in our income-tax laws that large families cost more to support than small and grant exemptions for dependents. But these provisions are of little benefit to those who need help most, namely the families that are too poor even to be subject to income tax.

Fifth, whereas some people get little or inadequate protection from our social-security programs, others get favorable treatment because they can benefit from more than one public program. Some workers are able to draw benefits from both the OASDI and from the special programs for veterans. A smaller number draw benefits both from the federal disability-insurance system and from workmen's compensation.

Sixth, I suspect that before too long we shall have to reconsider the methods by which we finance our social-insurance programs. Up to now, our policy has been to insist that the entire costs of social insurance should be carried by wage and/or payroll taxes, and that there should be no contribution from the general revenues. We even go so far as to say that the cost of the unearned benefits extended to those who were already old when the system began and the cost of the increases in benefits given to the already retired should also be financed in this manner. Although low in comparison with many European countries, these taxes are already quite high in absolute terms; the combined tax for OASDI will soon rise to 9.5 per cent of payroll. In addition, employers may pay up to 3.4 per cent for unemployment insurance, although thanks to experience-rating, most of them pay considerably less than this. Employers also make additional contributions, averaging about 1 per cent of payroll, for workmen's compensation. The enactment of hospitalization or health insurance will make additional wage and payroll taxes necessary.

These taxes, especially the worker's share, are quite regressive, unlike the income tax which falls relatively more heavily on those who are richer. But the social-security taxes have no exemptions or deductions—they levy the same rate regardless of the size of income, and they collect nothing at all from incomes above a certain level, currently 4,800 dollars. Thus the cost of the programs is largely concentrated on the lower-income groups. Organized labor has so far opposed the introduction of a contribution from the general revenues, a position that is very different from that of most labor movements in other countries. This is because of labor's desire to emphasize and protect the insurance character of this program in which workers have rights to specified benefits. They fear, wrongly in my opinion, if general revenues were used, that there would be a danger that appropriations might be inadequate in some years or that receipt of the benefits might be made conditional on passage of a needs- or means-test. The provisions in the new Health Bill for financing the health benefits received by people who are not technically insured from general revenues is the first sign of a departure from our old policy of exclusive reliance on wage and payroll taxes.

Finally, we have not yet clarified the appropriate roles of the public and the private social-security systems. The latter are to some extent subsidized from public funds because contributions made by employers can be treated as a business cost for tax purposes. The extent to which such schemes should be encouraged is, in view of the fact that they benefit mainly the more highly paid and more regularly employed workers, a question of public policy to which we do not as yet have any clear answer. The issue is complicated by the possibility that any significant expansion of fringe benefits may weaken the pressure for improvements in the public social-security systems. The main pressure for liberalizations of OASDI in the past has come from organized labor, and if the powerful unions are able to secure high benefits for their own members through collectively bargained plans, they may be less interested in fighting to improve the basic public program.

PROSPECTS FOR THE FUTURE

There are many reasons for anticipating that in the near future we shall come to grips with these as yet unresolved problems. The first is our rediscovery of, and preoccupation with, the problem of poverty. Until recently, we had been in danger of forgetting that large numbers of people have not shared in our rising prosperity and that this disadvantage has been perpetuated in our social-security system. It is almost as if we have two groups of people: those who are regularly employed and higher paid receiving higher social-security benefits and often also fringe benefits, on the one hand, and, on the other, the irregularly employed and low-paid getting low social-insurance benefits or only public assistance and who are unlikely to benefit from em-ployee-benefit plans. The persistence of this dichotomy has been sharpened by the absence of a political labor party dedicated to promoting the interests of the underdog. The concern about poverty ensures that we can no longer neglect the needs of those who have not shared in general prosperity.

Second, there are signs of weakening of the power of those who oppose further public action. In the past, the American Medical Association and the private insurance companies had, through a highly organized and effective opposition, succeeded in preventing the enactment of even the most modest health-insurance programs. Organized medicine's distrust of public inter-vention in the financing and the organizing of medical care is practically universal, but in no other country has it been so com-pletely uncompromising or prepared to devote so much energy and money to fighting the popular will. The passage of the federal hospital insurance program and the federally subsidized major medical insurance system for the aged is evidence that such opposition can no longer prevail.

Third, despite the strong feeling about "states' rights," there are signs of a growing acceptance of federal leadership in a wide range of policy areas. In the social-security field, legislative pro-posals for federal standards in unemployment insurance, for which organized labor has unsuccessfully fought for so many years, now have Administration support and may well be enacted. Even in public assistance, there is growing sentiment in favor of more rigorous and extensive federal standards.

Finally, we are becoming increasingly aware of the full nature and different causes of economic insecurity and of the risks against which we have not provided until now. We have con-centrated on *interruption or cessation* of income as our major problem. Inability to earn income because of old age, disability, or involuntary unemployment, or the death of the breadwinner have been facts that we could not ignore, and we are making increasingly adequate provision against such risks. But we are now beginning to grapple with the continuing existence of long-period unemployment. We now recognize that a major threat to the economic security of women and children is the break-down of the family or even the failure of parents ever to form a stable family. Our difficulty is that we do not wholly know what to do about it.

Progressively as we fill the gaps in public protection against loss or interruption of earnings, the other causes of economic insecurity become more visible. We are now beginning to recognize that, even when the breadwinner is employed, his family may be insecure because his earnings are insufficient to meet the needs of his family on account of its size. This is a problem that can hardly be met by enacting higher minimum-wage legislation, although it would help in some cases. Whether we shall resolve it in the end by adopting some system of children's allowances or by making use of negative income taxes to channel more income to larger families remains to be seen. But I am sure that this is a problem that we shall no longer be able to neglect.

Similarly, we are increasingly realizing that because of the high level and unequal incidence of medical expenses, even if our social-security benefits are very considerably liberalized, there will still be many people who will be insecure because they cannot meet heavy medical expenses. Some method other than increasing everyone's cash benefits must be sought. The great issue before us is whether this other method should be public assistance or social insurance. I think we shall choose social insurance.

As we complete the fabric of protection against loss by interruption of earnings, and as our knowledge of the causes of economic insecurity becomes more exact, it also becomes evident that some people are insecure because they earn very little even when working. This is partly because they are poorly educated and trained, or are sick; but it is also because some of them are barred from entering more highly paid jobs by prejudice or union-membership rules. We are already beginning to grapple with these problems. Anti-discrimination laws, measures to prevent school dropouts, expansion of training and education through such measures as the Manpower Training and Development Act or the Area Redevelopment and Appalachia Acts, and special programs to enhance the employability of the young, such as the recently enacted Employment Opportunity Act are all efforts to deal with these obstacles to economic security.

21 THE ECONOMIC INFLUENCE OF AMERICAN UNIONS

George H. Hildebrand

Economics is an observational rather than an experimental science. It lacks recourse to the laboratory. In consequence it cannot conduct experiments under ideally controlled conditions in which some single influence can be varied deliberately to discern its separate effects with all other determining forces held constant. Instead, it must rely on statistical procedures that, at best, are but imperfect substitutes for the method of controlled experiment. Failing these, it must fall back on descriptive insight and even a measure of intuition.

This is the underlying technical problem posed when one asks: what is the influence of labor unions on the American economy? The same difficulty besets an attempt to predict, in any precise way, the effect on GNP of a tax cut of 10 billion dollars. Many variables influence the behavior of GNP, of which tax levies are but one. Similarly, many variables affect relative wages, the share of wages in the national income, and the behavior of the levels of wages and of prices. Among them is the institution of unionism and collective bargaining, but it is only one. In consequence, the issue of union impact cannot be finally resolved. For the same reason, pronounced differences of opinion exist among the experts who have studied these questions. Nonetheless, there is a measure of agreement in some areas, and we are not entirely bereft of knowledge or of well-based opinions at some points.

IMPACTS OF UNIONISM ON THE FIRM

Probably the firmest ground involves the impacts of the union on the enterprise itself. When collective bargaining is introduced into a firm, the entire scope of its manpower policies falls under a jointly controlled system of rule-making and administration. This system will naturally embrace the structure of jobs, the tasks to be assigned to each job, the method by which wages are to be fixed, the wage rate for the job, the provision of supplements to basic wages (overtime premiums, vacation and sick leave pay), and an apparatus of work rules affecting the output of workers on these jobs. Beyond this, the system will also regulate the flow of labor through the job structure: hiring, assignment, promotion, transfers, demotions, layoffs from work, and discharge.

Four elements in this collection of manpower rules are particularly likely to exert some upward influence on production costs. One arises from regularly recurring demands for higher pay rates and for larger supplemental benefits. The "going annual increase" is now the rule in American industrial life. A second factor concerns negotiated controls over manning and speeds of machinery, in which the union by its nature finds itself on the side of tighter rules and lower output per worker. This source of cost inflation is not common, although it has proved an acute problem in the railroad, construction, and printing industries. A third element is the ancient principle of the standard job rate which requires that all workers in a given job must be paid the same basic rate, regardless of differences in personal efficiency. Finally, unions of factory workers generally insist that the choice of employees for promotion, or for demotion and layoff, must give great, if not exclusive, weight to seniority or length of service with the employer. To some undetermined extent, this restriction on managerial choice reduces its opportunities for rational selection to increase the efficiency of its work force.

Taken by itself then, the regulatory system imposed through collective bargaining operates to raise the cost of labor and, usually, to lower its productivity. In consequence, we can say with some confidence that the initial advent of collective bargaining for a firm brings higher average labor-cost per unit of product. But this is by no means the end of the matter. In its larger aspect, unionism introduces a challenge-and-response mechanism in which management is the central responding force. If efficiency was already poor at the start, the cost-raising impact of the union can exert an initial shock-effect that may force management to seek cost-saving economies. But the challenge is a continuing one, and most managements are not without means to meet it—by improving equipment, changing organization of the work force, revamping production methods, and raising product prices. All this occurs, of course, within a context of continuing economic change as well, making it difficult to isolate the impact of the union as a separate force. But, there can be no doubt that collective bargaining decisively shapes and constrains the efforts of management to make profits.

At the same time, the attempt of a union to gain cost-raising benefits from a management depends on a variety of circumstances. If the union has failed to organize all of the firm's competitors, it will be weakened in pursuit of its objectives. If the industry is undergoing a long-run decline of its markets, the union will have to struggle with a host of special problems involving labor displacement. If general business conditions are prosperous, union demands will normally be larger and will be advanced with more militancy, while the employer will be less willing to "take a strike." In times of slump, the situation will be reversed.

PENETRATION INTO MANAGEMENT DESIGN-MAKING

Because the very essence of collective bargaining consists of substituting joint union–management rule-making and enforcement for exclusive managerial control over the use of manpower within the firm, it obviously reduces management's freedom to make decisions. To many businessmen, particularly those who are new to the bargaining system, this penetration into managerial affairs seems unlimited in ambitions and, thus, ultimately intended to replace all areas of unilateral control by full co-determination of enterprise policies. This view is mistaken. In the great majority of cases, management alone continues to decide on methods of production, types of products, selling prices, finance, location of plants, dividend and reinvestment policy, and capital outlays. There is compelling reason for this, and it is inherent within American unionism itself.

In the United States, the union is a market-oriented organization, viewing itself as an attack group to get more for its employee-members. For this purpose, it requires a profitable enterprise as much as a fish needs water. But it leaves it to management to provide the water. Accordingly, the union shuns any role that would make it jointly and explicitly responsible for the success or failure of the enterprise because the very assumption of that responsibility would turn the union into an agency of management, concerned no longer with gains for its members, but with increasing the efficiency of the business itself. In the nature of the case, the union is an organization deliberately created to protect and promote the interests of employees as employees, and not to advance the management's competing interest in higher business efficiency. In this conception of the relationship, the pursuit of efficiency is the responsibility of management, while the task of the union is to win a share of the fruits of higher efficiency at the bargaining table. For this reason, American unions have always zealously guarded their independence and have always viewed schemes for union–management cooperation with suspicion if not outright hostility. To some observers, this attitude seems perverse and unreasonable. Actually, it is the rational expression of the functional purpose that the unions have long since defined for themselves, and which they have pursued with notable success over the years.

To be sure, there have been rare occasions when a union has departed tacitly from principle, making concessions on wages and working rules to firms finding themselves in extreme difficulty. But even here, concessions are not always the rule. On the contrary, the national leadership of the organization will frequently insist that it is improper for the organization to permit local weakening of standards, that instead it is preferable to let weak firms go under and to bring about thereby a shift of their shares of the market to the more profitable and better wage-paying competitors. Thus, the thrust of American unionism has been to favor increasing concentration of the product market in the hands of fewer and stronger producers.

The traditional refusal of the unions to share responsibility for the efficiency of the business has had some large consequences that do much to explain the peculiar nature of the American labor movement. Vis-à-vis the enterprise, it centers the union's interest on a limited objective: an authoritative voice in the making of manpower policy, rather than in the conduct of the business as a whole. Furthermore, the union asserts this interest as an independent organization, responding to employee rather than managerial objectives. Even more, its objectives are shaped and guided by the national union with which the local unit is affiliated. This external tie strengthens the independence from management enjoyed by the local body. At the same time, it means that the local organization itself loses some discretion. The reason is that the national union is a syndicate that deals with many competing employers, hence formulates its local policies with this wider set of external interests in mind.

The very success of the American economic system has meant that the principle of collective bargaining for limited objectives has been able to yield a rich, recurring harvest. Simply because the principle works and works well, it continues to dominate the objectives of organized labor. In turn, this fact does much to account for the movement's complete lack of interest in classical socialist ideas. But this is not all. Concentration on bargaining has meant that for many decades the national unions, which now number over 200, have been the real centers of power, rather than the over-all labor federation. In consequence, this dispersion of power has led to decentralization and diversity of rule-making in the field of manpower policy. Except in the broadest sense, there is no typical pattern. And finally, the preoccupation of American unions with their private sectional interests means that any consensus on a national policy for wages and incomes is unlikely to emerge—an element of weakness from the broader standpoint of government efforts to achieve full employment and adequate growth without inflation.

IMPACTS OF UNIONISM ON THE WHOLE ECONOMY

So much for the direct impact of collective bargaining on the firm: let us now move outward and consider what we know about the influence of unions on the American economy as a whole. In doing so, we must bear in mind that the unions account for only 30 per cent of all nonagricultural employees; that their areas of strength center in manufacturing, mining, transportation, and construction; and that mainly, they represent "blue-collar" or production workers, rather than professional, technical, and clerical employees. Furthermore, these general characteristics have remained typical ever since the last great upsurge of unionism, which took place in the late 1930's. Finally, as we have just contended, American unionism takes its *raison d'être* from bargaining struggle, not class struggle. That is, it relies primarily on collective bargaining with private employers for the definition and pursuit of its objectives. True, it employs political pressures as well, but it does so mainly to strengthen and supplement its bargaining activities in the labor market. It has not created a national party; it does not seek nationalization of any industry; and it is not attempting to bring about a system of government price control.

RELATIVE SHARES IN NATIONAL INCOME

Consider, now, the influence of unionism on the share of wages and salaries in the national product. The long-run trend of labor's percentage share has been slowly upward. But no expert who has studied the problem contends that unionism has had much if anything to do with this shift. Rather, the main forces have been the rapid growth of government employment, the unexpected rising importance of labor-intensive industries in total production, and the decline of the small entrepreneur. Even more, the rise in the wage share has not cut permanently into the share of profits, primarily because American management has been remarkably successful in offsetting the cost-raising impacts of collective bargaining through extensive innovations in production methods. At this point, the argument takes a different form: it is contended that wage-fixing by collective bargaining has prevented labor's share from otherwise falling. But there is no convincing reason why labor's share should fall over the long run. For many years capital stock has increased more rapidly than the supply of labor, and this relationship has worked to raise real wages and labor's relative share, not the reverse.

RISE IN REAL LEVEL OF WAGES

This is but another way of saying that competition itself works to raise both the productivity and the wages of workers generally, union and nonunion alike. This very fact makes it extremely difficult to gauge the independent contribution of unionism to wage advances. Official statistics show that between 1947 and 1963, output per man-hour and real wages per employee-hour in the nonagricultural business sector both rose at a compound annual rate of about 3 per cent. In comparison, money-wages per hour rose at about 5 per cent yearly, meaning that most of the gains in productivity were being distributed through higher wages rather than falling prices. But to what extent was the rise in money and real wages together affected by unionism and collective bargaining?

One point of view holds that only a minority of unions has the power to force up wages beyond the normal competitive rate of advance. This group consists of the so-called craft unions that have exclusive control over some particular function or skill and can make this type of labor artificially scarce by restricting the entry of apprentices into the trade. By contrast, the "industrial" or mixed unions embrace many different occupations, some requiring little or no skill. Since they have no effective way to limit the entry of new workers, it is argued that they cannot force up wages. And because the craft unions embrace not more than a quarter of all unionized workers, their impact upon the over-all wage level is negligible.

In my opinion, the craft unions do have net wage-raising power, although I doubt that it can be measured with precision. These organizations are strong in building construction, printing and publishing, entertainment, and on the railroads. These same industries have been the leaders in wage gains since the end of

World War II, and even comparatively unskilled groups within the sector are highly paid.

However, the ability to limit entry into a trade is not the sole source of a union's economic power. Otherwise it will be difficult to explain the large gains won by open industrial unions such as the United Automobile Workers and United Steelworkers. Many of these organizations have certainly kept pace with the crafts ever since the war and today rank at the top or very close to it in wages and benefits paid. But at no time have they been able to prevent the entry of new workers. The real secret of their strength lies in a combination of factors: complete organization of all firms, restricted competition in the product market, the ability to mount very effective strikes, and a willingness to trade off some gains in employment to win large wage benefits for the existing membership. Moreover, these unions have been the most important innovators in the field, introducing private pension schemes, supplemental unemployment-benefit plans, early retirement provisions, severance pay, long vacations, the cost-of-living escalator, an automatic tie between wage rates and productivity, and a joint union–management job-evaluation plan.

It must be admitted that not all of the open industrial unions enjoy such strength because of inability to organize all firms, adverse movements in product demand, or rapid displacement of labor through mechanization. Nonetheless, within the manufacturing sector there has been a remarkable parallelism in postwar wage gains from contract-round to contract-round. More than this, the parallelism has helped advance gross hourly earnings of production workers by between 4.5 and 5.0 per cent yearly (simple average) throughout the decade after 1953, despite a contraction of nearly a million jobs in the field. Indeed, gains of similar or even larger magnitude have been won in several highly unionized industries both inside and outside of manufacturing in these years, despite an over-all loss of 2 million jobs—evidence that points directly to the wage-raising power of labor organizations. If they lack this power, we could expect wages in these fields to rise no faster than 2.5 to 3 per cent yearly, and perhaps even less.

The contention that many unions do have net wage-raising power is also supported by a highly interesting comparison of wage movements during 1923–1929 as against the postwar years, group by group. Except for the very small extent of unionization in the twenties, over-all economic conditions were quite similar in the two periods: low rates of unemployment, rather rapid gains in labor productivity and in gross and per capita real output. Yet blue-collar workers obtained much greater advances in real and money wages in the post-World War II years, the period in which unionism had emerged strong and had become widespread.

WAGE-PUSH INFLATION

But again we must remind ourselves that American unionism today embraces only 30 per cent of all nonagricultural employees (17.2 million members out of 57.3 million total in 1962). Does it have the power to impose an inflationary rate of increase on the entire wage level and, through this, on the price level as well? This is the problem of cost-push inflation, and it is an issue over which there is extensive professional disagreement.

According to the "classical" position, only the craft unions can really push up wages, and their impact is negligible for the whole economy. What really governs the entire wage and price levels is the rate of expansion in the money supply. If this rate is too rapid, demand inflation follows, pulling up both wages and prices. In such circumstances, all unions can win large increases, although this showing of power is claimed in truth to be illusory. The real source of the wage advances originates from money, not from bargaining power. But illusory as the power may be, it may yet convince political leaders that it is real, and so they may yield to union demands for an inflationary monetary and fiscal policy to preserve full employment. This is another way of saying that the monetary managers in the country have somehow become the captives of organized labor.

This "demand-pull" model works well in explaining the American inflations during World War II, 1945–1948, and the Korean War. Also, its proponents can point to the lack of long-run evidence that wages in the union sector have been steadily widening their advantage over those in the larger nonunion sector; if unions really do force up wages, one would expect it to widen.

Nonetheless, there is an alternative view, and it is one that has been gaining currency among several experts in recent years. According to this position, the demand-pull model of inflation cannot explain wage and price movements since 1953, for in this decade the American economy has at no time experienced excess total demand. Indeed, it has undergone three mild recessions and has had unemployment rates of over 5 per cent of the labor force continuously since 1957. Yet between 1953 and 1960, wages in manufacturing continued to rise rapidly enough to force up labor cost per unit of product, despite slack demand. As for the failure of union wages to widen their spread, it is argued that gains won in the union sector spill over to the nonunion sector as well for good reason: acting out of fears of unionization and from a desire to prevent a costly rise in labor turnover and training expense, most nonunion employers will match the rate of advance developing in the union sector. Thus the two sectors march along closely together, although the unionized one is the real leader, and the over-all rate of advance in wages tends to be faster than it would be if there were no unions anywhere in the economy.

A recent careful study shows rather conclusively that wage agreements in manufacturing are highly and directly responsive to upshifts in profits. As expansion gets under way, profits soon move upward, whereupon contract settlements become much costlier. Together with spill-over, this cost-push process soon causes wage increases to outrun advances in labor productivity. In consequence, labor-cost per unit of product begins to rise, squeezing profit margins and forcing up prices. In those industries in which competition is quite limited, sellers may raise prices even more than the collateral increases in unit labor-cost. In any case, the advance of prices brings the threat of reduced exports and rising capital outflows, which worsen the international payments deficit.

On this reasoning, the pursuit of full employment may be obstructed by the early advent of troubles with the foreign balance, with the latter originating from the side of wage-and-price policy costs. For this reason, the Council of Economic Advisors introduced a wage-and-price "guideposts" policy in early 1962, in hopes that managements and the unions would confine their wage- and price-making decisions within noninflationary limits. Whether this is an effective approach to the cost-push problem remains to be seen. In my judgment, however, the guideposts are needed and are well conceived, for I think the American economy does have an inherent inflationary bias for which union wage-policy bears important, although not solo, responsibility.

ECONOMIC GROWTH

What impacts have the unions had on the growth of the American economy? In part, but only in part, the growth of total output depends directly on increase in the quantity of man-hours available. In turn, the latter is governed by the rate of growth in the population, the extent to which the population of working age enters the labor force, and the hours of work which each member of the force stands ready to provide per day, week, year, and over a lifetime.

Over their lengthy history, it is safe to say that the unions have followed policies that have slowed the growth of available man-hours in total impact. In the main, they have done so in pursuit of other objectives. In the earlier period, their goals were the shorter workweek and workday, more secondary education, and thus a later school-leaving age, prevention of child labor, and an earlier age of retirement—goals that the unions achieved directly through collective bargaining and indirectly through successful pressure for legislation. Moreover, they were attained only gradually. And, in part, the restraining effect on the potential growth of man-hours for work was offset by the favorable effect of these measures themselves, which increased the efficiency and productivity of the labor force. In the past quarter-century, the unions have concentrated on shortening the workyear, as the indirect consequence of winning or extending paid vacations and paid holidays. Here the ensuing gains in productivity have probably been too small to offset the reduction in available working time.

Economic growth is also promoted by labor mobility, which redistributes the labor force from less to more productive uses. Here the union impact has been mixed. On the one hand, unionism generally improves the efficiency of the labor market, by providing labor exchanges and better job information. On the other, where it forces up wages and creates or adds to unemployment, the very fact that wages are made comparatively high operates to hold workers where they are no longer needed, instead of inducing them to shift elsewhere.

Finally, of course, growth is promoted by investment and managerial efficiency. From their inception, the American unions have fought consistently for subsidized public education at all levels. This investment in human capital is, economists now believe, a powerful force for lifting worker productivity. As for investment in plant and equipment, the unions have had a limited and probably adverse influence. The reasons are that they have favored heavy taxation of profits, and their cost-raising policies have both reduced profit margins and, in some cases, compelled investment that might otherwise more profitably have been made elsewhere. In the area of business efficiency, the general impact of collective bargaining has been somewhat adverse because it regulates and constrains management. But against this, it must be recognized also that in its fuller development, collective bargaining may contribute something to worker morale which would favor higher efficiency.

SUMMARY

To sum up, the American unions have helped to bring into being a pluralistic form of democratic society, in which worker interests come into more effective competition with those of owners, managers, and consumers. We cannot say that a perfect balance has been achieved, but it is reasonable to conclude that rough justice has been attained. Without trade unions, the competing claims of workers as workers would be less likely to receive their due consideration. Notwithstanding the pressures exerted by unionism, and indeed partly because of those very pressures, the American economy has demonstrated dramatically over the years its capacity to grow and to distribute its fruits generously and widely over the whole population. By the broad success of collective bargaining as a localized system of private rule-making jointly between employers and unions, it has proved possible to hold down the burden of government regulation of industry, and to bring together power and responsibility for guiding the manpower policies of the organized sector of the business community. This peculiar system may not be readily exportable, but there is little doubt that it has worked well in the United States. If it can maintain the flexibility and adaptability that it has shown in the past, it will continue to perform effectively in the future.

22 THE INTERNATIONAL ACTIVITIES OF AMERICAN TRADE UNIONS

Victor Reuther

In 1965 it was taken for granted that an important part of the world's work falls to international organizations and institutions and that international conferences, international travel, and the exchange of personnel among the nations of the world are routine and accepted features of the daily scene.

An increasing number of American trade unionists work at what are called "international labor activities" today, either for the AFL-CIO, international organizations sponsored by the AFL-CIO in Africa and Latin America, for the International Confederation of Free Trade Unions, for the International Trade Secretariats, or for their own unions. At least a dozen American unions have a full-time staff detailed to international labor assignments. Unions conduct frequent conferences on what are called international labor problems. Almost at any time during 1966, there will be American trade unionists in Europe, Africa, Asia, Latin America, and among the Pacific nations on official union missions. They will be taking part in training institutes in the Caribbean, organizing vocational training centers in Africa, consulting on joint programs with Histadrut at the Afro-Asian Institute in Tel-Aviv. They will be working with labor research personnel in Tokyo at the newly established International Wage Research Center in that city, they will be attending steel conferences in Europe, speaking at Common Market autoworker meetings, helping to organize housing cooperatives in Mexico or Venezuela, giving technical assistance on union health programs in the Argentine, discussing international trade questions in Paris or Geneva, teaching at labor-training institutes in two dozen countries, studying the problems of trade unions in Vietnam, or consulting with the Peace Corps in Guinea on counterpart training in tractor repair-stations.

WORLD-WIDE SOCIETY

Trade unions are, of course, not unique in this ecumenical interest. Without a single exception, each of the hundred largest corporations that the UAW bargains with has overseas investments and operations. What is true in the auto industry is equally true in steel, in the electrical industry, in petroleum, in chemicals, and even in retail distribution. When American trade unionists go overseas on international missions, they invariably encounter U.S. university personnel, representatives of farm organizations, doctors, lawyers, and travelers from an entire range of American professions, industry, and institutions. The 1960's, which has been inadequately tagged as the Decade of Development or recently as the Decade of Despair, should more properly be characterized as the Decade of International Organization, for this development is both new in scale and significant historically. It marks the emergence of an international society that will inevitably engage the concern and prospects of more and more Americans as well as of Australians, of Englishmen, and of Africans, of Bolivians, and, for that matter, of Chinese and of Russians.

Yet it should be emphasized that what appears new is new only in scale and its institutionalized equipment. International interrelationships have, of course, always existed. In the labor movement, as in American society, there has never been a time when the nation has been totally insulated from the world.

EUROPEAN AID TO AMERICAN UNIONS

Like practically every other American institution, the American labor movement had its origins in European historical developments. In the metal trades some of the earliest U.S. labor organizations were branches of English unions. Thus in 1867, the Amalgamated Engineers Union had eleven local affiliates in the

U.S. American garment unions owe their origins and institutional character in large measure to the reformist zeal of eastern European political organizations. In subsidizing trade-union organizational activities in Asia, Africa, and Latin America, U.S. unions are only following a little-known precedent by which European democratic worker-organizations gave subventions to young trade-union leaders in the United States. European trade unionists not only influenced the American labor movement, they helped organize it. Certainly the organizational facility and bargaining skills displayed by the new CIO unions in the thirties were a result, in some measure, of the experience that many of the local union leaders had acquired in the English and Scottish trade unions. American unions were not only influenced from abroad, but were influential reciprocally. The fervor of the Knights of Labor found roots in Belgian and British lodges. The Industrial Workers of the World left ideological and organizational traces throughout the world, but especially in Latin America, and in the Scandinavian countries.

Yet although it is quite proper to insist that the American trade unions have always had some international ties, both coming and going, it would be misleading to suggest that there is not a profound difference between the present organizational effort overseas by American trade unions and the largely undirected and formless relationship which prevailed until World War II. Historically, modern international labor relations for U.S. unions coincide with the inauguration of the postwar aid program of the U.S. government through the Marshall Plan and took organizational shape in the founding of the International Confederation of Free Trade Unions.

THE DEVELOPED UNIONS HELP NEW UNIONS

During the past twenty years, American labor ventures overseas have received so disproportionate a share of the attention of scholars and journalists that there is an impression that this area of activity is, with only minor exceptions, exclusively American and is an expression of American egocentricity, or of American arrogance, or of American imperialism, or of some kind of American self-righteous missionary zeal. In reality, there is no

well-established national labor movement which does not engage
to some degree in an overseas program including both the traditional activities associated with the international labor organizations and the modern enterprises which have come to be
associated with technical assistance. The most recent entrants
into the international field are the Italian and the Japanese
trade unions. The British trade unions were, of course, in a
sense, the first on the scene; but today Germans, French, Swedes,
Norwegians, Danes, Swiss, Austrians, Israelis, and Arabs all carry
on activities which generally can be classified as international
labor programs. With the important distinction that their international labor activities, unlike those of free unions, are administratively government activities, Russians, Chinese, Czechs,
Cubans, and East Germans similarly busy themselves in labor
affairs outside their own borders.

BASIC MOTIVES OF LABOR PROGRAMS OVERSEAS

Press headlines have also tended to distort the basic motives
for international labor activities, which however much they have
been obscured by the weight of international government aid
programs and the Cold War, are substantially unchanged from
the first ventures one hundred years ago. The fact is, that for
the entire history of the labor movement in Western countries, it
has always been possible to go before a meeting of workers at
their local or branch union gatherings and to get a unanimous
vote for a contribution to fellow trade unionists caught in an
extremity, whether as the result of a strike, a mine disaster, or
government oppression wherever they are, in South Africa, in
Paraguay, in Georgia, in Germany, or Japan. U.S. workers, in an
instinctive reaction, send help to striking miners in France;
Japanese workers voted funds in support of the steel strike in
the U.S. several years ago; Indian workers demonstrated in Bom-
bay, Madras, and other cities, on behalf of General Motors
strikers in the U.S.

Solidarity in the union and in the world is a vital basis for
building and maintaining the strength of workers' organizations
and for achieving their social and economic aspirations. Most
wage-earners the world over believe in the right of workers every-

where to organize in autonomous unions, have a deep sense of compassion for fellow workers in trouble, and believe that ultimately the achievement of freedom and well-being by workers in any country depends on the attainment of these goals for workers everywhere. In addition, international labor efforts have been concerned with attempts to stop traffic in strikebreakers, securing recognition of journeyman cards for wandering unionists, and attempts to maintain wages from erosion through competition based on substandard scales.

CHANGES IN SCALE

Recognizing the historical persistence of the solidarity tradition in international labor affairs, it would still be impossible to understand the international labor scene today without acknowledging the decisive changes in scale, in method, in personnel, and in rationale which have transformed international labor cooperation from a fundamentally utopian endeavor into a major strand in the web of relationships which constitutes the whole texture of international economic, social, and government affairs.

Without weighting or according any one development primacy, the factors which contribute to the present importance of international labor activities are (1) the increased importance of unions in the community and in the government of most free countries, and especially the vital role that unions played in the achievement of independence in the new nations; (2) the acceptance in the Western countries of the trade-union movement as a legitimate and accredited voice for wage-earners; (3) the importance of economic aid, which tends to acknowledge in overseas activities the new status of trade unions in their own countries; (4) the institutionalization of the labor movement in each country which brings with it access to financial resources and the command of professional personnel; (5) communist foreign policy with its emphasis on penetration and subversion of trade unions, which necessarily provokes an intensive counter-effort by both the free nations and the free and democratic trade unions; (6) the expansion and growth in importance of international organizations, especially the United Nations, the Common Market, International Labor Organization (ILO), and General Agreement on

Trade and Tariffs (GATT), which accelerated the evolution of a parallel structure in the labor movement for representation and coordination of trade-union activities on the international level; (7) and finally, without exhausting the list of influences, the internationalization of corporate business activities which is fostering coordinate relations among various national unions dealing with these companies.

THE MEASURE OF IMPORTANCE

Two illustrations—the new representation of individuals drawn from trade-union ranks in the foreign offices of government and the financial commitment of the unions themselves to international affairs—measure the scale of the transformation. In almost every country where the United States maintains a mission, there are labor attachés and labor reporting officers. Within the State Department itself, there is a labor advisor to the secretary and labor advisors for each region. In the Agency for International Development (AID) in almost every mission overseas, there are labor advisors recruited from the present labor movement. The United States Information Agency's (USIA) staffs also include labor information specialists in some countries. Except for notable exceptions, such as the participation of Samuel Gompers in the Versailles meeting after World War I and the AFL representation at ILO after 1934, the role of unionists in international governmental affairs before World War II was nonexistent. Increased financial resources have also made a difference. In the first ten years of the existence of the International Secretariat of Trade Union Centers, which was the first in a series leading to the contemporary International Confederation of Free Trade Unions (ICFTU), 700,000 dollars was distributed in strike relief. This was the greater part of its total expenditures. Today the scale is quite different: 25 per cent of the total budget of the AFL-CIO is allocated to international affairs activities. Similar heavy commitments have been undertaken by the Swedes, Germans, and others.

Inevitably the structure of the labor movement in each country determines the method of its operation. In the United States, relations with the ICFTU, the United Nations, and other international governmental organizations; participation in governmental programs; relations with national labor federations overseas; and the administration of the two largest aid efforts to labor in Latin America and Africa are the responsibility of the AFL-CIO.

Among these initiatives, by far the most extensive overseas undertaking is that of the American Institute for Free Labor Development (AIFLD). This organization is governed by a board of directors composed of AFL-CIO officials and employer representatives. Contributions to its operating funds come from both the AFL-CIO and the employers; however, the largest portion of the budget represents U.S. government appropriations. The AIFLD is divided organizationally into two major activities. The Social Projects Division is concerned with the building of workers' housing, credit unions, and various other cooperative enterprises and has had, to date, a measure of success in initiating some worthwhile projects. Criticism has generally been directed at the AIFLD's other major activity—its role in trade-union training and education. Serious reservations have been expressed about its structure and orientation, from its inception, by trade unionists in the U.S. and in Latin America.

As AIFLD was originally conceived, the American labor movement together with a select group of responsible community leaders committed to social development would organize a nonprofit agency which would finance democratic development programs through contributions from the labor movement, grants from foundations, governmental grants, and AID contracts. Its objective was to meet an urgent need for a flexible, effective agency capable of mobilizing the energies, experience, and talents of the American labor movement and community organizations with expertise in economic and social development for the specific purpose of strengthening democratic institutions in the American hemisphere and to ensure that a proper share of American aid under the Alliance for Progress was allocated to social programs in the recipient countries.

The AIFLD has developed, in accordance with this original conception, with one unfortunate and critical departure—the decision to appoint American business leaders with interests in Latin America to the Board of Directors. Their presence on AIFLD's Board seriously compromises its trade-union training and educational role. Its structure exposes it to the charge of conflict of interest and is a propaganda gift to the enemies of free-trade unions who effectively characterize these businessmen as symbols of Yankee imperialism and enemies of social progress in Latin America.

It is to be expected, of course, that in a democratic society there will be differences of opinion over any policy which seeks to represent the different views of almost 140 autonomous national unions and some 14 million people. However, it is note-worthy that there are almost no reservations in the American labor movement with respect to the union-to-union activities that the affiliated unions of the AFL-CIO carry on under the auspices of the International Trade Secretariats to which they are affiliated.

UNION-TO-UNION

The United Steelworkers which for many years has assisted Venezuela and West Indian workers in primary iron and aluminum industries to negotiate contracts which are hardly inferior to those in the United States is extending similar assistance to workers in the metal extractive industries in Africa. A steelworkers mission in Japan several years ago demonstrated how Japanese steelworkers in the event of a strike could shut down a steel plant without damage to the installation which might jeopardize their jobs when the strike was settled. U.S. railroad workers helped Argentine railroad workers organize an important strike effort in that country by sharing their strike administrative experience. The American Newspaper Guild shares in the responsibility for seminars in Latin America for the purpose of explaining the technique of collective bargaining to journalists.

The International Union of Electrical Workers has been meeting over a period of years with Denkei Roren, the Japanese union in the electrical trades, for the purpose of coordinating their bargaining efforts with General Electric and Westinghouse, and today operates under the terms of mutual-assistance agreement with that union. U.S. union engineers and time-study specialists have given technical advice on problems relating to incentive systems and time study to unions in most of the free countries of the world. The International Ladies Garment Workers sponsors a vocational training center jointly with the unions in Kenya where Kenyans are trained in manufacturing garments. U.S. oil workers have helped the employees of the giant oil companies organize in unions from the Red Sea to the Caribbean. The International Association of Machinists is cooperating in the administration of an auto mechanics' training program in Nigeria. The ICFTU training schools in Africa, in India, and in Mexico draw on the American unions for teachers.

UAW AND THE INTERNATIONAL CORPORATIONS

The UAW, which is the largest affiliate of the AFL-CIO, is perhaps the union in the U.S. whose international activities have received the most public attention. Last year, wide publicity was given to participation by the union in the World Auto Conference which was presided over by President Walter Reuther (UAW) and had been called by the International Metalworkers' Federation (IMF) in Frankfurt. The beginning of a new era in international affairs for the union, this meeting was attended by international working parties in Ford, General Motors, Chrysler-Fiat-Simca, and Volkswagen and was a culmination of fifteen years of evolution.

At this Frankfurt meeting, one hundred twenty representatives of two million autoworkers from some thirty countries made a recommendation, adopted a week later by the IMF World Congress in Vienna, to establish continuing world councils of autoworkers in each of the international auto companies as well as in the other international manufacturing corporations. Unquestionably, this emphasis on international coordination of bargaining activities will be at the center of UAW overseas activities in the future. This concern, which also has found expression in the international oil industry, will probably be reflected in the programs of other trade secretariats and free unions. In this area, the UAW has, because of its resources, formulated explicitly both in its resolutions and in its activities the rationale and the program goals, not only of the American unions, but of free unions throughout the world.

Like workers everywhere in the free world, UAW members are apprehensive concerning the threatening advances by automation to their job security within their own plants and are deeply concerned over the international boundary-leaping activities of the giant world-wide corporations. The forward thrust of the twentieth-century technological revolution is internationalizing the tools of production in a complex world economy.

THE UAW PROGRAM

Yet parallel to the ability of the world corporations to operate outside the limits of national societies, the free-trade unions also have demonstrated that they have a potential for effective international action commensurate with the problems wage-earners face. By improving the lives of wage-earners and their families, by expanding job opportunities within the society, by demanding housing, health, education, and other socially necessary programs, unions deal directly with the national discontents that are the source of social instability, unrest, and war. The international solidarity of free-trade-union members is not an abstraction. It expresses the hopes and aspirations that workers hold in common throughout the world.

THE TECHNIQUE OF SOLIDARITY

Workers in the same international corporations and in the same international industrial sectors can cooperate in and coordinate their collective-bargaining programs. To put this principle into practice, UAW delegates to the union's eighteenth constitutional convention created the UAW International Free World Labor Defense Fund. By an overwhelming vote they revised the UAW constitution to provide that the interest accruing to the UAW strike benefit fund shall be utilized exclusively for projects and activities expressing their sense of solidarity with auto, metal, and other workers around the world. By their action, they committed a minimum of 1 million dollars per year toward developing the bonds of friendship and solidarity.

International Business Machines gives its name to processes at work in every country of the world. General Motors manufactures products in more than twenty-three countries. Ford production workers draw wages not only in the United States and Canada, but also in Brazil, Bermuda, Australia, the Republic of South Africa, Southern Rhodesia, New Zealand, the Congo, the United Arab Republic, France, Italy, Portugal, Belgium, Switzerland, Germany, Norway, Finland, Sweden, Denmark, and the Netherlands. Recently a Ford Motor Company Committee went to Japan to look the situation over. Massey-Ferguson, International Harvester, Chrysler, Borg-Warner, Sperry-Rand, Kelsey Hayes, American Motors, and General Electric, Westinghouse, switch orders, jobs, and production on international control boards. American companies are going overseas, and foreign companies are coming to the United States and Canada: Volkswagen, Saab, Renault, Fiat, Olivetti.

As Frederick G. Donner, board chairman of General Motors, told a world meeting of accountants at the Waldorf-Astoria Hotel in New York, modern corporations are "no longer adequately described as Dutch, German, French, Italian, British or U.S. corporations . . . the emergence of the modern industrial corporation . . . is creating a new kind of capitalism."[1]

Organizationally the chief solidarity effort of the UAW has been through the International Metalworkers' Federation. Responding to a UAW challenge to raise 1 million dollars a year for international solidarity activities among metalworkers around the world, IMF affiliates have already collected more than 750,000 dollars of which the UAW contributed a fourth.

As the result of a UAW Mission to Japan led by President Reuther, an International Wage Research Center has been established in Tokyo with the support of the labor movement of the free world, and sponsored by the four Japanese labor federations in a unique display of cooperation. In this pioneering venture, the ICFTU, the IMF, major European centers, the AFL-CIO, the Industrial Union Department of the AFL-CIO, and the UAW are joined together to promote the creation of a research center that will have an impact on collective bargaining throughout the world.

As a first task, focusing on the metal industry, the research center will supply economic data, labor-cost statistics, and comparisons which will enable unions to strengthen their common

[1] Frederick G. Donner, chairman of General Motors Corporation (September 27, 1962), New York, N.Y.

efforts to increase wages and improve working conditions. For the first time, data will be assembled to provide economic arguments for upward harmonization of wages, hours, and social benefits. The first world-wide conference of aerospace workers has already met to plan for stabilizing employment in this highly erratic industry. Steel unions, electrical unions, ship unions, and foundry workers meet regularly under the auspices of the IMF.

UAW IN AFRICA

UAW has shared in other ICFTU programs intended to help women win equal pay for equal work, equal rights, and equal opportunities on the job and in the community and in the struggle for freedom on the African continent.

UAW support has also gone to specific programs on the African continent:

(1) an apprenticeship training school in Austria where African youths learn skilled trades necessary for the development of their nation;

(2) a free-press activity which finances democratic trade-union publications in Africa, trains writers and printers, and provides basic printing equipment;

(3) organizational assistance to the struggle for freedom in Northern Rhodesia;

(4) scholarships to provide Arab refugees apprentice training in tractor, truck, and auto maintenance to meet an important manpower deficiency in the Arab countries;

(5) aid through the American Committee on Africa to the legal defense and relief of the victims of apartheid in South Africa and medical care to the fighters for freedom in Angola;

(6) assistance to the Afro-Asian Institute in Tel-Aviv where young African and Asian union leaders receive training in the operations of unions, cooperatives, and other democratic institutions;

(7) support to ICFTU Documentation Center for Arab Trade Unions in Lebanon.

New potentialities for solidarity undertakings in Africa have also been explored by the ten-member UAW Africa Mission which met in 1964 with the heads of state and trade-union leaders in sixteen countries of Africa and the Near East.

WHY IS SOLIDARITY VITAL?

But what seems self-evident to union members still provokes questions from some people: why does a trade union in the U.S. or in Europe engage in vocational training in Africa, in the support of cooperative housing in Latin America, or in technical assistance to Turkish unions? The answer goes back to the ideological idealism of the trade-union movement itself which compels the union, whatever the pressure or temptation to be practical, to insist on its central moral purpose. Every democratic trade unionist in the world ratifies and applauds UAW President Walter Reuther's expression of this conviction and commitment in New Delhi before the Indian Council on World Affairs on April 5, 1956.

Free labor understands and acts in the knowledge that the struggle for peace and the struggle for human freedom are inseparably tied together with the struggle for social justice. Free labor understands the social dynamics of our changing world. We understand the struggle of those who are hungry in their search for bread, of those who are oppressed in their search for freedom. We have geared our struggle not to be a negative program of anti-Communism but rather to a positive program for social justice. We believe that it is not enough to fight against the things that we oppose—we must fight with equal courage and equal dedication for the things that we believe in.

The language echoes one hundred years of resolutions. The difference is that today there are institutional and financial means to take the declarations out of resolutions and to put them to work in a day-to-day international trade-union effort.

23 WHITHER LABOR: RECENT DEVELOPMENTS IN THE STRENGTH AND PHILOSOPHY OF AMERICAN LABOR

A. H. Raskin

Some thirty years have gone by since the passage of the Wagner Act and other elements of Franklin D. Roosevelt's New Deal put a solid legal foundation under collective bargaining and opened the way for unionization of the mass-production industries. Ten years have passed since the two great power centers of United States unionism—the American Federation of Labor and the Congress of Industrial Organizations—pooled their economic, political, and social strength and merged into a single organization of 15 million members.

When Roosevelt entered the White House there were fewer than 3 million workers in unions. Today there are roughly 17 million. But it would not be accurate to present this as a picture of uninterrupted growth. On the contrary, the great upsurge was concentrated in the first half of the period. Since 1950, the number of workers in union ranks has stood still, even though total employment in nonfarm jobs has risen from 52 million to a present total of 66 million. The explanation for this sudden halt in the expansion of the American labor movement lies principally in the dramatic change that has taken place in the last decade in the character of the American economy.

The industries that have been the traditional backbone of union strength—manufacturing, mining, and transportation—have had such an increase in productivity that they can generate a much greater volume with many fewer workers. This decline in the goods-producing sectors of the economy has been more than offset by a growth in employment in the service sectors. The proportion of workers engaged in production fell below 50 per cent for the first time in 1955; it is now down to 45 per cent and still falling. Indeed, the prospect of large-scale installation of automated equipment in the next twenty years makes it certain that much more of the productive burden will be shifted from men to machines, with an even faster shrinkage in goods-producing employment.

To complicate the problem for unions, even within the production sector, the nature of jobs is changing in ways that necessitate fundamental revisions in union approach. Blue-collar workers are being replaced by white-collar workers and technicians—groups for whom unions have never had any great appeal. Whether labor will demonstrate enough imagination and resourcefulness to adapt its programs to the needs of these new groups in the service, clerical, and professional fields is one of the unresolved questions on which its future as a vital force in American democracy depends. There are reasons for both optimism and pessimism on this score, but before attempting to evaluate them, I should like to consider in some detail what seems to me the outstanding basic accomplishment of United States unions in recent years.

This accomplishment relates to the very substantial gains labor has made to guarantee lifetime income security for industrial workers. Over the years, nothing has contributed more to undermine the peace of mind and the economic well-being of hourly rated workers and their families than the unremitting uncertainty that they have had about how much money they would bring home each week and how long their jobs would last. Automation has vastly sharpened these fears of job loss, but it has also provided a powerful new instrument to do something about overcoming such worry.

New protective walls are being built around the pay check and, thus, are helping to take workers off the rollercoaster of feast-or-famine employment. This new development is, in many respects, an extension of the unique system of social security with a union label that began in the coal fields and the needle trades immediately after World War II. Employers accepted the idea that they had an obligation to workers "too old to work and too young to die."

Programs of health, hospital, and life insurance were established to protect workers, then, extended to cover their wives and children. Now they embrace everything from pregnancy to psychiatric care, and the benefits become more generous with each cycle of collective bargaining. Industry-financed pension programs encourage early retirement, with the triple purpose of adding to the dignity of old age, ensuring greater regularity of employment for the existing work force, and opening up more work opportunities for youngsters entering the job market.

A worker at General Motors, Ford, or Chrysler will receive 70 per cent of his normal wages, up to a maximum of 400 dollars a month, if he chooses to retire at sixty. All that he needs to qualify for this program is ten years of service. Workers with thirty years on the payroll will be free to retire as early as age fifty-five at a pension of 200 dollars a month. When the original UAW pension contracts were negotiated in 1949, the minimum retirement age was sixty-five, and the benefit was 100 dollars a month, including federal social security.

To add to the safety of such pension programs, the government is currently putting its influence behind widespread adoption of the idea that a worker should be able to take his nest egg with him if he moves from one company or one industry to another. Under such a system, he is not anchored to his job, but can pick up where he left off in piling up credits toward old-age protection when he finds a new place to work.

The contracts just signed in the can industry increased the level of retirement benefits by more than two-thirds, all as the result of a single negotiation. Only a short time has passed since the average factory wage crossed the 100-dollar a-week Rubicon— an event that Secretary of Labor Wirtz hailed as a milestone in labor's march toward relative affluence. Yet, there are already several key industries in which the worker can count on a regular income of 100 dollars a week for himself and his wife in retirement, quite apart from any savings that he has put aside on his own.

Inevitably, the acceptance of the concept that a worker's pay should be safeguarded against the hazards of old age and sickness gave birth to a movement for a third prop under income—this time to offset the hardship of unemployment by plugging the gap between standard wages and state job–insurance benefits. Idle production and maintenance workers in the automobile companies now get 50 dollars to 56 dollars a week above their state payments for periods up to a year. The can industry's agreement goes much further. It provides a supplemental benefit equal to 70 per cent of usual pay. This continues for five years in the case of workers on the payroll ten years or longer. Those with two to ten years of service qualify for two years of benefits.

A companion program takes much of the financial punishment out of irregular work schedules in auto, steel, and other major industries. If a worker is called in to work less than forty hours a week, he is guaranteed three-quarters of his customary weekly wage. In the can companies, a new provision prohibits the employer from reassigning the worker to another job that cuts his pay by more than 5 per cent from the average that he received in the preceding twelve months.

But a still newer extension of the security principle carries blue-collar workers closest to the "promised land" of lifetime job security. Put in its simplest terms, this is the principle that no regular employee will be pushed off the payroll because a machine takes his job. No matter how great the labor savings made by technological innovation, the worker is protected against unemployment. His job may go, but he stays. This is the concept known as "attrition," and it is becoming widely accepted as the most socially responsible method that collective bargaining can devise for meeting the problems of technological displacement. In effect, it provides for drawing a circle around the existing work force in a plant, enterprise, or industry and giving assurance that nobody inside that circle will be fired because of automation or other changes made in the interest of increased efficiency. The workers remain employed until they die, retire, or leave of their own accord.

Attrition has become the favorite answer of industry, labor, and government to the prime headache on today's labor front: what to do with people in an era of dynamic technological advance? It is a cornerstone of the long-range sharing plan at Kaiser Steel Company's big mill in Fontana, California. The union has given wholehearted cooperation in helping to cut the production cost of steel through more automatic machinery, greater care in the use of materials, reduced absenteeism, and other aids to efficiency. This cooperation has been accompanied by a management promise that no worker will be dismissed because the efficient new equipment has made him superfluous. If there is no other job immediately available for a displaced employee, he goes into a reserve labor pool—at full pay—until a spot is found. The Kaiser formula does not stop there. It also gives the entire work force at Fontana—white-collar as well as blue-collar—a cash stake in higher productivity. Nearly one-third of every dollar that the company saves through lower unit costs goes into a fund to be divided every month among the workers. Last year this premium averaged about twenty-five cents an hour on top of normal wages and benefits.

Dock workers on both the Atlantic and Pacific coasts are covered by pioneering contracts that also rest on the attrition principle, coupled with a sharing of the gains made possible by automation. The West Coast agreement, now nearing the end of its five and one-half year term, gives the employers full freedom to install modern ship-loading machinery; it also gives lifetime income assurances to the members of the International Longshoremen's and Warehousemen's Union.

Every worker must receive at least thirty-five hours' pay each week, which means a weekly wage floor of 116 dollars, no matter how little work there is to do. Unionists who elect to retire at sixty-two get a monthly pension of 220 dollars. However, if the volume of shipping dips so low that a squeezeout of workers becomes necessary to maintain the income guarantee for those on the active list, retirement at sixty-two would become compulsory—but the benefit would go up to 320 dollars a month. Thus far, there has been no drain on the fund and no pressure for forced retirement.

On the Atlantic and Gulf coasts, the International Longshoremen's Association has ranked low in internal democracy or concern for the welfare of its rank-and-file for many years. An investigation by the New York State Crime Commission in 1952 disclosed so many abuses in the union and in the conduct of labor–management relations in the Port of New York that a special Waterfront Commission was established to bar gangsters from the piers and to outlaw corrupt hiring practices. The AFL was so affronted by the underworld penetration of the ILA that it expelled it from the federation.

Four years ago it had cleansed itself sufficiently to be readmitted; but the union continued to take a backward view of new technology, and its record was marred by numerous wildcat strikes and extortionate practices. However, the ILA has now joined with the shipping employers in a four-year contract which many observers believe will do much to enhance the efficiency of the industry and also the job security of the longshoremen. They are now assured of permanent employment with a minimum annual guarantee of 1,600 hours' pay. This means dock workers will have at least 5,856 dollars a year in wages, plus liberalized vacations, improved medical benefits for the union members and their families, and a sharply increased pension, available any time after workers pass their sixty-second birthday.

Perhaps the most surprising place to find the attrition idea putting a foundation of solidity under jobs is in the railroads which have suffered a precipitous decline in employment in recent years. After World War I, there were 2 million railroad workers—three times as many as there are now. And even with that drastic shakeout, there are still more workers than are needed to run trains, man stations, and perform other useful services.

What to do about those who are not needed got to be so tortured an issue in the case of locomotive firemen that, in 1963, Congress passed the first compulsory arbitration law in America's peacetime history to force a solution. The arbitrators decided that only 10 per cent of the firemen were needed, but they ordered the railroads to keep 90 per cent employed on some basis until they could retrain them for other jobs or induce them to take separation payments. Attrition agreements have since been signed on a voluntary basis covering several hundred thousand rail workers in other categories. One such agreement protects workers against the ups and downs of the business cycle, as well as against technological unemployment. The railroads must stay within the boundaries of normal turnover in any shrinkage of total jobs, whether the cause of the cut is automated equipment or a decline in rail traffic.

But attrition is a threat as well as a safeguard for unions. In the first place, it represents a form of slow death for the organization. As the total number of jobs in the bargaining unit shrinks, so does the empire over which the union leader presides. His members are protected, but his organization dwindles. That is not the most insidious element in the threat, however. The union finds itself in the position of doing more and more for a smaller and smaller group of workers at the very time that young people are shouldering their way into the scramble for jobs at a rate never previously matched in the United States. Just to keep pace with this inflow, the U.S. will have to create 25,000 new jobs every week for the next decade.

To the extent that the job-contracting effect of new technology and the failure of the economy to grow with sufficient speed combine to bar that needed rise in jobs, youngsters may conclude that attrition plans are contributing to their exclusion from work opportunities. The same sense of irritation against being frozen out of jobs by the priorities that unions establish to protect those already in them may also afflict Negroes, Puerto Ricans, and others who count on the equal employment section of the new Civil Rights Act to increase their chances of finding work.

Now, obviously, this is an unfair accusation to direct against organizations that came into being for the primary purpose of protecting their members against exploitation and insecurity. What unions are doing through attrition programs is precisely what they were set up to do; yet the very success with which they fulfill their mission makes them vulnerable to attack by those who are on the outside clamoring to get in. The perverse fact is that the effect of automation in many industries is to make jobs fewer, easier to perform, and much more attractive in terms of wages and fringe allowances. This is fine for those who have the jobs; it merely intensifies the resentment of those who have no jobs and little prospect of getting any.

In a real sense, these outcasts are society's responsibility, but the have-nots are not always judicious in allocating blame. The danger is that those on the other side of the job wall will express their frustration in an unreasoning assault on unions and corporations as co-conspirators in a plot to build higher and higher fences around the workplace.

The defense against this danger lies much more in political action than it does in strikes or ingenuity at the bargaining table. The transcendent problem for labor is to apply all of its political effectiveness—alone and in association with the broadest possible coalition of allies—to bring about a full-employment economy so that a black worker will not have to elbow aside a white worker to get a job, so that a youngster will not have to regard his father as the barnacle in the way of his progress.

It is precisely in this area of political mobilization that American unions encounter a particularly difficult problem. This is not because they are strangers to politics. Ever since Samuel Gompers coined the slogan, "Reward your friends and punish your enemies," they have recognized that politics is an important part of union affairs. In fact, the earliest unions were so limited by legal disqualifications that they formed their own workingmen's parties and played an important role in establishing free public education and other reforms. But under Gompers, the accent shifted from direct political action on a class basis to politics as a means of defending gains won at the bargaining table. His successors, William Green and George Meany, summed up their political philosophy in the idea that labor could lose in the legislative halls the victories that it won on the picket line. Even for unionists like David Dubinsky of the ILGWU and Walter P. Reuther of the UAW, who began their careers as Socialists, the concept of labor in politics is a nonideological one. The head of the movement, Meany, once summed up his view with the blunt statement, "Ideology is baloney." As a child of the New Deal, the CIO was, from its inception in the mid-thirties, closely involved with government. The AFL, with a more conservative tradition, always emphasized its aloofness from the state. Yet, from the time of the enactment of the Taft-Hartley Act of 1947 which restricted many of labor's activities, both branches of American labor developed full-time political organizations. These have now been merged into the AFL-CIO Committee on Political Education. Through this committee and through parallel organizations operating in many individual unions, labor has become a significant force in politics at the federal, state, and municipal levels in most parts of the country. In presidential years, total union spending on politics probably exceeds 10 million dollars. Union officers are frequent visitors at the White House. A former union lawyer, Arthur J. Goldberg, was made Secretary of Labor by President Kennedy, then an Associate Justice of the Supreme Court, and was later appointed Ambassador to the United Nations by President Johnson. Unionists have been appointed public members of dozens of presidential commissions, and their advice is sought on many issues of public policy.

The political program of labor has spread from narrow bread-and-butter questions of direct interest to unions, and now embraces a broad spectrum of social improvement. Where "Repeal the Taft-Hartley Slave Labor Law" used to be almost the beginning-and-end of the program, the accent is now on all the elements of what President Johnson hopes to make his Great Society. In fact, through most of the last four years, labor has given legislative priority to subjects that had much more general application than they did specific reference to union welfare. Thus, it successively endorsed the Trade Expansion Act, the Civil Rights Act, and a Kennedy-Johnson tax program that gave more relief to corporations and the rich than it did to the poor. Only in 1965 did the AFL-CIO shift back to first emphasis on a Congressional matter of primary interest to its own unions. This is the proposal to take a clause that gives the state the power to enact so-called "right to work" laws prohibiting the union shop out of the Taft-Hartley Act.

In general, however, labor is ardently in support of the War on Poverty, expanded public works, universal education, and other elements of the Great Society. The difficulty is that it is a follower in all these fields, not an initiator of programs or a mobilizer of broad support behind them. The unemployment rate has stayed close to five per cent or higher for seven years. Yet, there has been no focused union campaign to translate into reality the full-employment concepts that have theoretically been a fundamental part of federal obligation since the passage of the Employment Act of 1946.

One reason for its ineffectuality as a catalytic agent for broad social movements is that its own leadership has grown old and barren of ideas. Even the young rebels who came out of the New Deal are now approaching sixty. The executive council of the AFL-CIO has an average age of nearly sixty-five. Nine of the

Federation's vice presidents are no longer presidents of their own unions. Meany himself is past seventy.

But more important than age, approaches to unionism and to public problems remain unchanged from the depression years of three decades ago. Labor has no training schools for new leaders. Few of its top men ever went to college, and there is little desire to recognize that changing technology has made many of the concepts that served unions well in their organizational days obsolete. Even now, power is so narrowly held that when an internal upheaval sweeps out one set of leaders and installs another, as recently happened in the million-member United Steelworkers of America, the change is more one of personality than of substance.

The shortcomings of the present high command are reflected in its failure to develop any persuasive recruiting appeal to the millions of white-collar and professional workers who are becoming the dominant factor in the labor force. Only among teachers and government employees has there been any important growth in recent years. Part of this is the product of fresh leadership in the American Federation of Teachers and the American Federation of State, County and Muncipal Employees; part stems from executive orders fostering collective bargaining and union organization issued by labor's friends in public office. But outside these fields, labor is standing still.

Even among the strongly unionized elements of the blue-collar work force, there have been some significant symptoms of dissatisfaction with the routineness of union function and the remoteness of union leadership. In the auto plants especially, controversies over local grievances have taken precedence over the over-all national patterns worked out by Reuther and his associates. General Motors was shut down for a month in 1964 by a strike called over plant problems after all national issues had been satisfactorily adjusted. Underlying the strike was a sense, on the part of the rank-and-file, that its day-to-day problems were being submerged in the monolithic structure of a giant national union.

The urgency of finding solutions for the challenge of drift is heightened by the ways in which automation is stripping labor of much of its economic muscle. The UMW, which was the fountainhead of the CIO in the leonine days of John L. Lewis, has become the shadow of a union under the impact of large-scale mechanization and the inroads of competitive fuels into the market for coal. The union had 700,000 members in the soft-coal fields after World War I. Now it is down to 100,000.

Other unions have found that technology has made their employers immune from any economic hurt through strikes. Thus, in the great telephone network of AT&T, union leaders learned that communication can go on uninterrupted, no matter how many union members go on strike. Automatic processes have had the same effect in electric utilities. A similar situation exists in oil refineries, and the list will grow as more and more industries go on push-button flow.

Philosophically, most American unions accept automation, although it is an exaggeration to pretend they welcome it. At the AFL-CIO convention in 1963, Meany admitted that he found it more of a curse than a blessing. But no union leader deludes himself with the notion that automation can be stopped, or that the United States would be able to maintain either its standard of living or its industrial pre-eminence if it were. Up to now, however, labor has had few ideas on how the enormous potential of technology for social betterment can be used more effectively to serve the total good. This is the great challenge that confronts it—and the country.

24 AMERICAN LABOR IN A CHANGING WORLD

Joseph A. Beirne

We who are entrusted with leadership positions in the American labor movement with more than 15 million men and women who make up our free and democratic trade unions are very proud of it—proud of the role we play in American life and proud of the responsibilities that we bear. In my lifetime, the American trade-union movement has come to occupy an accepted and respected place in the life of our nation, recognized in responsible places as one of the vital forces in the political, economic, and social life of our country.

When one considers that it was barely thirty years ago that American trade unionists were virtually universally condemned by all the newspapers in this country, that we were engaged in violent physical battles merely in defense of our right to exist— this is a considerable achievement.

It is an achievement, I think, not only of the American labor movement but an achievement of the American system and American society. We have demonstrated our capacity to grow. American society demonstrated its capacity to accept change and adjust to the necessities of a changing world.

It is this characteristic of America—its ability to achieve change—sometimes drastic and radical change within the framework of government that gives the nation strength and the ability to move forward. Perhaps it is a characteristic of youth. Perhaps it is a remnant of the days, not too many years ago as history is reckoned, when there were still vast miles of unoccupied land for restless people to move to. Whatever the reason, it is one of our characteristics and a valuable one, I think.

There is, in addition, one basic fact with regard to America and the American trade-union movement that must be understood if our country and the labor movement in our country are to be understood. And that basic fact is that neither our political parties nor our trade-union movement is committed to any hard and rigid political ideology.

As foreign observers have noted, our political parties are to some extent parties of opportunism. There is nothing in their structure—or indeed their history—that prevents them from responding to a great need, either expressed or felt. This is most evident today in the southern part of our country where political parties which once shunned identification with certain groups are now vying with each other for the support of these groups.

The same lack of rigidity is true of our labor movement. Within the American labor movement, there is a smattering of the socialist tradition that remains from the days when our labor force was essentially an immigrant labor force—when it was composed of people newly arrived on our shores who brought with them the ideologies of Europe and fused them with the American philosophy.

There are, I suppose, a handful of Communists scattered throughout the labor force—though there are none, so far as I am aware, that are even on the fringes of a trade-union leadership position. Because of their behavior in the past, because of their obvious first loyalty to foreign powers, and because of the vigilance and experience of our responsible trade-union leadership, the American communists are without doubt the most discredited group of outcasts in the trade-union organization.

The vast majority of American trade unionists—and by that I mean over 95 per cent—are either Democrats or Republicans, and a significant number of them may shift their political allegiance from one party to another in any election year. Most manual workers have, however, a predisposition to vote Democratic, a tendency which their trade unions have reinforced since the Democratic party in most states has shown a greater receptiveness to labor's legislative demands than has the Republican party.

We do not have competing unions based on political ideology, and our trade-union movement is definitely not the handmaiden of any political party. In the United States, this is the course of wisdom.

What is, then, the ideology of the American labor movement, and what are the methods by which we seek to achieve our objectives? Basically, the ideology of the American labor movement is the pragmatic one. We want to know: "Will it work?" "Will the men and women who belong to the ranks of the American labor movement be better off, and will our country be a better country?" Our purpose is not to take away from those who are wealthy. Rather, our purpose is to make every family wealthy, and if this permits the rich to acquire even more money, we are not unduly concerned with this by-product of an expanding economy that brings tangible benefits to millions of our families. We do think, however, that as total national wealth grows, that increase must be distributed more equitably throughout the population. The whole economy would benefit from the lower 40 per cent of the income spectrum's having more purchasing power.

To my mind, there is a great difference between *money* and *wealth*. A lot of money and the acquisition of a lot of money often rob a person of precious time and opportunities to follow paths that might be productive and creative. Wealth, on the other hand, means simply the possession of sufficient money for necessities, for pleasures, for serenity. It means sufficient resources to permit the person who possesses them to extend and expand his spiritual side—to learn, to paint, or to follow whatever pursuits take his fancy. Such a person is wealthy, regardless of the amount of riches that he possesses.

It is in these terms that we in the American labor movement seek, in this last third of the twentieth century, to make our members wealthy. It is to these terms that we have reference when we talk in the most speculative fashion, to be sure, of re-examining the nature of work. Most Americans, I know, and most people in the world I am sure, grow up with the notion that one must work in order to eat. Yet in our country today, this is not entirely true. We can produce enough of the basic necessities of life with a much shorter workweek than our present average forty hours. And, with automation and improving

technology, we are capable of increasing the pace of our production of food and manufactured articles. *does not*

That is why the American labor movement today is committed
to reducing the hours of work and, eventually, the number of
days of work. Men were born, we believe, to be the masters of the
machine and not its servants.

To the extent that we free man from the machine, and that we
free the human race from the necessity of exerting energy merely
to provide food, clothing, and shelter—to that extent we create
wealth. This is the thrust that American labor seeks to give to
American society. And I do not believe that it is incompatible
in any way with the pragmatism which is the basic philosophy
that prevails in the United States. The trade-union movement
cherishes concepts of a better life for all Americans. We speak
for the poor—the lower-income fifth—few of whom are union
members, and vigorously support the programs and aspirations of
the civil-rights movement.

American labor regards itself as an internal part of American
society, not as a hostile element within it. We believe that we
have a contribution to make and that we have the resources, the
capacity, and the dedication to increase the pace of progress in
our country.

I have asked people from other walks of life: businessmen,
people from the academic world, clergymen of all faiths, government officials, if they can name any other single private organization that has the resources, the strength of purpose, and
the dynamic will that the labor movement possesses for better-
ing the public welfare. I have met no one who can name an organization that matches us in this respect. Only the labor movement has this breadth, depth, and concentration in every aspect
of the public good.

The job of the American labor movement is two-fold. First, it
must maintain itself against those on the left and right who would
tear it down, so that we can continue to render service. Second,
we have a responsibility to stimulate progress in the field of social
sciences that will match our progress in the physical sciences. In
our generation we have seen fantastic progress in the physical
sciences. We have moved from old production-line techniques into
an atomic age, complete with electronic controls, thermonuclear

weapons, automation, and walks in space. We know more, far more about the nature of the world in which we live than any group that has preceded us in history. Yet our knowledge of ourselves lags far behind, and it sometimes seems that we know even less about the organization of our society than our forefathers did.

In spite of our capacity to produce, there are vast areas in the world and even areas in the United States where people go to sleep at night hungry, where people live without shelter and with only one tattered garment to wear. Thus we have much still to learn and to do.

Technical wisdom not withstanding, we have been unable to reduce the level of unemployment below 5 per cent. Expanded federal aid to school and hospital construction will create additional employment, but many people in the labor movement believe that still more federal spending is necessary. We do not know enough about what to do with people who are thrown out of jobs through plant shut-downs or automation. The federal government is moving toward solutions in its Manpower Development and Training Program and some of the newer projects under the Economic Opportunity Act. But more, much more is needed to achieve our mutual goal of an integrated, positive manpower policy.

We have not provided decent housing for large numbers of our people, nor have we been able to give our educational system the capacity to offer a higher education to all those who desire it and are capable of benefiting by it. We have not learned how to overcome prejudice against certain races and certain religions, nor have we learned how to prevent some sections of our great cities from becoming antisocial jungles. We know as much as anyone does about the diseases that afflict the body and mind of man, but we do not yet have the knowledge of how to apply what we know to those most in need of it.

These are some of the challenges that face us in the field of social science. The American labor movement regards these challenges as its own as much as that of any other group, for these are the areas of work to which we are dedicated.

Yet within the American society, there remain groups that are still hostile to the labor movement—that seek to confine its activities to ever smaller spheres, to drain its resources in futile side skirmishes, that continue to conduct guerrilla warfare against our organizations. Another job, therefore, that faces the American labor movement is to contain and beat back these assaults on it and to free ourselves for the creative tasks that confront us. To accomplish this job will require some changes within the labor movement itself. It will require, among other things, a recognition that the character of the American work force is changing. More and more, American workers today earn their living in what we call white-collar jobs, that is, in jobs that do not require much if any physical exertion. The majority of Americans who work for a living are in this category. Yet among the trade unions, the person who performs this kind of white-collar work constitutes only about 15 per cent of the membership.

Until fairly recently, clerical workers regarded unionism with less enthusiasm than did the men and women who worked in the shop. They tended to feel that, because they were in the front office, they were, somehow, more closely identified with management. This feeling has diminished as clerical workers have discovered that work at a desk in a room full of several hundred other people performing the same tasks is not essentially different from work in the shop, with the exception that they don't get their hands dirty and their pay is often somewhat less.

The union's problem is to make clear the identity of the clerical worker's interest with the man in workclothes and to bring him the understanding that although his grievances may not be of the same nature, the solution lies along the same road. It is my belief that the American labor movement stands on the verge of a great breakthrough in this field.

Another problem that confronts us is the fact that in the early days of this century, a large number of American trade unionists were either immigrants or first-generation Americans. Today the vast majority of American unionists are either second- or third-generation Americans with different orientations and different traditions. This changing constituency will obviously require a change in the tone of the American trade union, leading it to more and more social-welfare and political activities, as well as to more and more complex collective-bargaining arrangements. This will place a different kind of burden on the union officer requiring wider knowledge and the services of a more professional staff.

In addition to the changing character of the work force, there is, of course, the increasing automation of industry and the decreasing reliance on human labor. Obviously, this has had a great impact on the collective-bargaining process and on labor's ultimate weapon, the strike.

Let me cite an instance from the history of my own organization, the Communications Workers of America which, as the title indicates, includes all workers in the communications industry with the exception of the post office. In the telephone industry, which is far more automated than most, our last major strike took place ten years ago against a company that operates in nine southeastern states. The company is one of the largest employers of labor in the industry, with nearly 50,000 people on its payroll. It reaches into the booming cities of the new South as well as into sleepy back-country towns and farms.

For seventy-seven days in the spring and summer of 1955, we conducted a highly effective strike, judged by average standards. In an area where many unions had felt public hostility, we had public support. The members of our organization had a magnificent sense of unity, and they maintained the picket lines through good weather and bad, day and night. We presented our case well to the public and succeeded in securing a public understanding of the fact that the company had refused to accept the union fully or to bargain with it sincerely. The end result of the strike was a net gain for our organization. We won a number of the points at issue and the management's attitude underwent a substantial change.

But in a number of other ways, the strike was less than successful. It was impossible for us, as it would be for any other union in a similar situation, to achieve the first objective of a strike—a cessation of the employer's business or, at least, a substantial reduction of the employer's revenues. In spite of the strike, the automated telephone system kept functioning, hour-by-hour and day-by-day. Local and long-distance calls went through with only slight delays. Deterioration of service through lack of maintenance never seriously materialized. It was not a satisfying discovery for us to realize that a major weapon in collective bargaining was less than devastatingly effective. It caused us to undertake some serious rethinking.

I cite this instance because it is typical of what many other organizations are either now facing or will face in the very near future. Let me add two cautions. The first is that certainly the strike will continue to be used as an effective weapon in localized service industries and in other industries in which the technology is relatively less advanced, or the labor–management relationship is unusually hostile. The second caution is that it is essential in every industry, regardless of its size or character, that unions retain the right to strike and the right to use the strike threat as an instrument of collective bargaining.

Without that right, the union's strength at the collective-bargaining table is certainly diminished. It is all too easy for a sense of arrogance to develop in even the most charming and well-bred persons, when, representing rich and entrenched corporations at the collective-bargaining table, they deal with weak unions or unions without recourse to effective counteraction. The strike threat is a most satisfactory method of causing even the most secure and complacent of industrial relations vice presidents to roll up their sleeves a little higher and work a little harder at seeking a more satisfactory agreement.

Let me add a third caution. I hope no one will interpret my remarks as a suggestion that the level of collective bargaining in the United States today would be as high as it is if it had not been for the militancy of our movement and the leadership of such men as John L. Lewis, Sidney Hillman, Philip Murray, and a host of others. We owe much of our present status and strength to them.

But history has moved on. The American industrial machine has become more complex, and old methods are inevitably becoming obsolete. The skill of union and management negotiators that permits them to bargain hard is now the prime requisite in collective bargaining. There is a tendency in some industries where bargaining has been on a single company basis toward multi-unit bargaining. Unions in the same or related industries are also moving toward coordinating their programs. The federal government, through the President's Council of Economic Advisors, interests itself in the impact on the whole economy of the dozen or more crucial, periodic negotiations. This is then the direction in which industrial relations are moving. It calls for a greater reliance by both labor and management on rational approaches to problems and less reliance on trials by strength.

Two changes that I have mentioned—the change in the character of the work force and in the nature of industry—are only two of many. They are sufficient, however, to indicate the nature of the problem that American unions face—because, certainly, if they are to survive and prosper, they must also adapt to stay alive. I believe we will be successful in this because we are not circumscribed by an ideology based on events and observations, however perceptive, that took place many, many decades ago. We are not confronted with the job of trying to fit new problems into old solutions—a process as fraught with peril as the familiar one of putting new wine in old bottles.

If we are to be true to the best interests of our members, we who lead labor unions must be willing to change with the times, just as we insist that corporate executives must "think modern." We have a responsibility to point out the shortcomings of government and industry and to ask for a better performance. We have a responsibility to act as gadflies and irritants, if need be, to prevent complacency and stagnation from slowing down our progress toward a better society. But it is equally important that unions and their members and the families of their members drop worn-out slogans and outdated thinking, if we are truly to make the most of our opportunities.

History has recorded that the human suffering involved in the nineteenth-century industrial revolution was essentially a failure in social and economic innovation. We cannot afford, in these latter years of the twentieth century, to permit a new round of failure in social and economic innovation in the new revolution that confronts the world. All of the elements in our national life, business, labor, and government, must recognize the primacy of our long-range national interests over the short-range advantages which might possibly be obtained. And this recognition involves a recognition by each group of the legitimate role played by the other in our national life.

In our lifetime, we have seen the inability of strong trade-union movements to stem the rise of totalitarianism—an inability attributed by some scholars to a preoccupation by those organizations with narrow, day-to-day problems. This led, in turn, to isolation from the national community and inability to exert leadership when such national leadership was vital to the life of the entire nation.

In my view, the American community, including American labor, faces a somewhat similar challenge—to rise above the structural limitations, the bargaining procedures and above all, the attitudes, that were shaped in bygone days. Successful adjustment to change will permit American labor, in the years that lie ahead, to fulfill its responsibilities to its own members and to the whole nation.

With courage and imagination, we can meet our challenge and our appointment with the future. And if we fully utilize the creative intelligence that we possess, we can help make not only the United States but the entire free world a more interesting, more satisfying, more wholesome place for ourselves, our children, and the as yet unborn generations to come.

That is the challenge to democratic American labor. And that is the challenge that I, as an American trade-union leader, accept as my responsibility to my members, my country, and indeed the people of the entire world.

Index

Ackley, Gardner, 95
ad hoc arbitrators, see under voluntary arbitration
AFL, see American Federation of Labor
AFL-CIO, 132, 133, 153–154, 163 ff, 189, 198, 208, 227, 243 ff, 261, 263, 318, 319, 321; Civil Rights Committee, 245; international organizations, 298 ff; see also American Federation of Labor; Congress of Industrial Organizations
African labor, 298 ff
Agency for International Development (AID), 303, 304
agriculture, see farming, decreasing importance of
AID, see Agency for International Development
AIFLD, see American Institute for Free Labor Development
Alliance for Progress, 304
Amalgamated Clothing Workers Union, 151
Amalgamated Engineers Union, 299
Amalgamated Meat Cutters Union, 145
American Economic Association, 145
American Federation of Government Employees, 163
American Federation of Labor (AFL), 16, 107–109, 112–114, 127, 138, 139, 144 ff, 187, 254, 257–260, 311, 316; early racial policies, 241 ff; membership gains, 116–118; merger with CIO, 119, 153,

243–246; see also AFL-CIO; Congress of Industrial Organizations
American Federation of State, County and Municipal Workers, 163, 320
American Federation of Teachers, 320
American Institute for Free Labor Development (AIFLD), 304
American labor movement, see labor movement
American Medical Association, 282
American Newspaper Guild, 305
American Nurses Association, 168
American Railway Union, 137, 144–145
anthracite coal strike (1902), 140
Appalachia Act, 275, 284
Arab Trade Unions, 309
arbitration, see voluntary arbitration
Asian labor, 298 ff
automation, 189, 324, 326; enhanced white-collar job opportunities, 167–168; growth of, 73–75, 86–87; see also technological change
Automobile Workers, see United Automobile Workers

Baer, George, 176
Barnett, George, 145
blue-collar workers: decline of, 85, 159–161, 163; predomination in unions, 123, 131; vulnerability to industrialization, 91–92
Boulware, Lemuel, 172

333

Boulwareism, 172
Bridges, Harry, 151, 157
Brown, Thomas H., 150
Bureau of Labor Statistics, 49, 122

Carey, Henry C., 45–46
Carnegie, Andrew, 16
Census of Housing (1960), 52
Chrysler Corporation, 116, 166
Churchill, Winston L. S., 129
CIO, see Congress of Industrial Organizations
civil rights, see minorities in labor movement; Negroes in labor
Civil Rights Act (1964), 9, 64, 66, 212, 245, 246, 249, 317, 319; see also Negroes in labor
Civil War, American industrialization since, 42, 144, 256
class and class consciousness, 12–44; affluent worker, 28 ff, 58 ff; authority, 35–36; criteria, 34 ff; education, 35–36; ethnicity, 36–38; ideological diversity, structural roots of, 26 ff; limits of class analysis, 26 ff; locality, 36–38; Marxian, 14–16, 17, 19–21, 26, 34, 36–37, 42, 44; middle-class culture, 28 ff; mobility, 38–41; occupational group, 35–36; poverty, 32–34; race, 36–38; relations of production, 14; social class, idea of, 13–14; today, attitudes toward, 16–22
Clayton Act (1914), 226
collective bargaining, 16, 26, 50, 55, 155, 165 ff, 178, 183, 198 ff, 230 ff, 285 ff, 329; economic values, 213; ethical values, 212; philosophical values, 211–212; political values, 213; as a reflection of social values, 213–214; Section 7(a), 112–115, 147, 149; system, 211–214; see also grievance procedure; unions; voluntary arbitration
Committee on Equal Employment Opportunity, 248– 249

Committee on Political Education (COPE), 260, 261 ff
Committee on the Unemployment Statistics (1962), President's, 99
Committee to Appraise Employment and Unemployment Statistics, President's, 99
Common Market, 298, 302
Communications Workers of America, 328
Communism, Conformity, and Civil Liberties (Stouffer), 35
Congress of Industrial Organizations (CIO), 19, 118, 127, 258–260, 311, 321; created by John L. Lewis, 114, 150; early racial policies, 242–243; membership gains, 116–117; merger with AFL, 119, 153, 243–246; see also AFL-CIO; American Federation of Labor
Congress of the United States, 97, 110, 111, 130, 140, 152, 188, 222, 226, 229 ff, 261, 265, 316; House of Representatives, 262; Senate, 175
Constitution of the United States, 212–213, 236; First Amendment, 136; Fifteenth Amendment, 212
Consumer Price Index, 49
consumption of goods, current high level of, 45, 51–53, 55, 88, 90
Coolidge, Calvin, 146
COPE, see Committee on Political Education
Council of Economic Advisors, President's, 83, 89–92, 93, 95, 100, 204, 294, 329
Curran, Joe, 151
cybernation, see automation; technological change

Debs, Eugene V., 144
Democratic party and labor, 23 ff, 263–267; see also New Deal; Roosevelt, Franklin D.
depression, see Great Depression

Donner, Frederick G., 308
Dubinsky, David, 150, 318

Economic Opportunity Act (1964), 65–66, 67, 275, 326
education: importance in American labor force of, 4, 18, 29 ff, 40–41, 55, 93–94; *see also* class and class consciousness; unemployment
Eisenhower, Dwight D., 23 n, 153, 249
Electrical Workers, *see* United Electrical Workers Union
Employment Act (1946), 66, 97, 319
European labor, 27, 40, 47, 58, 62, 132, 143–144, 183–184, 188, 193, 198, 201–202, 230, 298 ff; unemployment, 99

Fair Employment Practices Committee, 247
Fair Labor Standards Act (1938), 111, 117, 188
farming, decreasing importance of, 2, 3, 40, 85, 99–100
Federal Bureau of Labor, 48
Feminine Mystique, The (Friedan), 186
Fifteenth Amendment to the Constitution, 212
First Amendment to the Constitution, 136
Fortune Magazine, 80
Frankfurter, Felix, 226
Frenning, Harvey C., 150
Frey, John P., 146, 149
Friedan, Betty, 186

General Agreement on Trade and Tariffs (GATT), 302–303
General Electric Company, 172–173
General Motors Corporation, 152, 153, 301, 307–308, 320; 1964 strike, 179
GNP, *see* Gross National Product
Goldberg, Arthur J., 319
Goldwater, Barry, 266

Gompers, Samuel, 141, 144, 257–258, 261, 303, 318
government's role in union activities: anti-injunction measures, 226; compulsory arbitration, 230; early judicial control, 224–225; enforcement of collective bargaining, 235; featherbedding, 232–233; functions of National Labor Relations Board, 227 ff; future policy considerations, 237; grievance arbitration, 235–236; labor injunction, 255; national emergency strikes, 234; organization of government employees, 232–233; picketing and free-speech decisions, 228–229; post-World War I changes, 230; Railway Labor Acts, 106, 127, 229–230; regulation of internal union affairs, 236–237; Sherman Anti-Trust Act (1890), 225–226; Taft-Hartley Act (1947), 119, 153, 231, 233, 236; unfair labor practices, 231–233; union immunity from anti-trust laws, 228; unions' political contribution, 236
Grand Consolidated Trades Union (England), 144
Grazia, Sebastian de, 192
Great Depression (1930's), 50, 124, 128, 130, 144, 178, 213, 269
Great Society, 23, 319
Green, William, 148, 150, 151, 153, 318
greenbackism, 15
grievance procedure, 235–236; attitudes toward administration of, 217–218; multi-step, 216–217; types of, 215–218; *see also* collective bargaining; voluntary arbitration
Gross National Product (GNP), 54, 69, 97, 285

Harris, Louis, 24
Haymarket Square bomb explosion, 15

health, improving, effect on labor of, 3
Heller, Walter W., 89–91
Hillman, Sidney, 150, 329
Homestead strike (1892), 16, 137
Hoover, Herbert C., 109, 145
hours, working, 16, 187–191; case for reduction, 192 ff; effects on unemployment, 189; shorter-hour movement, 187–188
Howard, Charles P., 150
Hoxie, Robert F., 121, 128
Hutcheson, William, 149

ICFTU, see International Confederation of Free Trade Unions
ILGWU, see International Ladies Garment Workers Union
ILO, see International Labor Organization
ILWU, see International Longshoremen's and Warehousemen's Union
IMF, see International Metalworkers' Federation
income distribution of labor: forms of income earned, 59–62; form of income received, 59–62; inequality, 61 ff; rich and poor, characteristics of, 64–67; trend toward equality, 61; war on poverty, 65–67
industrialization, see technological change
Industrial Man (Kerr), 193–194
industrial unionism: craft unions, 143–144, 149 ff; definition, 143; evolution, 143–148; government, 156–157; laws favoring unions, 148–149; organizing, 151–152; post-World War I decline, 145–147; rebirth under Roosevelt, 147–148; revolution, 154–156; stabilized, 152; see also labor force; labor movement; unions
Industrial Workers of the World (IWW), 108, 145, 146
International Association of Machinists, 306

International Confederation of Free Trade Unions (ICFTU), 118, 298, 300, 303, 306, 308–309
International Labor Organization (ILO), 188, 302, 303
International Ladies Garment Workers Union (ILGWU), 108, 147, 151, 305–306, 318
International Longshoremen's and Warehousemen's Union (ILWU), 151, 157, 315
International Metalworkers' Federation (IMF), 306, 308
International Secretariat of Trade Union Centers, 303, 305
International Union of Electrical Workers, 305
IWW, see Industrial Workers of the World

Johnson, Lyndon B., 23, 38, 189–190, 248–249, 266, 319; and "war on poverty," 33, 65–67

Kaiser Steel Company, 171, 173; long-range sharing plan, 314
Kennedy, John F., 165–166, 248–249, 263, 319
Kerr, Clark, 193
King, Martin Luther, 245
Knights of Labor, 15, 16, 108, 144, 256–257, 258, 300
Korean War, 83, 119, 125, 128–129, 293
Kuznets, Simon, 61

Labor, United States Department of, 1, 9, 158, 160, 163, 205
labor and management, see management, American
labor force in America: added-worker hypothesis, 4; aggregate demand, 4–6; civilian, 1 ff; discouraged-worker hypothesis, 5–6; effects of World War II on, 5, 10, 50, 51, 61, 64, 67, 83, 85, 100, 118, 119, 124–125, 128–129, 152, 159,

160, 168, 229–230, 248, 300, 312; female, 2–3, 6–9, 54–55, 63–64, 119, 123, 168, 186; growth of, 1, 10; growth problems, 10–11; importance of education, 4, 88, 93–94, 103; industrial composition, 3–4; occupational composition, 3–4; opportunities, 10–11, 92, 103; participation, 2 ff; projected growths, 9–10; rates of participation, 4–6; *see also* labor movement; unions

labor in politics, *see* politics, American labor in

Labor Management Relations Act, 221

Labor Management Reporting and Disclosure Act, 119

labor movement: absence of involved philosophy, 134–135; AFL-CIO merger, 119, 153, 243–246; American economy, 141–142; bases of union growth, 125; changes in tactics, 142; collectivist theories, 135–138; concentration of membership, 122–124; future outlook, 130–132; growth of, forces influencing, 121 ff; historical growth of, 124–125; New Deal and labor standards, 110–112, 118; New Deal view, 109–110; philosophy of, 133 ff; political action, 139–141; position of minorities in, 238–251; recent problems, 119–120; Section 7(a), 112–115, 147, 149; secular force, 126–127; size and shape, 122; Wagner Act (1935), 114–116, 119, 124, 130, 148–149, 178, 226–228, 231, 235; in war, 127–130; weaknesses before 1933, 105–106; *see also* American Federation of Labor; Congress of Industrial Organizations; industrial unionism; labor force; minorities in labor movement; technological change; unions

Labor's League for Political Education (LLPE), 260

Labor's Non-Partisan League, 259

La Follette, Robert M., 257

La Follette Committee hearings (1936), 115

Landrum-Griffin Act (1959), 247

Latin American labor, 298 ff

Leiserson, William M., 149

leisure, *see* hours, working

Lewis, John L., 24, 114, 116, 118, 149–150, 152, 242, 258–259, 264, 321, 329

Little Steel strike (1937), 137, 152

living standards in labor: aftermath of World War I, 49–50; automobile ownership, 53; changing, 45 ff; consumer credit, 53; consumption, current high level of, 51–53, 55, 88, 90; contribution of immigrants, 48–49; disadvantaged poor, 55–56; future outlook, 55–56; the Great Depression's effect, 50; historical importance of, 45–46; housing, 52–53; industrialization period, 46–47; insurance, 54; leisure, growth of, 55; 1950's, 50–51; 1960–1961, 51–52; working wives, 54–55; *see also* technological change

LLPE, *see* Labor's League for Political Education

Lonely Crowd, The (Riesman), 193

McCarthy, Joseph R., 35

McClellan, John L., 175

management, American: business reliance on private property, 178–179; competition as a way of life, 180–181; concepts of function, 176; conflict with union goals, 181–183; diversity of attitudes, 171–173; human-relations training, 173–174; philosophy toward labor, 171–184; union goals, short and long-run, 183–184

Manpower Training and Development Act (1962), 66, 275, 284, 326

Marx, Karl, 14; predictions of increasing misery for the masses,

61; *see also* class and class consciousness, Marxian
Massachusetts Bureau of Labor, 46,
Meany, George, 153, 245, 318
Medicare, 272
Michigan University Survey Research Center, 62
middle class, *see* class and class consciousness
Milton, John, 212
Mine Workers, *see* United Mine Workers of America
minorities in labor movement: AFL-CIO merger, effects of, 243–246; CIO's early racial policies, 242–243; exclusion from membership, 246–247; internal union affairs, 249–250; segregation, 247–249; union racial patterns, 246–249; unions and Negroes, 239–242; *see also* Negroes in labor
Murray, Philip, 153, 329

National Association for the Advancement of Colored People (NAACP), 244, 246
National Association of Manufacturers, 189
National Education Association (NEA), 169
National Industrial Recovery Act (1933), 110–111, 112–113, 147, 148, 178, 227, 258
National Labor Reform Party, 256
National Labor Relations Act, *see* Wagner Act
National Labor Relations Board (NLRB), 114–115, 149, 156, 227 ff, 247
National Labor Union, 256
National Maritime Union, 151
National Mediation Board, 229
National War Labor Board, 129
NEA, *see* National Education Association
Negro American Labor Council, 244
Negroes in labor, 8–9, 23, 25, 32, 34,

36–37, 42, 44, 55, 58, 64–67, 102, 104, 118, 127, 156, 238; AFL-CIO merger, effects of, 243–246; AFL's early racial policies, 241 ff; CIO's early equalitarian policies, 242–243; exclusion from membership, 246–247; internal union affairs, 249–250; relations with unions, 239–242; segregation, 247–249; union racial patterns; *see also* Civil Rights Act of 1964; minorities in labor movement
New Deal, 16, 23, 105, 109 ff, 118, 124, 146–147, 150, 151, 311; *see also* labor movement; Roosevelt, Franklin D.
New Deal-Fair Deal coalition, 23
New York Journal of Commerce, 177
New York State Crime Commission, 315
NIRA, *see* National Industrial Recovery Act
NLRA, *see* Wagner Act (1935)
NLRB, *see* National Labor Relations Board
Norris-La Guardia Act (1932), 105, 226, 228

OSADI, *see* Old Age, Survivors, and Disability Insurance
Of Time, Work, and Leisure (de Grazia), 192
Old Age, Survivors, and Disability Insurance (OASDI), 270, 272, 274, 277 ff
Owens, Robert, 144

PAC, *see* Political Action Committee
Pacific Maritime Association, 157
Peace Corps, 298–299
Perkins, Frances, 110
Perlman, Selig, 146
permanent arbitrators, *see under* voluntary arbitration
Philadelphia & Reading Coal and Iron Company, 176
Piel, Gerald, 195–196

Pinkerton detectives, 16

Political Action Committee (PAC), 259–260

politics, American, labor in: contemporary activities, 260–265; future outlook, 266–267; in the nineteenth and early twentieth centuries, 254–257; labor vote, 264–265; organization, 263–264; as a pressure group, 253–254; *see also* American Federation of Labor; Congress of Industrial Organizations

Presbyterian Ministers Fund, 46

Public Health Service, U.S., 46

Pullman Company strike (1894), 137, 145

Railway Labor Acts: (1926), 106, 229–230; (1934), 227, 229–230, 247

Randolph, A. Philip, 246

Republic Steel Corporation, 152

Retail Clerks International Association, 163

Reuther, Walter, 153, 246, 306, 310, 318

Reynolds, Malvina, 29

Riesman, David, 193–194

Roosevelt, Franklin D., 16, 22, 109–110, 112, 118, 124, 129, 145, 242, 247, 259, 311; resurgence of industrial unionism under, 147–148; *see also* New Deal

Roren, Denkei, 305

Rubber Workers, *see* United Rubber Workers Union

Sarnoff, David, 80

Schnitzler, William, 245

Scientific American, 195

Section 7(a), *see under* collective bargaining

Sherman Anti-Trust Act (1890), 225–226, 228

shorter-hour movement, *see under* hours, working

skidders in labor, 39–40

Skidmore, Thomas, 136

Smith, Adam, 177

Socialist Labor party, 107–108

Social Security Act (1935), 66, 76, 111, 269

social security in America, 268: background, 269–271; characteristics of public programs, 271–272; evaluation, 277–281; future prospects, 281–284; individual programs, 271–275; private employee-benefit systems, 275–277; public systems, 269–275

Spanish-American War, 124, 128

Steelworkers, *see* United Steelworkers of America

Steel Workers Organizing Committee (SWOC), 151–152

Stouffer, Samuel A., 36

Supreme Court of the United States, 64, 116, 140, 152, 181, 222, 225, 228–229, 230 ff, 250

SWOC, *see* Steel Workers Organizing Committee

Taft, Robert, 233, 264

Taft-Hartley Act (1947), 119, 153, 231, 233, 236, 247, 260, 318–319

tax-reduction and reform legislation, recent, 66, 83–84, 90, 96, 102–103, 319

Taylor, Myron, 152

Teamsters Union, 123, 133

technological change, 91–92, 102; attrition, 314 ff; complexities, 77–78; disengagement of man, 72; Frankenstein syndrome, 73–74; implications for the future, 78–81; physical burden, easing of, 72–73; role of labor unions, 69–70; searching for security, 76–77; workers' attitude toward machines, 70–71; *see also* automation

Trade Expansion Act, 319

Truman, Harry S, 22, 129

UAW, *see* United Automobile Workers

UMWA, *see* United Mine Workers of America

unemployment, 1, 4–6, 7, 10, 28, 32 ff, 55, 82–84; changing job mix in factories, 86; classifying unemployed, 92–93; consumer spending changes, 88; counting unemployed, 92–93; decline of agriculture, 2, 3, 40, 85, 99–100; effects of working hours, 189; excess since 1957, 101; impact of automation, 86–87; job market changes (1950–1962), 84–85; Johnson's new emphasis on, 96; lagging adjustment to change, 88–90, 93–95; pattern of improvement, recent, 101–104; President's Council of Economic Advisors and, 89–92, 93, 95, 100; progress since 1947, 97; public policy and, 6; recent developments, 95; statistical differences, 98–100; structural differences, 98–100; teenage rate, 104; unemployable, 101–103

unions: bases of growth, 125 ff; before 1933, 105 ff; Communist infiltration, 108, 118, 156–157, 323; conflict of goals with management, 181 ff; craft, 143–144, 149 ff; economic influences, 285–297; European aid to, 299–300; fringe benefits, 313 ff; government regulation of activities, 224–237; impacts on American economic growth, 290, 295–296; impacts on the firm, 286–287; influence on national income, 290–291; international activities, 298–310; membership during defense and war periods, 119, 124–125; penetration into management decisions, 287–289; politics and labor, 252–267; position of Negroes, 239–242; predominancy of blue-collar workers, 123, 131; predominancy of males, 131; racial patterns, 246–249; recent memberships, 122–123; and rise in real wages, 291–293; rise of industrial unionism, 143–157; role in technological change, 69–70; solidarity, 307–308, 310; strikes, 15, 16–17, 137, 140, 145, 152–153, 179, 230, 233–234, 301, 328; unionization of white-collar workers, 158–170; wage policies, 197–210; wage-push inflation, 293–295; *see also* collective bargaining; government's role in union activities; industrial unionism; labor force; labor movement; technological change; voluntary arbitration

United Automobile Workers (UAW), 113, 116, 123, 151, 153, 165, 166, 179, 200, 208, 264, 292, 306–307, 318; in Africa, 309–310

United Electrical Workers Union, 123, 151

United Mine Workers Journal, 147

United Mine Workers of America, 108, 109, 113, 133, 144, 147, 153, 208, 243, 259

United Nations, 302, 303

United Rubber Workers Union, 151

United States Information Agency (USIA), 303

U.S. Public Health Service, 46

United States Steel Company, 116

United Steelworkers of America, 123, 137, 165, 171–172, 208, 292, 320

USIA, *see* United States Information Agency

Van Buren, Martin, 187

Vocational Education Act (1963), 66

voluntary arbitration: acceptance of awards, 221–222; *ad hoc* arbitrators, 219–221; issue of arbitrability, 222; permanent arbitrators, 219–221; variation of procedures, 218–219; *see also* collective bargaining; grievance procedure wage policies of unions: detriments, 199–201; general wage adjustments, 203–205; structure of bargaining, 201–203; wage structure, 205–209

wages, better, 16, 28 ff, 59 ff

Wagner, Robert F., 110

Wagner Act (1935), 114–116, 119, 124, 130, 148–149, 178, 226–228, 231, 235

Walsh-Healey Public Contracts Act (1936), 111

War Labor Board, 229–230

wealth distribution, 60 ff

Western Federation of Mines, 145, 258

Wharton, Arthur, 149

white-collar workers, 29, 36, 119, 131, 327; AFL-CIO response to growth, 164–165; challenge of unionism, 162–163; government employment, 161–162; growth of, 3–4, 18, 86–87, 158 ff; improved job opportunities, 91, 167–168; likely increase in organization, 170; opportunities through automation, 167–168; present status in unionism, 163; problems and prospects in unionism, 165–167; rise in manufacturing industries, 86–87; unionism outside AFL-CIO, 168–170; unionization, 158–170; *see also* labor force; labor movement

Williams, G. Mennen, 25

Willkie, Wendell L., 24, 259, 264

Woll, Matthew, 149

working class coalition with lower-middle class, 23; *see also* class and class consciousness

working hours, *see* hours, working

World Auto Conference, 306

World War I, aftermath in labor of, 49–50, 124, 127–129, 145–147, 152, 174–175, 230, 303, 316, 321

World War II, effect on labor of, 5, 10, 50, 51, 61, 64, 67, 83, 85, 100, 118, 119, 124–125, 128–129, 152, 159, 160, 168, 229–230, 248, 300, 312

Wright, Carroll D., 46–47

Young, Edward, 47

Young, Owen D., 145

Zaritsky, Max, 150